The Expectant Father

Facts, Tips, and Advice for Dads-to-Be

"Just as your wife suspected, Mr. Sanders. You have a very little boy growing inside you."

The Expectant Father

Facts, Tips, and Advice for Dads-to-Be

SECOND EDITION

Armin A. Brott and Jennifer Ash

Abbeville Press • Publishers
New York • London

To Tirzah and Talya, who make the world a better place and me a better dad. And to Liz, who makes me a better man.—A.A.B.

For Joe, Clarke, and Emmy, and my parents, Clarke and Agnes Ash, with love and affection.—J.A.

EDITOR: Jacqueline Decter
DESIGNER: Celia Fuller
PRODUCTION EDITOR: Abigail Asher, Ashley Benning
PRODUCTION MANAGER: Louise Kurtz

 The text of this book was set in Bodoni Book. Printed and bound in the United States of America.

Second paperback edition
20 19 18 17 16

Cover photograph by Milton Heiberg. For cartoon credits, see page 271.

Library of Congress Cataloging-in-Publication Data
Brott, Armin A.
The expectant father : facts, tips, and advice for dads-to-be / Armin A. Brott and Jennifer Ash.
p. cm.
Includes bibliographical references and index.
ISBN 0-7892-0538-6
1. Fathers. 2. Pregnancy—Popular works. I. Ash, Jennifer. II. Title.
HQ756.B76 2001
649'.1'0242—dc21 00-052586

Contents

Acknowledgments

So many people have had a hand in creating this book—both the first and second editions—that it's nearly impossible to thank them individually. Andrea Adam read all the early drafts, encouraged me, and helped hone my ideas while adding a few of her own. David Cohen and Jackie Needleman and Matt and Janice Tannin also contributed stories, recipes, advice, and friendship to the first edition. And then, of course, there are the hundreds of expectant and new dads (and plenty of new moms too) who contacted me with their suggestions and comments and anecdotes—this book wouldn't be what it is without them.

Behind the scenes, Jackie Decter did the editing, correcting my mistakes and massaging my prose while leaving my ego intact. Celia Fuller is the brains behind the wonderful design. Marion Appellof did a fine job proofreading. Jim Levine and Arielle Eckstut were there from the beginning and hooked me up with Jennifer, which ultimately made the whole thing possible. And finally, huge thanks to the team at DrSpock.com and, in particular, to Marjorie Greenfield, M.D., for her bluntness in reviewing everything and anything medical in the text.

Armin Brott

While awaiting the arrival of our first baby, I vowed to read every piece of printed advice on pregnancy and motherhood. It quickly became apparent that nine months wasn't sufficient time to digest all that was available for expectant mothers. However, my husband's bedside table remained bare, not for lack of interest but for want of resources. A heartfelt thanks to Joe, who convinced me men do want to know more about pregnancy and thus encouraged me to embark on this project. I'm also grateful to my brothers, Eric and Jim, and to the many friends who candidly discussed impending fatherhood and made insightful suggestions. Virginia Webb's and Esther Williams's advice about newborns was invaluable.

Sincere thanks to everyone at Abbeville, especially Alan Mirken, who supported this project from the onset. The enthusiasm of Bob Abrams and Mark Magowan kept it on track. Jackie Decter deftly guided the book to completion and her friendship made the journey a joy. Thanks to Armin Brott for agreeing to provide the narrative, which breathed male life into the book. Laura Straus made the inclusion of cartoons possible, and Celia Fuller's inspired design brought all of this to life.

Jennifer Ash

J. GREER

Introduction

When my wife and I got pregnant with our first child, I was the happiest I'd ever been. That pregnancy, labor, and the baby's birth was a time of incredible closeness, tenderness, and passion. Long before we'd married, my wife and I had made a commitment to participate equally in raising our children. And it seemed only natural that the process of shared parenting should begin during pregnancy.

Since neither of us had had children before, we were both rather ill-prepared for pregnancy. Fortunately for my wife, there were literally hundreds of books and other resources designed to educate, encourage, support, and comfort women during their pregnancies. But when it finally hit me that I, too, was expecting, and that the pregnancy was bringing out feelings and emotions I didn't understand, there simply weren't any resources for me to turn to. I looked for answers in my wife's pregnancy books, but information about what expectant fathers go through (if it was discussed at all) was at best superficial, and consisted mostly of advice on how men could be supportive of their pregnant wives. To make things worse, my wife and I were the first couple in our circle of close friends to get pregnant, which meant that there was no one else I could talk to about what I was going through, no one who could reassure me that what I was feeling was normal and all right.

Until fairly recently, there has been precious little research on expectant fathers' emotional and psychological experiences during pregnancy. The very title of one of the first articles to appear on the subject should give you some idea of the medical and psychiatric communities' attitude toward the impact of pregnancy on men. Written by William H. Wainwright, M.D., and published in the July 1966 issue of the *American Journal of Psychiatry,* it was called "Fatherhood as a Precipitant of Mental Illness."

As you'll soon find out, though, an expectant father's experience during the transition to fatherhood is not confined simply to excitement—or mental illness; if it were, this book would never have been written. The reality is that men's emotional response to pregnancy is no less varied than women's; expectant fathers feel everything from relief to denial, fear to frustration, anger to joy. And for anywhere from 22 to 79 percent of men, there are physical symptoms of pregnancy as well (more on this on pages 64–68).

So why haven't men's experiences been discussed more? In my opinion it's because we, as a society, value motherhood more than fatherhood, and we automatically assume that issues of childbirth and childrearing are women's issues. But as you'll learn—both from reading this book and from your own experience—this is simply not the case.

Who, Exactly, Has Written This Book?

When Jennifer Ash (who is not my wife) approached me about collaborating with her on *The Expectant Father,* we agreed that the goal was to help you—the father—understand and make sense of what you're going through during your pregnancy. The rationale was simple: the more you understand about what you're going through, the better prepared you'll be and the more likely you'll be to take an interest in—and stay involved during—the pregnancy. Research has shown that the earlier fathers get involved (and what could be earlier than pregnancy?), the more likely they are to be involved after their children are born.

All that's very nice, of course, but it's clearly dependent on your partner's *being* pregnant. So a good understanding of *her* perspective on the pregnancy—emotional as well as physical—is essential to understanding how *you* will react. It was precisely this perspective that Jennifer, along with my wife and a number of other expectant and new mothers I interviewed, provided. Throughout the process of writing the book, all of these women contributed valuable information and comments, not only about what pregnant women are going through but also about the ways women most want men to stay involved and the impact that that involvement had on the entire pregnancy experience.

A Note on Structure

Throughout the book I try to present straightforward, practical information in an easy-to-absorb format. Each of the main chapters is divided into four sections, as follows:

What's Going On with Your Partner

Even though this is a book about what you as an expectant father are going through during pregnancy, and how you can best stay involved, we felt that it was important to start each chapter with a summary of your partner's physical and emotional pregnancy experience.

What's Going On with the Baby

You can't very well have a pregnancy without a baby, right? This section lets you in on your future child's progress—from sperm and egg to living, breathing infant.

What's Going On with You

This section covers the wide range of feelings—good, bad, and indifferent—that you'll probably experience at some time during the pregnancy. It also describes such things as the *physical* changes you may go through and the ways the pregnancy may affect your sex life.

Staying Involved

While the "What's Going On with You" section covers the emotional and physical side of pregnancy, this section gives you specific facts, tips, and advice on what you can *do* to make the pregnancy "yours" as well as your partner's. For instance, you'll find easy, nutritious recipes to prepare, information on how to start a college fund for the baby, valuable advice on getting the most out of your birth classes, great ways to start communicating with your baby before he or she is born, and tips about how to be supportive of your partner and how to stay included in the pregnancy.

The book covers more than the nine months of pregnancy. We've included a detailed chapter on labor and delivery and another on Cesarean section, both of which will prepare you for the big event and let you know how best to help your partner through the birth itself. Perhaps even more important, these chapters prepare you for the often overwhelming emotions you may experience when your partner is in labor and your child is born.

We've also included a special chapter that addresses the major questions and concerns you may have about caring for and getting to know your child in the first few weeks after you bring him or her home. If someone hasn't bought you them already, I'd recommend that you rush right out and get copies of *The New Father: A Dad's Guide to the First Year* and *A Dad's Guide to the Toddler Years.* These books pick up where this one leaves off and continue the process of giving you the skills, knowledge, confidence, and support you'll need to be the best possible dad.

We end this book with a chapter called "Fathering Today," in which you'll learn to recognize—and overcome—the many obstacles contemporary fathers are likely to encounter along the road to being an actively involved dad.

As you go through *The Expectant Father,* remember that each of us brings different emotional baggage to the whole pregnancy process, and that none of us will react to the same situation in exactly the same way. You may find that some of the feelings described in the "What's Going On with You" section in the third-month chapter won't really ring true for you until the fifth month, or that you already experienced them in the first month. You may also want to try out some of the ideas and activities suggested in the "Staying Involved" sections in a different order. Feel free.

A Note on Terminology

Wife, Girlfriend, Lover, He, She . . .

In an attempt to avoid offending anyone (an approach that usually ends up offending everyone), we've decided to refer to the woman who's carrying the baby as "your partner." And because your partner is just as likely to be carrying a boy as a girl, we've alternated between "he" and "she" when referring to the baby.

Hospitals, Doctors . . .

Naturally, not everyone who has a baby delivers in a hospital or is under the care of a medical doctor. Still, because that's the most frequent scenario, we've chosen to refer to the place where the baby will be born as "the hospital" and to the people attending the birth (besides you, of course) as "doctors," "nurses," "medical professionals," or "practitioners"—except, of course, in the sections that specifically deal with home birth and/or midwives.

As a rule, today's fathers (and prospective fathers) want to be much more involved with their children than their own fathers were able to be. It's my firm belief that the first step on the road toward full involvement is to take an active role in the pregnancy. And it's our hope that when you're through reading *The Expectant Father*—which is the book Jennifer wishes she could have bought for her husband when she was pregnant and the one I wish I'd had both times my wife and I were pregnant—you'll be much better prepared to participate in this important new phase of your life.

Some Special Additions to This Edition

It's hard to believe that it's already been five years since the first edition of *The Expectant Father* was published. Over that time I received hundreds of letters and e-mails from readers offering comments and suggestions for how to make this book better. I've incorporated many of those suggestions into this edition and believe that the book is greatly improved as a result.

Throughout, for example, we've added information for adoptive fathers. Although your partner may not actually be carrying a baby, the two of you are still very much "psychologically pregnant." There's a lot of research, in fact, that suggests that in the months leading up to the adoption of their child, expectant adoptive fathers deal with many of the same emotional and psychological issues that biologically expectant fathers do.

In addition, we've added some information specifically geared toward expectant fathers of multiples—twins, triplets, and so forth—and we've greatly expanded the Resources section to include the latest from the Internet and elsewhere.

We Need Your Help

I'd love to hear your experiences, feelings, comments, and suggestions, and I'll try to incorporate them into future editions of this book. You can contact me in writing c/o Abbeville Press (the address is on the copyright page of this book), or by e-mail at armin@MrDad.com. And please check out my Web site (www.mrdad.com).

Good luck as you start this new and wonderful chapter in your life!

The First Decisions

Among the first major questions you and your partner will face after learning you are pregnant are *Where are we going to have the baby?*, *Who is going to help us deliver it?*, and *How much is it all going to cost?* To a certain extent, the answers will be dictated by the terms of your insurance policy, but there are nevertheless a range of options to consider. As you weigh all your choices, give your partner at least 51 percent of the votes. After all, the ultimate decision really affects her more than it does you.

Where and How

Hospitals

For most couples—especially first-time parents—the hospital is the most common place to give birth. It's also the safest. In the unlikely event that complications arise, most hospitals have specialists on staff twenty-four hours a day and are equipped with all the necessary machinery and medications. And in those first hectic hours or days after the birth, the on-staff nurses monitor the baby and mother and help both new parents with the dozens of questions that are likely to come up. They also help fend off unwanted intrusions. If you have a choice among several hospitals in your area, be sure to take a tour of each of them before making your decision. In many cases, though, your decision will be made for you—either by your insurance company or by the doctor or midwife who'll be delivering your baby. Some couples choose another option; they select a practitioner who's associated with the hospital where they want to deliver their baby.

Many hospitals now have birthing rooms that are decorated to look less like a hospital and more like a bedroom at home, although the effect is really more like a nice motel room. The cozy decor is supposed to make you and your partner feel more comfortable. But with nurses dropping by every hour or so, and with the wood furniture cleverly concealing sophisticated monitoring equipment and the cabinets full of sterile supplies, it's going to be hard to forget where you are. And remember, at some hospitals birthing rooms are assigned on a first-come-first-served basis, so don't count on getting one—unless you can convince your partner to go into labor before anyone else does that day. In other hospitals *all* the labor rooms are also birthing rooms, so this won't be an issue.

Birthing Centers

Staffed by certified nurse-midwives (CNMs), these facilities tend to offer a more personal approach to the birthing process. They look and feel a lot like home and are generally less rigid than hospitals and more willing to accommodate any special requests your partner or you might have. Birthing centers are designed to deal with uncomplicated, low-risk pregnancies and births, so expect to be prescreened. And don't worry: if something doesn't go exactly as planned, birthing centers are always affiliated with a doctor and are usually either attached to a hospital or only a short ambulance ride away from one. If you can't find one on your own or through friends or family, contact the National Association of Childbearing Centers in Perkiomenville, PA, (215) 234-8068, or ReachNACC@BirthCenters.org.

Home Birth

With all their high-tech efficiency and stark, impersonal, antiseptic conditions, hospitals are not for everyone. So, if you or your partner don't feel particularly comfortable in hospitals, and you're not anticipating any complications during pregnancy, home birth can be a more relaxed option to consider. Home birth has been around forever but has been out of favor in this country for a long time. It is, however, making something of a comeback as more and more people (most of whom aren't even hippies) decide to give it a try. Here are some of the reasons why you might want to consider a home birth:

- The surroundings are more familiar.
- You've already had one or more uncomplicated hospital births.
- Helpers (usually nurse-midwives) are experienced mothers; nurses in hospitals may have no personal experience with birth. Keep in mind that

you may not be able to have a certified nurse-midwife at the birth. Many can't get malpractice insurance unless they work at a hospital or birthing center.
- The birth is more likely to go exactly as you want it than it might anywhere else.
- Your partner is going to be treated less like a patient than she would be in a hospital.
- The two of you can pay attention to the spiritual aspects of the delivery, an intimate matter that you might be discouraged from, or feel embarrassed about, in the hospital.
- It's cheaper. (This, however, should not be your only reason.)

If you're thinking about a home birth, be prepared. Having a baby at home is quite a bit different from the way it's made out to be in those old westerns. You'll need to assume much more responsibility for the whole process than if you were using a hospital. It takes a lot of research and preparation. At the very least, you're going to need a lot more than clean towels and boiling water.

My wife and I thought about a home birth for our second baby but ultimately decided against it. While I don't consider myself particularly squeamish, I just couldn't imagine how we'd avoid making a mess all over the bedroom carpet. What really clinched it for us, though, was that our first child had been an emergency Cesarean section; fearing that we might run into problems again, we opted to be near the doctors.

Making the decision to give birth at home does *not* mean that your partner can skip getting prenatal care or that the two of you should plan on delivering your baby alone. You'll still need to be in close contact with a medical professional to ensure that the pregnancy is progressing normally, and you should make sure to have someone present at the birth who has plenty of experience with childbirth (no, not your sister or your mother-in-law, unless they happen to be qualified). So if you're planning on going this route, start working on selecting a midwife right now (see the Resources section for help in finding a midwife and page 19 for some questions to ask).

Natural vs. Medicated Birth

In recent years giving birth "naturally"—without drugs, pain medication, or any medical intervention—has become all the rage. But just because it's popular doesn't mean it's for everybody. Labor and delivery are going to be a painful experience—for both of you—and many couples elect to take

When *Not* to Have your Baby at Home

There's a lot of research indicating that an uncomplicated, planned home birth (as opposed to the unplanned kind) is at least as safe as a hospital birth. Still, home birth isn't for everyone, because things can happen during your pregnancy that might make giving birth at home unnecessarily risky. If, for example, your partner goes into labor prematurely, if she's carrying twins (or more), or if you find out that the baby is breech (feet down instead of head down), you'll probably want to reconsider the hospital. The same is true if your partner develops preeclampsia, a condition that affects about 10 percent of pregnant women and that can have very serious complications if it's not detected and treated early (see page 57 for more on this).

You'll have to think about the hospital option if your partner suffers from diabetes, has a heart or kidney condition, has had hemorrhaging in a previous labor (a quick blood transfusion can be conducted at the hospital), has had a previous Cesarean section, or smokes cigarettes regularly. While plenty of people with these and other conditions have delivered perfectly healthy babies at home, the chances that complications can develop are significant, and you and your partner should make every effort to ensure the safest possible delivery.

advantage of the advances medical science has made in relieving the pain and discomfort of childbirth. Whichever way you go, make sure the decision is yours. Proponents of some childbirth methods (see pages 135–37) are almost religiously committed to the idea of a drug-free delivery, to the extent that they often make women who opt for some kind of pain medication feel as though they're failures. So don't let your friends, relatives, or anyone else pressure you into doing something you don't want to do.

And be flexible. You and your partner may be planning a natural childbirth, but conditions could develop that necessitate intervention or the use of medication (see pages 190–91). On the other hand, you may be planning a medicated delivery but could find yourself snowed in someplace far from your hospital and any pain medication, or the anesthesiologist may be at an emergency on the other side of town.

What to Ask Your Prospective Practitioner

Besides a medical school degree, OB/GYNs may share little in common. Each will have a slightly different philosophy and approach to pregnancy and birth. The same (except for the medical school part) can be said for midwives. So before making a final decision about who's going to deliver your baby, you should get satisfactory answers to the following questions:

ESPECIALLY FOR OB/GYNS

- How do you feel about family members and/or coaches attending the delivery? Are you enthusiastic about it or just tolerant?
- Do you recommend any particular childbirth preparation method (Lamaze, Bradley, and so on)?
- At which hospital(s) do you deliver your babies?
- Are you board certified?
- Do you have any specialties or special training?
- How many partners do you have and how often are they on rotation? What percent of your patients' babies do you deliver? What are your backup arrangements if you can't be there?
- How many sonograms do you routinely recommend?
- Do you perform amniocentesis yourself?
- What percentage of your deliveries are Cesarean?
- Do you permit fathers to attend Cesarean sections?
- What is your definition of a "high-risk" pregnancy?
- What is your policy on inducing labor?
- How often do you perform an episiotomy?
- How do you feel about the mother lifting the baby out herself if she wishes?

Who's Going to Help?

At first glance, it may seem that your partner should be picking a medical practitioner alone—after all, she's the one who's going to be poked and prodded as the pregnancy develops. But considering that more than 90 percent of today's expectant fathers are present during the delivery of their children, and that the vast majority of them have been involved in some significant way during the rest of the pregnancy, you're probably going to be spending a lot of

- How do you feel about the father assisting at the birth?
- Do you routinely suction the baby during delivery?
- Do you usually hand the naked baby straight to the mother?
- Do you allow the mother or father to cut the umbilical cord?

ESPECIALLY FOR MIDWIVES

- Are you licensed?
- How many babies have you delivered?
- Which physicians are you associated with?
- How often does a physician get involved in the care of your patients?
- What is the role of the physician in your practice?
- What position do most of the women you work with adopt for the second stage of labor?

FOR BOTH OB/GYNS AND MIDWIVES

- What are your rates and payment plans?
- What insurance, if any, do you honor?
- What percentage of your patients had natural, unmedicated births in the past year?
- Are you willing to wait until the umbilical cord has stopped pulsating before you clamp it?
- Can the baby be put to the breast immediately after delivery?
- Are you willing to dim the lights when the baby is born?
- How much experience have you had with twins or more? (This is a very important question if you and/or your partner have a family history of multiple births or if you suspect that your partner is carrying more than one baby.)

time with the practitioner as well. So if at all possible, you should feel comfortable with the final choice, too.

Private Obstetrician

If your partner is over twenty, she probably has been seeing a gynecologist for a few years. And since many gynecologists also do obstetrics, it should come as no surprise that most couples elect to have the woman's regular obstetrician/gynecologist (OB/GYN) deliver the baby.

Private OB/GYNs are generally the most expensive way to go, but your insurance company will probably pick up a good part of the bill. Most private OBs, however, aren't strictly private; they usually have a number of partners, which means that the doctor you see for your prenatal appointments might not be the one in attendance at the birth. So make sure that you are aware of and comfortable with the backup arrangements—just in case your baby decides to show up on a day when your doctor is not available. Labor and delivery are going to be stressful enough without having to deal with a doctor you've never met before.

Researcher Sandra Howell-White found that women who view childbirth as risky, or who want to have a say in managing their pain or the length of their labor, tend to opt for obstetricians.

Family Physician (FP)

Although many FPs provide obstetrical care, not all do, so check with yours to see whether he or she does. If not, he or she will refer your partner to someone else for the pregnancy and birth. One of the big advantages of going with your family doctor is that after the birth, he or she often can see your partner and baby on the same visit. The time saved running around from doctor to doctor will be welcome.

Like most doctors, FPs are frequently in group practices, and there's no guarantee that the doctor you know will be on call the day the baby comes. So, if you can, try to meet with the other doctors in the practice, as well as with any OB/GYN your family doctor might work with.

Midwife

Although midwives are not as common in the United States as they are in Europe, they're becoming increasingly popular. And you might want to consider bringing one into the process, even if your partner has a regular OB.

In Howell-White's study, women who expect their partners to be actively involved in labor and delivery and who place a high value on getting information on the birth process are more likely to opt for a midwife. Interestingly, so are women who have no religious affiliation.

Certified nurse-midwives (CNMs) are licensed nurses who have taken a minimum of two or three years of additional training in obstetrics and passed special certification exams. They can deliver babies in hospitals, birthing centers, or at home. But because their training is usually in uncomplicated, low-risk births, CNMs have to work under a physician, just in case something comes up.

Some states have created a new designation, certified midwife (CM), which allows practitioners who aren't nurses, but who go through the same training and take the same exams as CNMs, to work as midwives.

Many standard OB/GYN practices, recognizing that some of their patients might want to have a midwife in attendance at the birth, now have a CNM (or in some cases a CM) on staff. Officially, then, your partner is still under the care of a physician—whose services can be paid for by insurance—but she'll still get the kind of care she wants.

If you're considering using a CNM or a CM, the American College of Nurse Midwives can put you in touch with one in your area and fill you in on any applicable regulations. Call 1(888)MIDWIFE or check out their Web site, www.midwife.org.

There are also plenty of midwives out there who are neither certified nor licensed. Lay midwives have a lot of experience working with pregnant women and may even have a lot of specialized training. But they're not regulated and may not have passed any specific midwife exams, which means that in most cases they aren't certified to work in hospitals or birthing centers, but only in home settings. Like CNMs or CMs, lay midwives must work with a physician, in case of an emergency. The Midwives Alliance of North America, at www.MANA.org, can help you find out more about lay midwives and make contact with one near you.

And finally, whether you're considering a midwife or not, you still might want to start thinking about a doula at this point. If you don't already know what a doula is, see pages 138–40.

Bills

Having a baby isn't cheap. Even if you have good insurance, the 20 percent (plus your deductible) that most policies make you pay can still add up in a hurry. In the sections that follow, you'll get an idea of how much a typical—and a not-so-typical—pregnancy and childbirth experience might cost. It's a good idea to look over your insurance policy, find out about how much it will be picking up, and start figuring out now how you're going to pay for the rest of it.

Putting together a budget can be important even if you're adopting. In many cases, adoptive parents are in close contact with the birth mother throughout her pregnancy and delivery. You and your partner might go to the doctor's appointments, see the ultrasound, hear the baby's heartbeat, and pick up the bills—most of which won't be reimbursed by your insurance company—for

"Listen, are you absolutely sure *you want to have kids?"*

everything. If you're doing an international adoption, you won't have to worry about covering the birth mother's medical expenses, but you'll probably need to budget in the cost of several overseas trips. In addition, you'll need to take into account the many other adoption-related expenses you're likely to incur, including agency fees, attorney's fees, and the home study you'll have to go through.

Pregnancy and Childbirth

Most doctors charge a flat fee for your partner's care during the entire pregnancy. This generally covers monthly visits during the first two trimesters, biweekly visits for the next month or so, and then weekly visits until delivery. But don't make the mistake of thinking that that's all you'll pay. Bills for blood and urine tests, ultrasounds, hospital fees, and other procedures will work their way into your mailbox at least once a month. Here's what you can expect to pay (before your insurance pays its part) for having your baby:

OB/GYN

$2,500 to $6,500 for general prenatal care and a problem-free vaginal delivery. Most doctors will meet with you to discuss their rates and the services they provide. For a list of important questions to ask, see pages 18–19. In addition, be sure to discuss which insurance plans, if any, they participate in (it might actually be easier to start with the doctors your insurance covers and choose from there). You should also ask whether they'll bill your insurance company directly or will want you to make a deposit (most will want to collect about 25 percent of the anticipated bill up front); whether you can make your payments in installments; and whether they expect their fee to be paid in full before the delivery.

MIDWIFE

The average cost of a delivery by a midwife is $1,500 to $4,000, but it can vary greatly depending on where you live. If you're delivering at home, you'll also need to add the cost of the supplies the midwife thinks you'll need for the birth (sterile pads, bandages, and so on).

Lab and Other Expenses

- Blood: Over the course of the pregnancy, you can expect to be billed anywhere from $100 to $1,000 for various blood tests.
- Ultrasound: At least $200 each. In an ordinary pregnancy, you'll have between none and three.

Prenatal Testing

If you and/or your practitioner decide that you're a candidate for amniocentesis or any other prenatal diagnostic test, you can expect to pay $800 to $1,200. In most cases genetic counseling is required beforehand, and that costs an additional $300 to $500. If you're having any prenatal testing done just because you'd like to find out the sex of the baby or want reassurance of its well-being (and not because you're in a high-risk group), your insurance company may not pay for it. But if your partner is 35 or older, they probably will pay for testing.

At the Hospital

- If you're paying for it yourself, a problem-free vaginal delivery and a twenty-four-hour stay in a hospital will run anywhere from $1,500 to $2,500, depending on where you live.
- If you're planning to spend the night in the hospital with your partner, add about $200 per day.
- Anesthesiologists usually charge from $750 to $1,500, depending on what they do and the time spent doing it.

If Your Partner Needs a Cesarean Section

If your partner ends up having a C-section, all bets are off. It's considered major surgery, and it is expensive. The operation, which your OB/GYN will

Your Rights to Free and Subsidized Medical Care

Many state health departments operate free health clinics. In addition, hospital emergency rooms are required by federal law to give you an initial assessment—and any required emergency care—even if you can't afford to pay.

perform, is not included in his or her flat fee, and you'll have to pay for at least two other doctors to assist, plus a pediatrician, who must be in attendance to care for the baby. In addition, a C-section entails a longer recovery period in the hospital—usually four to five days—as well as extra nursing care, pain medication, bandages, and other supplies. If the baby is in good health, you can probably take him home while your partner stays in the hospital, but chances are you'll want the baby to stay with your partner, especially if she is breastfeeding. The baby's additional time in the nursery costs more, too. In our case, by the time all the bills had been paid, we (actually, mostly our insurance company) had shelled out more than $15,000 for the birth of our first child. That alone was just about enough to make us decide on a home birth for the second one (although we ultimately opted against it).

An Important (and Possibly Profitable) Word of Advice

Make sure that you and your partner check your birth-related bills very carefully. Hospitals can make mistakes, and they are rarely in your favor. After we'd recovered from the shock of the C-section bills (which started off at closer to $17,000), we asked a doctor friend to go over them with us. He found that we'd been charged for a variety of things that hadn't happened and overcharged for a lot of the things that had. For example, we'd been billed $25 for a tube of ointment that the hospital's own pharmacy was selling for $1.25. And for the second pregnancy, our nit-picking review of the bills cut about 20 percent off the total.

Now here's the profitable part. Since your insurance company will probably be paying for most of your bills, they'll be ecstatic if your review ends up saving them money. In fact, some insurers are so thrilled that they'll actually give you a percentage (sometimes as much as half) of the money they save. Naturally, though, you'll have to ask for your reward. So, read your policy carefully and, if you still have questions, talk to your agent or one of the company's underwriters.

And while you're reading your insurance policy, here are a few other things to look out for:

- **How long before the birth does the insurer need to be notified about the pregnancy and estimated due date?** Not complying with the carrier's instructions could mean a reduction in the amount they'll pay for pregnancy and birth-related expenses.
- **When can the baby be added to the policy?** Until the baby is born, all pregnancy- and birth-related expenses will be charged to your partner. After the birth, however, your partner and the new baby will be getting separate checks (all baby-related expenses, such as medication, pediatrician's exams, diapers, blankets, and various other hospital charges, will be charged to the baby). Some carriers require you to add the baby to your (or your partner's) policy as far in advance as thirty days before the birth; most give you until thirty days after. Again, failing to follow the insurer's instructions carefully could result in a reduction of coverage.

Low-Cost Alternatives

Obstetrical Clinics

If you live in a city where there is a large teaching hospital, your partner may be able to get prenatal care at its obstetrical clinic. If so, you'll spend a lot less than you would for a private physician. The one drawback is that your baby will probably be delivered by an inexperienced—yet closely supervised—doctor or a medical student. This isn't to say that you won't be getting top-quality care. Clinics are often equipped with state-of-the-art equipment and the young professionals who staff them are being taught all the latest methods by some of the best teachers in the country.

Notes:

THE 1ST MONTH

Salad Days

What's Going On with Your Partner

Physically

- Morning sickness (nausea, heartburn, vomiting)
- Food cravings or aversions
- Dizziness, irritability, headaches
- Fatigue
- Breast changes: tenderness, enlargement

Emotionally

- Thrilled—or stunned or even a little frightened—that she's pregnant
- A heightened closeness to you
- Apprehension about the nine months ahead
- Mood swings and sudden, unexplained crying

What's Going On with the Baby

It's going to be a busy first month. About two hours after you had sex, the egg is fertilized, and after a full day or so there is a tiny bundle of quickly dividing cells. By the end of the month the embryo will be about ¼-inch long and will have a heart (but no brain), as well as tiny arm and leg buds.

What's Going On with You

Thrills

I still have the white bathrobe I was wearing the morning my wife and I found out we were pregnant the first time. I stood nervously in the kitchen, the countertop cluttered with vials of colored powders and liquids, droppers, and the small container filled with my wife's "first morning urine." (Fortunately,

Morning Sickness

About half of all pregnant women experience morning sickness. Despite the name, the nausea, heartburn, and vomiting can strike at any hour of the day. No one's quite sure what causes morning sickness. Some suggest that it's the pregnant woman's reaction to changing hormone levels. Others, such as researcher Margie Profet, contend that morning sickness is the body's natural way of protecting the growing fetus from *teratogins* (toxins that cause birth defects) and *abortifacients* (toxins that induce miscarriage). Whatever the cause, for most women morning sickness disappears after about the third month. Until then, here are a few things you can do to help your partner cope:

- Help her maintain a high-protein, high-carbohydrate diet.
- Encourage her to drink a lot of fluids—although milk may be a problem; some women with morning sickness can't tolerate it. You might also want to keep a large water bottle next to the bed. She should avoid caffeine, which tends to be dehydrating, and she might want to start the day with a small amount of non-acidic juice, such as apple or grape, or flat soda; the sweet flavor will probably encourage her to drink a little more than she might otherwise.
- Be sensitive to the sights and smells that make her queasy—and keep them away from her. Fatty or spicy foods are frequent offenders.
- Encourage her to eat a lot of small meals throughout the day—every two or three hours, if possible—and to eat before she starts feeling nauseated. Basic foods like rice and yogurt are particularly good because they're less likely to cause nausea than greasy foods.
- Make sure she takes her prenatal vitamins, if her doctor says to do so.
- Put some pretzels, crackers, or rice cakes by the bed—she'll need something to start and end the day with, and these are low in fat and calories and easy to digest.
- Be aware that she needs plenty of rest and encourage her to get it.

do-it-yourself pregnancy detection kits are a lot less complicated today than they used to be, but I'm not sure they're as much fun.) Feeling like a Nobel Prize-winning chemist on the edge of making a discovery that would alter the course of the entire world, I carefully dropped several drops of the urine into one of the vials of powder. I stirred the mixture with the specially provided swizzle stick, rinsed it, and slowly added the contents of the other vial.

"Young kids today don't know how good they have it . . . I remember the old days before home pregnancy tests."

In all honesty, the results we got twenty minutes later weren't a complete surprise. But that didn't make it any less thrilling. I'd always wanted to have children, and suddenly it seemed that all my dreams were finally going to come true. It was like hitting the million-dollar jackpot on the nickel slots.

Relief . . . and Pride

At the same time, I was filled with an incredible feeling of relief. Secretly, I'd always been afraid that I was sterile and that I'd have to be satisfied with taking someone else's kids to the circus or the baseball game. I also felt a surge of pride. After all, I was a man, a fully functional man—all right, a stud, even. And by getting my wife pregnant, I'd somehow lived up to my highest potential.

Irrational Fears

At some point after the initial excitement passes, a surprising number of men find themselves experiencing an irrational fear that the child their partner is carrying is not theirs. Psychologist Jerrold Lee Shapiro interviewed more than two hundred men whose partners were pregnant, and found that 60 percent "acknowledged fleeting thoughts, fantasies, or nagging doubts that they might not really be the biological father of the child." The majority of these men don't actually believe their partners are having affairs. Rather, Shapiro writes, these feelings are symptoms of a common type of insecurity: the fear many men have that they simply aren't capable of doing anything as incredible as creating life, and that someone more potent must have done the job.

Staying Involved

Exercise

If your partner was already working out regularly before the pregnancy, she won't need any extra encouragement to exercise, and if her doctor approves, she can probably continue her regular physical fitness routine. Be aware, though, that some health clubs—out of fear of getting sued—ask a pregnant woman to provide a letter from her doctor.

If your partner wasn't physically active before pregnancy, this isn't the time for her to take up rock climbing. That doesn't mean, however, that she should spend the entire pregnancy on the sofa. Getting sufficient exercise is critical. It will help improve her circulation, and it will keep her energy level high. Exercising during pregnancy may also help your partner keep her weight gain steady and reasonable, help her sleep better, improve her self-esteem, and reduce some of the normal pregnancy-related discomforts. In addition, it will improve her strength and endurance, which will be helpful during labor and delivery, and may even lessen the chance that she'll deliver prematurely or need a Cesarean section.

But because pregnancy can make even the most fit woman feel a little tired, she may not always feel like working out. One way to help motivate her to get the exercise she needs is to work out with her. (See page 31 for a list of good activities you can do together.) The most important thing is to start easy and not push her if you see she's feeling tired or winded. If your budget doesn't permit joining a health club, you can always buy pregnancy workout videotapes.

Whatever you do, remember that you and your partner will get the greatest benefit and least chance of injury if you exercise regularly—three times a week—rather than sporadically.

Workout No-Nos

- **High-impact sports** There's a lot of disagreement about whether or not it's possible to induce a miscarriage by falling. Dr. Robert Bradley, who has delivered over 30,000 babies, says that he has "never known a mother to have harmed a baby by any external trauma." (Severe, sudden impacts such as car crashes can sometimes cause a miscarriage, though.) Still, most high-impact activities should be avoided.
- **Any sport that might cause her to take a hard fall** This includes horseback riding, in-line skating, ice skating, and, starting in about the 7th month, bicycling.
- **Scuba diving and water skiing** Highly pressurized water can be squeezed through the vagina and cervix into the uterus.
- **Downhill skiing** Unless you're an expert, don't, and even then take it easy. My wife skiied when she was seven months pregnant but avoided the most challenging runs where she'd have risked a serious fall. Unless your partner's doctor prohibits it, cross-country skiing should be fine.
- **Hot tubs/steam baths/saunas** Research indicates that raising a pregnant woman's body temperature by more than two degrees could be dangerous to the fetus. To cool itself, the body moves blood away from the internal organs—including the uterus—and toward the skin.
- **Anything involving heavy lifting** This can put unnecessary pressure on internal organs.
- **Anything too exhausting** If she can't carry on a normal conversation while exercising, she's working out too hard.
- **Anything that could lead to overheating** Your partner shouldn't overdress, and she should keep her workouts moderate. Remind her to take plenty of breaks and drink lots of water before, during, and after the workout.

One final word of advice: *Do not panic* if your partner engaged in any of these activities before you found out she was pregnant. First of all, there's no going back to undo it, and second, the chances are slim that anything she did will have an impact on the baby in any significant way. Just be careful from here on out.

Exercises and Sports to Do Together

- Walking—fast or slow—is great exercise.
- Running—but do yourselves a favor: get good shoes and run on a soft surface.
- Swimming, water aerobics, snorkeling.
- Cycling—stationary or street is fine, but you should probably avoid those bumpy dirt-bike rides.
- Tennis.
- Light weight-lifting.
- Golf.
- Yoga—but avoid extreme stretches; this can cause damage to your partner's connective tissues, which are somewhat weakened during pregnancy.
- Low-impact aerobics and low-impact exercise machines such as stairsteppers, treadmills, and bicycles.

Before starting any kind of workout program, discuss the details with your practitioner and get his or her approval. If you're doing anything that will work up a sweat, be sure to get enough fluids. Both of you should drink a glass or so an hour before starting and another 4 to 8 ounces every fifteen to twenty minutes while you're working out.

Nutrition

The principles of good nutrition haven't changed all that much since you learned about the four basic food groups (or, if you're younger, the pyramid of food) in sixth grade. But now that your partner is pregnant, she'll need about 300 more calories a day than before. (Of course, if she was underweight before the pregnancy or is pregnant with twins, she might need a little more.) If she was overweight before getting pregnant, this is not the time to go on a diet. At the same time, the fact that she's "eating for two" is not a license to eat anything she wants. Your practitioner will undoubtedly suggest a diet for your partner to follow, but here are a few important nutritional basics to keep in mind:

PROTEIN

The average woman needs 45 grams of protein a day, but your pregnant partner should take in 75 to 100 grams per day. If she's pregnant with twins, however, she'll need to up her protein intake by about 20 to 25 grams a day, but not until she's in the fourth or fifth month. When the fetus is eight weeks old, it has about 125,000 brain-cell neurons. By the end of the nineteenth week, there are about 20 billion—the most he or she will *ever* have. Obstetrician F. Rene Van de Carr has found that a high-protein diet—especially during the first nineteen weeks of pregnancy—supports this surge in brain-cell growth in the baby. Lean proteins are always the best bet. Low-fat milk is one of the easiest sources of protein: one glass has about 8 grams. Other good sources are skinless chicken, lean meats, low-fat cheese, tofu (soybean curd), peanut butter, and cooked fish. Eggs (stay away from the raw ones) are another excellent choice; hard-boiled, they travel well and make a convenient between-meal snack.

IRON

If your partner doesn't get enough iron, she may become anemic and begin to feel exhausted. Spinach, dried fruits, beef, fortified cereals, and legumes are all good sources, but since much of your partner's iron intake is being used to manufacture the fetus's blood, she may need still more than she can possibly get from food alone. If so, her doctor will prescribe some over-the-counter supplements, but probably not until sometime after the third month. (The doctor may also have her take prenatal vitamins, which contain some extra iron.) If possible, your partner should take the tablets with a glass of orange juice—it (and other sources of vitamin C) helps the body absorb the iron. One warning: iron supplements frequently cause constipation.

CITRUS FRUIT (AND OTHER FOODS HIGH IN VITAMIN C)

Vitamin C is critical to the body's manufacture of collagen, the stuff that holds tissue together. It also helps ensure the baby's bone and tooth development. An inadequate level of vitamin C may weaken your partner's uterus, increasing the likelihood of a difficult labor. Your partner should have a total of at least seven servings a day of fruits and vegetables.

CALCIUM

Calcium is critical to the manufacture of the baby's bones. And since so much of your partner's intake of calcium goes directly to the baby, she needs to make sure she's getting enough for herself—about 1,500 mg per day. If not, the growing fetus will leach it from your partner's bones, which could increase her risk of developing osteoporosis later in life. The best sources of calcium are milk and other dairy products. But if your partner is allergic to milk, some doctors say she should stay away from it—especially if she's planning to breastfeed (her milk allergy could be passed to the baby). Good alternate sources of calcium include pink salmon (canned, with soft bones, is okay), tofu, broccoli, calcium-fortified orange juice, eggs, oyster-shell calcium tablets, and TUMS 500s.

GREEN AND YELLOW VEGETABLES

Besides helping form red blood cells, green and yellow vegetables (which, strangely enough, include cantaloupe and mango) are excellent sources of iron and vitamins A and B, which will help your partner's body absorb all that extra protein she'll be eating. Vitamin A may also help prevent bladder and kidney infections. These vegetables are also an excellent source of folic acid, which can help reduce the incidence of brain and spinal cord defects, especially in the early months of the pregnancy. The prenatal vitamins your partner is probably taking will help augment the folic acid she's getting from her food. The darker the green, the better it is for your partner. She should try to have a serving or two per day.

GRAINS AND OTHER COMPLEX CARBOHYDRATES

Grains (including breads and cereals) are basically fuel for your partner's body, and she should have at least four servings a day. Since her body will burn the fuel first, if she doesn't get enough there may not be enough for the baby. Grains are generally low in calories and high in zinc, selenium, chromium, and magnesium—all essential nutrients. They're also high in fiber, which will help your partner combat the constipating effect of iron supplements. Good

sources includes whole-grain breads (keep her away from white bread for a few months if you can), brown rice, fresh potatoes, peas, and dried beans.

WATER

As if she doesn't have enough to do already, your partner should try to drink at least eight 8-ounce glasses of water a day—more if she's doing a lot of exercise or if she's pregnant during the summer. This will help her to replace the water she loses when she perspires (which she'll do more during pregnancy), and to carry away waste products. Keep in mind that at any given moment, about half of the population is walking around somewhat dehydrated, which puts them at increased risk of developing all sorts of problems, including kidney stones and urinary tract cancers.

FATTY FOODS

Despite all the hype about low- or no-fat diets, the fact is that your partner, like everyone else in the world, needs to consume at least some fat. She'll probably be getting most of what she needs in the other things she's eating during the day. But no more than 30 percent of her total caloric intake should come from fat. Monounsaturated fats (avocado, peanuts, olive oil, canola oil) are best, followed by polyunsaturated fats (margarine, mayonnaise, walnuts). The worst kind are saturated fats (bacon, lard, butter, coconut oil).

Nutritional and Chemical No-Nos

- **Cigarettes** When a mother-to-be inhales cigarette smoke, her womb fills with carbon monoxide, nicotine, tar, and resins that inhibit oxygen and nutrient delivery to the baby. Maternal cigarette smoking increases the risk of low-birth-weight babies and miscarriage. There's also some recent research indicating that paternal smoking (exposing your partner and your baby to secondhand smoke) may have similar effects. Too many expectant dads don't realize how important this is; if you think the baby is somehow protected from your smoke by being inside your partner, or if you think that smoking doesn't matter this early in the pregnancy, you're dangerously wrong. Bottom line: if you're a smoker, quit now. If she is, encourage her to quit and help her any way you can. Interestingly, a lot of men put off quitting—or asking their partners to quit—out of fear that withdrawal might lead to some marital tension. Bad choice. The potential danger to your baby far outweighs the danger to your relationship.
- **Alcohol** Complete abstinence is the safest choice (although your partner's practitioner may sanction a glass of wine once in a while to

(continued on following page)

"Is it organic?"

(continued from preceding page)

induce relaxation). One binge, or even just a few drinks at the wrong time (such as when the baby's brain is developing), can cause Fetal Alcohol Syndrome, a set of irreversible mental and physical impairments. Even moderate social drinking has been linked to low-birth-weight babies, learning impairments, and miscarriages in the early stages of pregnancy. If you're worried about any drinking your partner may have done before you found out you were pregnant, talk to her practitioner about it.

- **Fasting** Unless she has a doctor's approval, your partner should never, *ever* go twenty-four hours without eating. This is especially important in the first nineteen weeks of pregnancy, when the baby's brain is developing.
- **Over-the-counter or prescription drugs** Consult your doctor before taking any medication, including aspirin, ibuprofen, and cold medicines—especially those containing alcohol or codeine.
- **Caffeine** Avoiding caffeine is especially important in the early months. Some studies have shown that pregnant women who drink a lot of coffee—more than four cups a day, for example—have a greater risk of having a miscarriage, of delivering prematurely, or of having a low-birth-weight baby.
- **Recreational drugs** Abstain during pregnancy—unborn children can be born addicted.
- **Certain foods** Raw meats and fish may contain *Toxoplasma gondii,* which can blind the fetus or damage its nervous system. Soft cheeses such as Brie may contain *Listeria,* another dangerous bacterium. Raw eggs and chicken may contain salmonella. Practitioners do disagree, however, on the magnitude of the risk involved. My wife's first OB/GYN was Japanese and had absolutely no problem with her eating sushi.
- **Cat feces** Although cat feces don't have much to do with nutrition, they do contain high quantities of the same parasite found in some raw meats. So if you have a cat, take over the duty of cleaning the litter box for the duration of the pregnancy.
- **Insecticides, weed killers, and the like** Prolonged and repeated exposure to such toxic substances is thought to be linked to birth defects. So, after you change the litter box, put on your gloves and do the gardening. And while you're at it, you might as well switch to

organic fertilizers and pesticides. Your partner should stay far away from other potential chemical contaminants, such as diazinon (a common cockroach killer), as well as no-pest strips, flea sprays and collars, and pesticide bombs. Two chemicals in particular—PCBS and DDE (an insecticide by-product)—can have some very negative effects. Kids exposed to those chemicals in utero tend to be taller (about 2 inches) and weigh more (an average of 11 to 15 pounds) as teens than kids who weren't exposed. Prenatal exposure to these and other chemicals may also be linked to the early onset of puberty. You and your partner might consider eating organic fruits and vegetables during the pregnancy to avoid any nasty chemicals that might have been sprayed on them. At the very least, wash your food carefully.

- **Hair dyes** Although no link to birth defects has been proven, the chemical solutions in hair dyes can be absorbed through the scalp into the bloodstream. The simple solution is for your partner to avoid dyeing her hair while she's pregnant. If you can't convince her that her hair looks wonderful just the way it is, vegetable dyes may be an alternative; they don't last as long, but they look as good as, and in some cases even better and less artificial than, the chemical variety.

You can get a comprehensive listing of domestic eco-hazards online from greenhome.com. Contact information is in the Resources section.

A WORD ABOUT A VEGETARIAN DIET

If your partner is a vegetarian, there's no reason why she and the baby can't get the nutrition they need—especially if she eats eggs and milk. But if she's a strict vegan, you should check with your doctor or a good nutritionist for special guidance.

A FINAL NOTE ON NUTRITION

Helping your partner eat right is one of the best things you can do to ensure that you'll have a healthy, happy baby (and a healthy, happy partner). But don't be too hard on her; while she'd undoubtedly be better off eating nothing but healthy foods all the time, an occasional order of fries or candy bar is unlikely to cause any serious problems. Finally, be supportive. This means that you should try to eat as healthily as she does. If you absolutely must have a banana split, do it on your own time (and don't brag about it).

A Special Note for Adoptive Dads
If you're one of the many expectant adoptive parents who has met your future baby's birth mother, do whatever you can to support her pregnancy without being annoying. Encourage her to exercise, stop smoking, eat right, take her prenatal vitamins, go to her regularly scheduled medical appointments, and so on.

The Hunger Campaign

One of the things I constantly underestimated while my wife was pregnant was how incredibly hungry she would get, and how quickly it would happen. Even though she might have had a snack before leaving the office, by the time she got home she'd be ravenous again.

If you've been doing most of the cooking at your house, things probably won't change much during the pregnancy. But if your partner has been doing most of the cooking, there are a few things you can do to simplify her life significantly:

- **Learn to cook simple, quick meals.** There are plenty of cookbooks specializing in meals that can be made in less than thirty minutes (two good ones are *The 15-Minute Vegetarian Gourmet* and *Desperation*

"Why have you brought me here?"

Stocking Up

If you keep the following items on hand, you or your partner should be able to throw together a healthy meal or snack any time.

- Unsweetened cereals
- Whole-wheat pasta
- Tomato or vegetable juice
- Whole-grain bread
- Skim milk
- Nonfat cottage cheese
- Low-fat, naturally sweetened yogurt
- Fresh eggs (and some hard-boiled ones too)
- Natural peanut butter
- Pure fruit jams
- Bottled water
- Crackers
- Fresh vegetables that can be eaten raw, including carrots, cucumbers, celery, and tomatoes
- Fresh fruit
- Frozen berries and grapes
- Raisins and other dried fruits

Dinners!: Home-Cooked Meals in 20 Minutes Flat). In addition, most major newspapers run columns featuring easy-to-cook meals using local and seasonal produce. You can also stock up on healthy microwavable dinners or order take-out meals, but that can get expensive pretty fast.

- **Do some meal planning.** This means you'll have to spend some time reading cookbooks, looking for things that sound good. As you're reading, be sure to write down the ingredients you'll need. Although meal planning doesn't sound all that difficult, it's time-consuming—especially when you add in the extra time you'll have to spend at the grocery store.
- **Do the shopping.** Even if your partner still plans the meals and makes out the shopping lists, your going to the store will spare her an hour or so a week of walking around on floors that are tough even on nonpregnant people's feet. In addition, many women who have severe morning sickness find that being in a grocery store, surrounded by so much food, is just too

much to stomach. If your partner did the shopping before the pregnancy, ask her to make a *detailed* list of the items she usually bought.

- **Make her a nutritious breakfast shake.** Let her spend a few more precious minutes relaxing in bed in the morning (see below for a good recipe).

Recipes

Power Shake

½ cup skim milk
1 banana
12 strawberries
juice of 2 oranges

Combine ingredients in a blender or food processor and serve over crushed ice or straight up chilled.

Basic Quick Snacks

- Peel and slice carrots and celery the night before for your partner to take to work for lunch.
- Boil eggs: put a few eggs in a pot with enough water to cover them, cover the pot, bring to a boil. As soon as the water boils, turn off the heat and let the eggs sit in the pot for 20 minutes. Then rinse with cold water and shell.
- Mix up some GORP (dried fruits, nuts, raisins, sunflower seeds).

Open-Face Mexican Omelet

3 eggs
1 teaspoon cilantro, finely chopped
1 small tomato, chopped
¼ cup green and/or red pepper, chopped
¼ cup red onion, diced
black pepper to taste

If eating the egg yolks aggravates your partner's morning sickness, use only the whites. Whisk eggs in a bowl or measuring cup and pour into a medium nonstick frying pan. Turn heat on low. As eggs begin to cook, add all other ingredients. Simmer until egg becomes firm, and slide omelet onto plate for serving.

Microwave Oatmeal

⅓ cup oats (you can use 1-minute, 5-minute, quick, or regular)
⅔ cup water
½ banana, sliced
dash cinnamon
⅛ teaspoon vanilla extract
milk
1 tablespoon wheat germ

Put the oats in a 1-quart microwave-safe bowl. Stir in the water, banana, cinnamon, and vanilla. Microwave on high for 2 to 3 minutes, or until the concoction starts steaming or bubbling. Take out and stir again. Add milk to taste. Sprinkle with wheat germ for extra vitamins and protein.

Chocolate Banana Pancakes

½ cup white flour
½ cup whole wheat flour
2 teaspoons baking powder
¼ teaspoon cinnamon
pinch salt
½ tablespoon white sugar
½ tablespoon brown sugar (if you're missing either kind of sugar, just use a whole tablespoon of the one you have)
1 egg
1 teaspoon vanilla extract (optional, but great)
1 tablespoon vegetable oil
a bit less than 1 cup milk
½ cup chocolate chips
1 tablespoon butter or margarine
3 bananas, sliced

Mix the dry ingredients in a large bowl. Add the egg, vanilla, oil, and milk. Mix into a smooth batter. Add the chocolate chips and mix again. Melt the butter on a heated griddle. Pour the batter onto the griddle in large spoonfuls. Then quickly place several banana slices on each pancake. When the bubbles that form on the surface of the pancakes pop, flip them over. Cook until the second side is as brown as the first, and remove from griddle.

Any of the following salads can be served as a main course for lunch or as a side dish for dinner.

Tomato and Basil Salad

The combination of these 2 ingredients makes a refreshing salad. When available, use fresh basil and local tomatoes for the best flavor.

2 vine-ripened tomatoes
6 to 8 basil leaves

Reading the Small Print

Getting healthy food isn't always as easy as it might seem, and even though labeling requirements are getting more stringent, most food manufacturers aren't about to do you any favors. So as you're pushing your cart around the grocery store, be sure to read the labels carefully. In particular, watch out for the following:

- **Ingredients** The first ingredient on the list is always the one there's the most of—no matter what you're buying. So, if that healthy ingredient (oat bran!!!) splashed all over the front of the box turns out to be at the bottom of the ingredients list, try something else.
- **Sugar—and all the synonyms** Watch out for fructose, corn syrup, corn sweeteners, sucrose, dextrose, and even honey. They're just fancy ways of saying "sugar."
- **Words like "drink," "flavored," or "cocktail"** Despite the healthy-looking label, most fruit "drinks" or fruit-"flavored" drinks contain less actual juice than you might guess—often as little as 10 percent, with the rest usually water and sugar.
- **Servings** This is one of the most potentially deceptive areas in food labeling. In most cases, the number of calories, grams of fat and protein, and other nutritional information is given *per serving*. That's all very nice, except that manufacturers don't all use the same serving size. For example, I recently saw an 8-ounce package of fairly healthy frozen lasagna. The calories, protein, and fat all seemed okay—until I noticed that the serving size was actually only 6 ounces. This means that since one person would eat the entire 8 ounces, there was really 33 percent more fat and calories than expected.

4 tablespoons balsamic vinegar
4 tablespoons extra virgin olive oil
freshly ground black pepper to taste

Slice tomatoes and arrange on serving plate. Shred basil leaves and sprinkle over tomatoes. Cover with the vinegar and oil. Add freshly ground pepper. Cover and refrigerate for at least 1 hour. Remove from refrigerator a half-hour before serving.

- **Percentage of calories from fat** Most nutritionists agree that pregnant women should limit their percentage of calories from fat to about 30 percent. Manufacturers are now required by law to make this calculation for you, so pay careful attention to the "nutrition facts" you'll find on any packaged food.
- **A word about additives** When it comes to ingredients, my rule of thumb has always been that if you can't pronounce it, don't eat it. In addition, even some easy-to-pronounce items don't belong in your partner's stomach. So while she's pregnant, keep her away from saccharine (a popular sweetener), nitrates and nitrites (preservatives commonly found in lunch meats and bacon), and monosodium glutamate (MSG, a flavor enhancer especially popular in Asian food and, for some odd reason, gefilte fish). All of these may have negative effects on your unborn child.
- **A word about fat substitutes** Olean and olestra are both fat substitutes that supposedly taste just like butter but pass through the body undigested. This means that they won't enter your partner's bloodstream, so—theoretically, at least—they won't affect your baby in any way. But they might affect your partner. As they pass through her system, these products may actually deplete her body of some valuable vitamins—A, D, E, and K—and interfere with her ability to absorb other important nutrients. Since pregnancy is a time to be increasing nutritional intake, not cutting back, your partner should probably eat as little of these fat substitutes as possible. In addition, olean and olestra have been shown to cause diarrhea and other stomach problems in some people, and your partner is already feeling nauseated enough as it is.

Mixed Green Salad with Balsamic Vinaigrette

Combining different types of greens, such as Boston, red leaf, radicchio, arugula, and endive, makes a green salad more interesting. Raw cucumbers, snow peas, French beans, shredded carrots, and cooked beets also add to the flavor, color, and nutrition of a mixed salad. Stay away from croutons, which are high in calories and low in nutrition.

Thoroughly wash and dry greens, place each serving on a plate, and arrange whatever selection of vegetables you like on top. Just before serving, pour about three tablespoons of balsamic vinaigrette dressing (see recipe below) over each salad.

BALSAMIC VINAIGRETTE

2 cloves crushed garlic
⅔ cup balsamic vinegar
1 teaspoon Dijon mustard
½ teaspoon chopped parsley
½ teaspoon chopped chives
½ teaspoon chopped basil
⅓ cup oil
salt and pepper

Mix garlic, vinegar, mustard, and herbs together. Whisk oil into the vinegar mixture. Add salt and pepper to taste.

Cucumber Salad

2 large cucumbers, sliced
1 medium Bermuda onion, diced
1 cup cider vinegar
½ cup nonfat plain yogurt
1 teaspoon fresh dill, chopped

If the cucumbers are not waxy, leave the skin on. Slice the cucumbers thinly (a food processor does the job best). Combine the diced onion with the cucumber slices in a large bowl that can be refrigerated. Pour the vinegar and yogurt over the mixture, cover, and leave in the refrigerator overnight. Serve cold as a side dish, garnished with the dill.

Low-Calorie Pizza

Create your own combination of toppings, including artichokes, olives, and squash, and use an assortment of cheeses, such as blue, cheddar, Swiss, and even low-fat cottage cheese.

4 soft tortillas (found in grocery freezer)
2 fresh plum tomatoes, sliced
3 cloves garlic, minced or crushed
1 cup mushrooms, sliced and sautéed
1 medium onion, chopped and sautéed
6 teaspoons fresh herbs (oregano, thyme, and basil), minced (or 3 teaspoons dried)
½ cup shredded cheese or low-fat cottage cheese

Preheat oven to 350° F. Place tortillas on a lightly greased cookie sheet. Cover with tomatoes, garlic, mushrooms, onions, and herbs. Add cheese. Bake for 20 minutes or until tortilla is crisp. Serve hot.

Low-Calorie Cream of Zucchini Soup

This recipe can be varied by substituting carrots, potatoes, or celery for zucchini.

3 medium-size zucchini, seeded and cut into ¼-inch slices
1 medium white onion, diced
1 small chicken bouillon cube (optional; bouillon cubes usually contain MSG)
1 cup nonfat plain yogurt
1 tablespoon fresh dill
salt and pepper

Put zucchini, onion, and bouillon cube in a saucepan. Add just enough water to cover. Bring to a boil and cook until soft (about 10 minutes). Let cool. Transfer to a blender or food processor, add yogurt and dill, and blend until smooth. Add salt and pepper to taste.

Quick and Easy Vegetarian Spaghetti Sauce

2 large onions, chopped
4 tablespoons olive oil
½ pound mushrooms, thinly sliced
2 16-ounce jars meatless spaghetti sauce
2 14.5-ounce cans stewed tomatoes
1 4-ounce can tomato paste
1 pound tofu, diced into ½-inch cubes
1½ teaspoons dried basil
generous pinch of cayenne pepper
1 bay leaf
salt and pepper to taste
1 teaspoon sugar
½ teaspoon garlic powder
1 tablespoon rice vinegar

In a saucepan, sauté onions in the olive oil over medium heat until they're translucent. Add mushrooms, and sauté for 5 more minutes (until the mushrooms begin to release their liquid). Add all the other ingredients and simmer for 40 minutes. If sauce won't be used immediately, let cool, pour into two-serving containers, and store in freezer. Defrost as needed.

Spa Potato Chips

3 baking potatoes, peeled and thinly sliced
nonstick cooking spray
paprika to taste

Preheat oven to 350° F. Slice potatoes as thinly as possible (a food processor is best). Spray a cookie sheet with nonstick cooking spray. Spread out potatoes evenly in pan. Sprinkle with paprika and bake for about 15 minutes, or until crisp.

Spicy Peanut Butter Pasta

1 pound angel hair pasta
1 tablespoon sesame oil
4 tablespoons peanut or safflower oil
6 cloves garlic, minced
1 generous pinch (⅛ teaspoon) red pepper flakes
10 scallions, thinly sliced
½ cup creamy peanut butter
6 tablespoons rice wine vinegar
6 tablespoons soy sauce
4 teaspoons white sugar
1 cucumber, peeled, seeded, and diced (optional)
cilantro to taste (optional)

Cook pasta according to directions on package. Drain and drizzle with the sesame oil. Set aside. Sauté garlic and pepper flakes in the peanut or safflower oil in a large frying pan. Add scallions. Turn heat to high and stir for one minute. Remove from heat. Add remaining ingredients and use a wire whisk to thoroughly mix into a thick sauce. Pour over pasta while sauce is still warm. Garnish with cucumber and/or cilantro, if desired.

Garlic Roasted Chicken

1 roasting chicken (3 to 4 pounds)
5 garlic cloves
1 carrot, sliced
2 celery stalks, sliced
4 small white onions
2 teaspoons olive oil
½ cup white wine (optional)
¼ cup water

Preheat oven to 450° F. Clean chicken and rinse thoroughly with water. Pat dry. Using fingers, make pockets under skin and stuff with garlic cloves. Place chicken in a deep baking dish. Stuff cavity of chicken with carrot and celery slices and onions. Drizzle olive oil on top of chicken. Pour wine and water over chicken. Bake chicken at 450° F for ten minutes to sear. Then reduce heat to 350° F and cook for 30 to 40 minutes, or until the juices run clear when the thigh is pierced with a fork.

Rack of Lamb

A festive, delicious dish that is easy to prepare.

¼ cup bread crumbs
3 cloves garlic, crushed
2 teaspoons parsley flakes
salt and pepper to taste
1 rack of lamb (ask the butcher to crack the rack, remove excess fat, and French-cut the ribs)
5 teaspoons Dijon mustard

Preheat oven to 450° F. In a small bowl, mix the bread crumbs, garlic, parsley, and salt and pepper. Place rack of lamb in a baking pan, meat side up. Spread mustard on top and bake for 10 minutes. Remove from oven. Using a fork, press the bread-crumb mixture into mustard, reduce heat to 350° F, and cook for about 20 more minutes, or until medium rare.

Fruit Salad with Creamy Yogurt Dressing

A refreshing, low-calorie dish for breakfast, lunch, or dessert. As a side dish or dessert, this recipe serves four. As a main course for lunch, it serves two.

1 green apple, cored and diced
1 banana, sliced
juice of 1 lime
1 small bunch of red or green seedless grapes
5 strawberries, halved
1 seedless navel orange (or other citrus fruit), sectioned
2 kiwis, peeled and sliced
1 cup low-fat vanilla yogurt (or nonfat plain yogurt)
1 teaspoon cinnamon
½ cup shredded coconut (optional)
4 to 8 fresh mint leaves (optional)

In a large mixing bowl combine banana and apple, pour lime juice over them, and mix. Add remaining fruit and mix again. In a separate bowl combine yogurt and cinnamon. Just before serving, mix the yogurt dressing and coconut into the fruit. If fresh mint is available, garnish each serving with one or two leaves.

THE 2ND MONTH

The Doctor Will See You Now

What's Going On with Your Partner

Physically

- Continuing fatigue
- Continuing morning sickness
- Frequent urination
- Tingly fingers
- Breast tenderness and darkening nipples

Emotionally

- Continued elation and at the same time some ambivalence about being pregnant
- Inability to keep her mind on her work
- Fear you won't find her attractive anymore
- Continuing moodiness
- Fear of an early miscarriage

What's Going On with the Baby

During this month, the baby will change from an embryo to a fetus. By the end of the month, he or she (it's way too early to tell which) will have stubby little arms (with wrists but no fingers yet), sealed-shut eyes on the side of the face, ears, and a tiny, beating heart (on the outside of the body). If you bumped into a six-foot-tall version of your baby in a dark alley, you'd run the other way.

What's Going On with You

The Struggle to Connect

Just about every study that's ever been done on the subject has shown that women generally "connect" with their pregnancies sooner than men do. Although they can't feel the baby kicking inside them yet, the physical changes they're experiencing make the pregnancy more "real" for them.

For most men, however, pregnancy at two months is still a pretty abstract concept. For me—as excited as I was—the idea that we were really pregnant was so hard to grasp that I actually forgot about it for several days at a time.

Excitement vs. Fear

But when I remembered we were pregnant, I found myself in the midst of a real conflict—one that would plague me for months. On the one hand, I was still so elated that I could barely contain myself; I had visions of walking with my child on the beach, playing, reading, helping him or her with homework, and I wanted to stop strangers on the street and tell them I was going to be a father. On the other hand, I made a conscious effort to stifle my fantasies and to keep myself from getting attached to the idea of being pregnant. That way, if we had a miscarriage or something else went wrong, I wouldn't be devastated.

Increased or Decreased Sexual Desire

It was during the times when I let myself get excited about becoming a father that I noticed that my wife's and my sex life was changing. Perhaps it was because I was still reveling in the recent confirmation of my masculinity, or perhaps it was because I felt a newer, closer connection to my wife. It may even have been the sense of freedom resulting from not having to worry about birth control. Whatever the reason, sex in the early months of the pregnancy became wilder and more passionate than before.

But not all men experience an increase in sexual desire during pregnancy. Some are turned off by their partner's changing figure; others are afraid of hurting the baby (a nearly impossible task at this stage of the game). Still others may feel that there's no sense in having sex now that they're pregnant. Whatever your feelings—about sex or anything else for that matter—try to talk them over with your partner. Chances are she's experiencing—or soon will be—very similar feelings.

Adoption Validation

If you're adopting, the time between your decision to adopt and the actual arrival of your child could be considered a "psychological pregnancy." Unlike a biological pregnancy, you won't, in most cases, know exactly how long it's going to take from beginning to end. But what's interesting is that most expectant adoptive parents go through an emotional progression similar to that of expectant biological parents, says adoption educator Carol Hallenbeck. The first step is what Hallenbeck calls "adoption validation," which basically means coming to terms with the idea that you're going to become a parent through adoption instead of through "normal" means.

This might seem straightforward, but it's usually not. For many parents, adoption is a second choice, a decision reached only after years of unsuccessfully trying to conceive on their own and after years of disappointments and intrusive, expensive medical procedures, says researcher Rachel Levy-Shiff. Infertility can make you question your self-image, undermine your sense of masculinity (how can I be a man if I can't get my partner pregnant?), may force you to confront your shattered dreams, and can take a terrible toll on your relationship. If you're having trouble coping with accepting the fact that you won't be having biologically related children, I urge you to talk to some other people about what you're feeling. Your partner certainly has a right to know—and she might be feeling a lot of similar things. In addition, the adoption agency you're working with will probably have a list of support resources for adoptive fathers. Give them a try.

Staying Involved

Going to the OB/GYN Appointments

The general rule that women connect with the pregnancy sooner than men has an exception: men who get involved early on and stay involved until the end have been shown to be as connected with the baby as their partners. And a surefire way to get involved is to go to as many of your partner's OB/GYN appointments as possible.

Although I always love being told that I'm healthy as a horse, I've never looked forward to going to the doctor. And going to someone else's doctor is even lower down on the list. But over the course of two pregnancies, I think I missed only two of my wife's medical appointments. Admittedly, some of the time I was bored out of my mind, but overall it was a great opportunity to have my questions answered and to satisfy my curiosity about just what was going on inside my wife's womb.

There's no doubt that you can get at least some basic questions answered by reading a couple of the hundreds of pregnancy and childbirth books written for women. But there are a number of other, more important reasons to go to the appointments:

- You will become more of a participant in the pregnancy and less of a spectator. In other words, it will help make the pregnancy "yours."
- It will demystify the process and make it more tangible. Hearing the baby's heartbeat for the first time (in about the third month), and seeing his or her tiny body squirm on an ultrasound screen (in about the fifth month) bring home the reality of the pregnancy in a way that words on a page just can't do.
- As the pregnancy progresses, your partner is going to be feeling more and more dependent on you, and she'll need more signs that you'll always be there for her. While going to her doctor appointments may not seem quite as romantic as a moonlit cruise or a dozen roses, being there with her is an ideal way to remind her that you love her and reassure her that she's not going to be alone.
- The more you're around, the more seriously the doctor and his or her staff will take you and the more involved they'll let you be (see pages 63–64 for more on this).

If you're planning to go to your partner's checkups, you'd better get your calendar out: most women see their health care provider at least once a month for the first seven months, twice in the eighth month, and once a week thereafter. Of course, taking time off from work for all these appointments may not be realistic. But before you write the whole thing off, check with the doctor—many offer early-morning or evening appointments.

Testing

Besides being a time of great emotional closeness between you and your partner, pregnancy is also a time for your partner to be poked and prodded. Most of the tests she'll have to take, such as the monthly urine tests for blood sugar and the quarterly blood tests for other problems, are purely routine. Others, though, are less routine and sometimes can be scary.

The scariest of all are the ones to detect birth defects. One of the things you can expect your partner's doctor to do is take a detailed medical history—from both of you. These medical histories will help the practitioner determine whether or not you are at risk of having a child with severe—or not so severe—problems (see page 54 for more on this).

If you're in one of the high-risk categories, your doctor may suggest some additional prenatal testing. Keep in mind that, with the exception of ultrasound, blood, and urine tests, each of the other prenatal diagnostics involves some potential risks either to your partner or to the baby. Ask your doctor about them and make sure the benefits of taking the test outweigh the potential risks.

ULTRASOUND (SONOGRAM)

This noninvasive test is painless to the mother, safe for the baby, and can be performed any time after the fifth week of pregnancy. By bouncing sound waves around the uterus and off the fetus, the procedure gives a pretty clear—to an expert anyway—picture of your baby and what he or she is doing. To the rest of us, ultrasound images of babies look remarkably like potatoes with stick arms and legs. In the first trimester, your doctor will probably recommend an ultrasound if your partner has experienced any bleeding, if there's any doubt as to the number of fetuses, or if he or she suspects an ectopic pregnancy (a pregnancy that takes place outside the uterus). In the second trimester, you may have an ultrasound to determine the sex of the baby (this one is optional), to get a more accurate estimate of the due date, or just because you're curious about what the baby looks like. During the last part of the pregnancy—and especially if the baby is overdue—your partner's doctor may order additional ultrasounds to determine the baby's position, to make sure the placenta is still functioning, or to confirm that there's still enough amniotic fluid left to support the baby.

MULTIPLE MARKER TEST

Until recently, pregnant women often had an Alpha-Fetoprotein test (AFP) to screen for potential abdominal wall abnormalities and a variety of neural-tube defects (defects relating to the brain or spinal column), the most common of which are spina bifida and anencephaly (a completely or partially missing brain). The problem was that AFP wasn't particularly accurate. As a result, many practitioners now prescribe the test only as part of the "Multiple Marker" test, which includes two or three other far more accurate screens for many of the same risks. These simple blood tests are conducted when your

Reasons Your Partner (or You) Might Be Considered at High Risk for Having a Baby with Birth Defects

- One of you has a family history of birth defects.
- One of you is a member of a high-risk ethnic group (African Americans, Native Americans, Jews of Eastern European descent, Greeks, Italians, and others (see "Tests *You* May Have to Take" below).
- Your partner is thirty-five or older.
- Your partner had a positive Multiple Marker or AFP test (see pages 53–54).

Other Reasons for Prenatal Testing

Prenatal testing is also available to people who, while not considered at risk, have other reasons for wanting it done. Some of the most common reasons include:

- Peace of mind. Having an amniocentesis or a Chorionic Villi Sampling (CVS) test can remove most doubts about the health of your child. For some people, this reassurance can make the pregnancy a much more enjoyable—and less stressful—experience. If the tests do reveal problems, you and your partner will have more time to prepare yourselves for the tough decisions ahead (for more on this, see pages 60–61).
- To find out the sex of the baby.

partner is 15 to 18 weeks pregnant, and the results are usually available within a week, sometimes even the next day. It's important to remember that a "positive" result on these tests is not necessarily an indication of the presence of an abnormality, just that the baby is at increased risk. Most turn out perfectly fine, but if your partner does get a positive result, she'll be asked to take additional tests, such as an ultrasound and amniocentesis, which should clear up any doubts you have. Since the Multiple Marker test is really designed to let your partner know whether she needs additional testing, she may not want to bother if she's planning to have an amnio or an in-depth ultrasound test.

TESTS *YOU* MAY HAVE TO TAKE

No, you're not pregnant, but there are still a few times when you may need to give a little blood to make sure all is well with your baby. A variety of genetically transmitted birth defects, for example, affect some ethnic groups more than others. So, based on your family histories, your partner's doctor may order one or both of you to get additional blood tests. Among the most common ethnically linked defects are:

- Sickle-cell anemia. If you're African American or if your family came from the Caribbean, Italy, Sardinia, or India, you should be tested whether your practitioner suggests it or not. If your partner knows she's negative, though, ask the doctor whether you should bother.
- Tay-Sachs and Cavanan Disease. If either you or your partner is of Ashkenazi (Eastern European) descent, get tested. Tay-Sachs is also found in some non-Jewish French Canadians. Interestingly, once your partner is pregnant, it is more accurate to test you for these conditions than to test her. If your results come back positive, she'll need to be tested, though.
- Thalasemia. Affects mainly families of Asian, Southeast Asian, African, Middle Eastern, Greek, or Italian origins.

You may also have to be tested if your partner has a negative Rh (for rhesus, like the monkey) factor in her blood. If you're positive (and most of us are) your baby might be positive as well. If this is the case, your partner's immune system might think the Rh-positive baby is some kind of intruder and try to fight it. This can lead to fetal brain damage or even death. Fortunately, this problem is preventable: your partner will have to get some anti-Rh injections, starting around the 28th week of the pregnancy.

AMNIOCENTESIS

This extremely accurate test is usually performed at 15 to 18 weeks, and can identify several hundred genetic disorders, including Down syndrome, anencephaly, and spina bifida. It can't, however, detect deformities such as cleft palate. (Amnio is also sometimes used in the third trimester of pregnancy to help doctors determine whether the fetus's lungs are mature enough to survive an emergency premature delivery, if they're worried about that.) It involves inserting a needle through the abdominal wall into the amniotic sac, where a small amount of fluid is collected and analyzed. Results are usually available in one to three weeks. Unless your partner is considered at high risk (see page 54), or either of you needs to be reassured that your baby is healthy, there's no real reason to have this test. The chances that a twenty-five-year-old woman will give birth to a baby with a defect that an amnio can detect are about 1 in 500. The chances that the procedure will cause a miscarriage, however, are 1 in 200. For a woman over thirty-five, though, amnio begins to make statistical sense: the chances she'll have a baby with abnormalities are roughly 1 in 190 and rise steadily as she ages. At 45, for example, they're about 1 in 20.

CHORIONIC VILLI SAMPLING (CVS)

Generally this test is performed at 9 to 11 weeks to detect chromosomal abnormalities and genetically inherited diseases. The test can be done by inserting a needle through the abdominal wall or by threading a catheter through the vagina and cervix into the uterus. Either way, small pieces of the chorion—a membrane with the genetic makeup identical to that of the fetus—are snipped off or suctioned into a syringe and analyzed. The risks are higher than with an amnio, though, and the two tests can identify pretty much the same potential abnormalities. The main advantage to CVS is that it can be done a lot earlier in the pregnancy, giving you and your partner more time to consider the alternatives.

PERCUTANEOUS UMBILICAL BLOOD SAMPLING (PUBS)

This test is usually conducted at 17 to 36 weeks and is sometimes ordered to confirm possible genetic and blood disorders detected through amnio or CVS. The procedure is virtually the same as an amnio, except that the needle is inserted into a blood vessel in the umbilical cord; some practitioners believe this makes the test more accurate. Later in the pregnancy, PUBS may be used to determine whether the fetus has chicken pox, *Toxoplasma gondii* (see page 36), or other dangerous parasites. Preliminary results are available within about three days. In addition to the risk of complications or miscarriage resulting from the procedure, PUBS may also slightly increase the likelihood of premature labor or clotting of the umbilical cord, and since it can't be performed any earlier than 17 weeks, it's not nearly as popular as amnio or CVS.

Dealing with the Unexpected

For me, pregnancy was like an emotional roller-coaster ride. One minute I'd find myself wildly excited and dreaming about the new baby, and the next I was filled with feelings of impending doom. I knew I wanted our babies, but I also knew that if I got too emotionally attached and anything unexpected happened—like an ectopic pregnancy, a miscarriage, or a birth defect—I'd be crushed. So, instead of allowing myself to enjoy the pregnancy fully, I ended up spending a lot of time torturing myself by reading and worrying about the bad things that could happen.

ECTOPIC PREGNANCY

About 1 percent of all embryos don't embed in the uterus but begin to grow in the fallopian tube, which is unable to expand sufficiently to accommodate the growing fetus. If undiagnosed, an ectopic pregnancy would eventually cause the fallopian tube to burst, resulting in severe bleeding. Fortunately, the vast majority of ectopic pregnancies are caught and removed by the eighth week of pregnancy—long before they become dangerous.

PREECLAMPSIA

This is one of the most common pregnancy complications—about 10 percent of pregnant women, most between eighteen and thirty, suffer from it. Basically, it's an increase in the mother's blood pressure late in the pregnancy. This can deprive the fetus of blood and other nutrients and put the mother at risk of a stroke or seizure. Women who have a history of high blood pressure or blood vessel abnormalities are especially prone, but most of the time it comes as an unpleasant surprise to everyone. In its early stages there usually aren't any symptoms, but it can be detected by a routine blood pressure check. If the condition worsens, the woman may develop headaches, water retention, vomiting, pain in the abdomen, and blurred vision. Interestingly, researchers now suspect that preeclampsia is actually a disorder in which the mother's immune system rejects some of the father's genes that are in the fetus's cells. They suspect that women may be able to "immunize" themselves *before* getting pregnant if they build up a tolerance by exposing themselves to their partner's semen as often as possible. This explains why preeclampsia is far more common during first pregnancies or at least the first pregnancy with a new partner. It also explains why fewer women over thirty develop this condition. A forty-year-old first-time mom is actually at greater risk than a thirty-year-old.

MISCARRIAGES

The sad fact—especially for pessimists like me—is that miscarriages happen fairly frequently. Some experts estimate that as many as one pregnancy out of five ends in miscarriage. In fact, almost every sexually active woman will have one at some point in her life. (In most cases the miscarriage occurs before the woman ever knows she's pregnant—whatever there was of the tiny embryo is swept away with her regular menstrual flow.)

Before you start to panic, there are a few things to remember: first, over 90 percent of couples who experience a single miscarriage get pregnant and have a healthy baby later. Second, many people believe that miscarriages—most of which happen within the first three months of the pregnancy—are "a blessing

If You're Expecting Twins

If your partner was carrying twins (or more), miscarrying one "does not seem to have negative implications regarding the health or genetic integrity of the surviving fetus," say doctors Connie Agnew and Alan Klein. Miscarrying a twin may, however, put your partner at a slightly higher risk of going into preterm labor.

in disguise." The authors of *What to Expect When You're Expecting* sum up this feeling quite well: "Early miscarriage is generally a natural selection process in which a defective embryo or fetus (defective because of environmental factors, such as radiation or drugs; because of poor implantation in the uterus; because of genetic abnormality, maternal infection, random accident, or unknown reasons) is discarded before it has a chance to develop." Still, if you and your partner have a miscarriage, you probably won't find any of this particularly reassuring.

Until very recently, miscarriage, like the pregnancy it ends, has been considered the exclusive emotional domain of women. Truth is that it isn't. While men don't have to endure the physical pain or discomfort of a miscarriage, their emotional pain can be just as severe as their partner's. They still have the same hopes and dreams about their unborn children, and they still feel a profound sense of grief when those hopes and dreams are dashed. And many men, just like their partners, feel tremendous guilt and inadequacy when a pregnancy ends prematurely.

Some good friends of mine, Philip and Elaine, had a miscarriage several years ago, after about twelve weeks of pregnancy. For both of them, the experience was devastating, and for months after the miscarriage they were besieged by sympathetic friends and relatives, many of whom had found out about the pregnancy only after it had so abruptly ended. They asked how Elaine was feeling, offered to visit her, expressed their sympathy, and often shared their own miscarriage stories. But no one—not even his wife—ever asked Philip what he was feeling, expressed any sympathy for what he was going through, or offered him a shoulder to cry on.

Psychologists and sociologists have conducted many studies on how people grieve at the loss of a fetus. But the vast majority of these studies have dealt only with women's reactions. The ones that have included fathers' feelings generally conclude that men and women grieve in different ways. Dr. Kristen Goldbach found that "women are more likely to express their grief openly,

Pregnancy after a Miscarriage

Getting pregnant after having lost a baby can bring up a jumble of feelings for both you and your partner. For example, you'll probably be feeling incredibly happy that you're expecting again. But you may also be worried that this pregnancy will end just as the last one did. That could keep you from allowing yourself to become truly engaged in and enjoy the pregnancy—at least until after you're past the point when the miscarriage happened last time. If your partner is feeling this, she may deliberately keep herself from bonding with the baby, trying to save herself the grief if the worst happens again. If it's been a while since the miscarriage, you might be angry—in an abstract sort of way—that you're still expecting, when by all rights you should be holding a baby in your arms right now. But if your partner got pregnant right away, you might be feeling guilty at not having let an appropriate (whatever that means) amount of time pass.

Everyone deals with post-miscarriage pregnancy differently, but there are a few things that may make it a little easier:

- Try not to worry. It may have happened before, but chances are it won't happen again. Only one in about 200 women are what are called "recurrent miscarriers," meaning that they have had three miscarriages and have never delivered a child.
- Don't pay attention to other people's horror stories (you'd be amazed at how insensitive some people can be).
- Don't tell anyone about the pregnancy until you're absolutely ready to and then tell only people you'd want to support you if something bad were to happen (see page 71 for more on this).
- Get some more ultrasounds or listen to the heartbeat—this might help to reassure you that all is well.
- Get some support. If your partner can help you, great, but she may be preoccupied with her own thoughts. Otherwise, find someone else who's been there and tell him or her how you're feeling.
- Support your partner. Encourage her to talk about what she's feeling and don't make any judgments about what she says. And try to keep her calm. As the pregnancy progresses, for example, and she can feel the baby's movements, she may become fixated on counting them—worried that there are either too many or too few. Just so you know, anywhere from 50 to 1,000 a day is normal.

while men tend to be much less expressive, frequently coping with their grief in a more stoical manner." This doesn't mean that men don't express their grief at all. Instead, it simply highlights the fact that in our society men, like my friend Philip, have virtually no opportunity to express their feelings.

BIRTH DEFECTS

If one of the tests discussed earlier in this chapter indicates that your baby will be born deformed or with any kind of serious disorder, you and your partner have some serious discussions ahead of you. There are two basic options for dealing with birth defects in an unborn child: keep the baby or terminate the pregnancy. Fortunately, you and your partner won't have to make this decision on your own; every hospital that administers diagnostic tests has specially trained genetic counselors who will help you sort through the options.

If you're considering terminating the pregnancy for genetic reasons, remember that communicating clearly and effectively with your partner is probably the most important thing you can do during this stressful time. The decision you make should not be taken lightly—it's a choice that will last a lifetime—and you and your partner must fully agree before proceeding with either option.

If your partner is carrying three or more fetuses, you may have to deal with the question of "selective reduction." Basically, the more fetuses in the uterus, the greater the risk of premature birth, low birth weight, and other potential health hazards. Simply—and gruesomely—put, all these risks can be reduced by reducing the number of fetuses. It's an agonizing decision that only you and your partner can make.

COPING WITH YOUR GRIEF

If you and your partner chose to terminate your pregnancy or reduce the number of fetuses, or if the pregnancy ended in miscarriage, the emotional toll can be devastating. That's why it's critical for the two of you to seek out the emotional support you are entitled to as soon as possible. While there's nothing that can be done to prepare for or prevent a miscarriage, telling your partner how you feel—either alone or with a member of the clergy, a therapist, or a close friend—is very important. And don't just sit back and wait for her to tell you what *she's* feeling. Take the initiative: be supportive and ask a lot of questions.

You and your partner do not have to handle your grief by yourselves: counseling and support are available to both women *and* men who have lost a fetus through miscarriage, genetic termination, or selective reduction. Going to a support group can be a particularly important experience for men—especially those who aren't getting the support they need from their friends and families. Many men who attend support groups report that until they joined the group, no one had ever asked how they felt about their loss. The group setting can also give men the chance to stop being strong for their partners for a few minutes and grieve for themselves. If you'd like to find a support group, your doctor or the genetic counselors can refer you to the closest one—or the one that might be most sympathetic to men's concerns.

Some men, however, are not at all interested in getting together with a large group of people who have little in common but tragedy. If you feel this way, be sure to explain your feelings tactfully to your partner—she may feel quite strongly that you should be there with her and might feel rejected if you aren't. If you ultimately decide not to join a support group, don't try to handle things alone—talk to your partner, your doctor, your cleric, or a sympathetic friend. Keeping your grief bottled up will only hinder the healing process.

Notes:

THE 3RD MONTH

Spreading the Word

What's Going On with Your Partner

Physically

- Fatigue, morning sickness, breast tenderness, and other early pregnancy symptoms beginning to disappear
- Continuing moodiness
- Thickening waistline

Emotionally

- Heightened sense of reality about the pregnancy from hearing the baby's heartbeat
- Continuing ambivalence about the pregnancy
- Frustration and/or excitement over thickening of waistline
- Turning inward—beginning to focus on what's happening inside her
- Beginning to bond with the baby

What's Going On with the Baby

By now, the little fetus looks pretty much like a real person—except that he or she (even a really sharp ultrasound technician would be hard pressed to tell you which) is only about two or three inches long, weighs less than an ounce, and has translucent skin. Teeth, fingernails, toenails, and hair are developing nicely, and the brain is not far behind. By the end of this month, the baby will be able to curl its toes, turn its head, and even frown.

What's Going On with You

A Heightened Sense of Reality

During the third month, the pregnancy begins to feel a little more tangible. By far the biggest reality booster for me was hearing the baby's heartbeat, even though it didn't sound anything like a real heart at all (more like a fast hoosh-hoosh-hoosh). Somehow, having the doctor tell us that what we were hearing was really a heartbeat—and a healthy one at that—was mighty reassuring.

Feeling Left Out

While becoming more aware of the reality of the pregnancy is certainly a good thing, it's not the only thing that you'll be feeling at around this point. Toward the end of this first trimester, your partner will probably begin to spend a lot of time concentrating on what's happening inside her body, wondering whether she'll be a good enough mother, and establishing a bond with the baby. She may be worried about the baby's health or concerned that every little ache and pain she feels is a sign of some horrible disease. She's probably internalizing her feelings about all this and may become a little self-absorbed. And if she has a close relationship with her mother, the two of them may develop a deeper bond as your partner tries to find good role models.

Everything she's going through at this point is completely normal. The danger, however, is that while your partner is turning inward or bonding with her own mother and the baby, you may end up feeling left out, rejected, or even pushed out of the way. This can be particularly painful. But no matter how much it hurts, you should resist the urge to "retaliate" by withdrawing from her. Be as comforting as you can be, and let her know—in a nonconfrontational way—how you're feeling (see the "Your Relationship" section, pages 74–77). Fortunately, this period of turning inward won't last forever.

Excluded—or Welcomed—by Your Partner's Doctors

For some men—especially those who are feeling emotionally left out by their partners—the joy they experience at the increasing reality of the pregnancy can be outweighed by the bitterness they feel at the way they're treated by their partner's doctors. Pamela Jordan, a nurse and a pregnancy expert, found that most men feel that their presence at prenatal visits is perceived as "cute" or "novel." Many men complain that medical professionals have a tendency to treat them as mere onlookers or intruders and consider their partners the only ones worth interacting with. If they were talked to at all, it was only to discuss how to support their partners. The fact that they had very specific and important needs and concerns didn't seem to occur to anyone.

Fortunately, this was not my experience at all. During both pregnancies, my wife's OBs went out of their way to include me in the process. They made a special point of looking at me when talking about what was happening with my wife and the baby, encouraged me to ask questions, and answered them thoroughly. Part of the reason for this was that from the very beginning I made it clear that I wanted to be involved and I asked a lot of questions, so it was almost impossible for them to ignore me. I'd suggest that you do the same, especially if you have even the slightest suspicion that your partner's practitioner is ignoring you or not taking you seriously.

Our first OB even invited me to take a look at my wife's cervix. I was a little put off by the idea, but getting to see the cervix—through which our baby would emerge just six months later—somehow made the pregnancy seem less mysterious and made me feel much more a part of the whole thing. If your OB doesn't offer you a look, ask for one—I highly recommend it. But be sure to ask your partner first. She might feel that it's a bit intrusive—especially since it's a part of her body that she may never see.

Physical Symptoms: Couvade

Although most of what you'll be going through during your pregnancy will be psychological, don't be surprised if you start developing some physical symptoms as well. Various studies estimate that as many as 90 percent of expectant American fathers experience couvade syndrome (from the French word meaning "to hatch"), or "sympathetic pregnancy." Couvade symptoms are typically the same as those traditionally associated with pregnant women—weight gain, nausea, mood swings, food cravings—as well as some not associated with pregnant women: headaches, toothaches, itching, even cysts. Symptoms—if you're going to have them at all—usually appear in about the third month of pregnancy, decrease for a few months, then pick up again in the month or two before the baby is born. In almost every case, though, the symptoms "mysteriously" disappear at the birth.

Considering that our society generally denies the importance (if not the very existence) of what expectant fathers go through during pregnancy, it's not surprising that some men express their concerns and feelings by developing physical symptoms. Among the most common reasons an expectant father might develop couvade symptoms are:

SYMPATHY OR FEELINGS OF GUILT FOR WHAT THE WOMAN IS GOING THROUGH

Men have traditionally been socialized to bite the bullet when it comes to pain and discomfort. And when our loved ones are suffering and we can't do anything to stop it, our natural (and slightly irrational) instinct is to try to take their pain away—to make it ours instead of theirs. This is especially true if we have even the slightest feeling—no matter how irrational—that we're responsible for the pain in the first place. If your partner has been suffering from morning sickness or has had any other pregnancy-related difficulties, you may feel that it's your fault. And if her symptoms have been particularly rough, she might even reinforce your subconscious guilt by reminding you that you're the one who "got her into all this" in the first place.

JEALOUSY

There's no question that your partner is going to be getting a lot more attention during the pregnancy than you are. And a lot of men who develop couvade symptoms do so in a subconscious attempt to shift the focus of the pregnancy to themselves. My father, who was pacing the waiting room while my mother was in labor with me, suddenly got a gushing nosebleed. Within seconds the delivery room was empty—except for my mother—as three nurses and two doctors raced out to take care of my poor, bleeding father. I'm sure he didn't do it on purpose, but for one brief moment during the delivery, Dad was the complete center of attention. The same, of course, holds true during the pregnancy. Similarly, physical symptoms could be a kind of public way of asserting paternity.

YOUR HORMONES COULD BE RAGING

No, I haven't got that backward. While she's pregnant, several of your partner's hormone levels gradually rise. These include prolactin, which helps get her breasts ready to lactate (produce milk), and cortisol, which appears to be associated with parent-child bonding. It used to be that everyone thought these hormone changes were triggered by the developing fetus. But in a fascinating study, researcher Anne Storey and her colleagues found something that may change some minds. Storey took blood samples from expectant mothers and fathers at various points during the pregnancy and found that expectant dads' levels of cortisol and prolactin (which you wouldn't think guys would even have) paralleled their partners'. "The differences for mums were much more drastic, but the patterns were similar," said Dr. Storey, who's Canadian—hence the cute "mums." Some guys seem to be more susceptible to this kind

"Just as your wife suspected, Mr. Sanders. You have a very little boy growing inside you."

of thing than others. In talking with the men in her study, Storey found that those who had experienced tiredness, weight gain, changes in appetite, or any other physical couvade symptoms had higher-than-average levels of prolactin and lower-than-average levels of testosterone compared to expectant dads who didn't have these symptoms. Fortunately, this doesn't mean that you'll be developing breasts anytime soon. Like your partner's, your hormone levels will return to normal not long after your baby is born, and your manliness will remain intact.

These hormone changes could also contribute to an extremely common, nonphysical type of couvade symptom. Most expectant dads find themselves somewhat more interested in children than before the pregnancy. Is it simply curiosity, or is it the body's way of preparing the expectant dad for his changing responsibilities? Hard to say. But studies have shown that the stronger an expectant dad's couvade symptoms, the better he'll care for his newborn. If any of this is hitting home, though, you may want to think twice before you let your partner read this page—especially if you've been making fun of her out-of-control hormones.

YOU MAY BE SENDING MESSAGES TO YOUR PARTNER

Generally speaking, women are more vulnerable during pregnancy and parenthood than men; *you* can always take off, she can't. (At the risk of sounding politically incorrect, a number of researchers have speculated that this is precisely why women have traditionally looked for men who will be "good providers.") As a result, expectant mothers are often particularly concerned about whether their partners are going to be there for them and whether they're really committed to being fathers. On one level, you can reassure your partner by telling her you love her, by going to all the prenatal doctor appointments, and by educating yourself and staying as involved as you possibly can.

Some evolutionary psychologists have speculated recently that on a far more subconscious level, expectant dads' physical couvade symptoms could be a chemically driven way of showing their partners just how committed they truly are. After all, you could be lying when you tell her you love her and that you're excited about being a dad. But it's a lot harder to fake a nosebleed or a backache or a weight gain. In short, your physical symptoms may be nature's way of giving your partner a means of evaluating your true feelings about her and the baby, as well as your reliability as a partner and fellow parent.

A LITTLE HISTORY

Most researchers today agree that in Western societies couvade symptoms appear unconsciously in those expectant fathers who experience them. But as far back as 60 B.C.E. (and continuing today in many non-Western societies), couvade has been used deliberately in rituals designed to keep fathers involved in the experience of pregnancy and childbirth. Not all of these rituals, however, have been particularly friendly to women. W. R. Dawson writes that in the first century A.D. mothers were routinely ignored during childbirth, while their husbands were waited on in bed. And more recently, in Spain and elsewhere, mothers frequently gave birth in the fields where they worked. They then returned home to care for the baby's father.

But in some other cultures, men tried to do the same thing they try to do today: take their partner's pain away by attracting it to themselves. In France and Germany, for example, pregnant women were given their husband's clothes during labor in the belief that doing so would transfer the wives' pains to their husbands. The eighteenth-century Scots believed that a nurse could use witchcraft to transfer the pain of childbirth from the wife to the husband.

Perhaps the most interesting aspect of ritual couvade is the importance attached to the supernatural bond between the father and the unborn child. Whatever the fathers did during the pregnancy was believed to have a direct impact on the unborn child. In Borneo expectant fathers ate nothing but rice and salt—a diet said to keep a new baby's stomach from swelling. In other countries a man who hammered a nail while his wife was pregnant was thought to be dooming her to a long, painful labor, and if he split wood, he would surely have a child with a cleft lip. Afraid of making his own child blind, an expectant father wouldn't eat meat from an animal who gave birth to blind young. He also avoided turtles—to make sure that his child would not be born deaf and anencephalic (with a cone-shaped head).

While it's pretty doubtful that couvade rituals actually reduced any woman's childbirth pains or prevented any deformities, they do illustrate an important point: men have been trying to get—and stay—involved in pregnancy and childbirth for thousands of years. As Bronislav Malinowski noted in his 1927 book, *Sex and Repression in Savage Society:*

> Even the apparently absurd idea of couvade presents to us a deep meaning and a necessary function. It is of high biological value for the human family to consist of both father and mother; if the traditional customs and rules are there to establish a social situation of close moral proximity between father and child, if all such customs aim at drawing a man's attention to his offspring, then the couvade which makes man simulate the birth-pangs and illness of maternity is of great value and provides the necessary stimulus and expression for paternal tendencies. The couvade and all the customs of its type serve to accentuate the principle of legitimacy, the child's need of a father.

Couvade for Adoptive Dads Too? Yep.

Given that couvade symptoms seem to be an expression of fathers' desires to get some confirmation of their special status in their children's lives, it shouldn't come as much of a surprise that adoptive fathers often experience them as well. In fact, according to adoption educator Patricia Irwin Johnson, "sympathetic symptoms of pregnancy" are fairly common. "One or both partners may experience repeated, and even predictably scheduled, episodes of nausea," says Johnson. "Food cravings and significant weight gain are not unusual. One or both may complain of sleep disturbances or emotional peaks and valleys."

Staying Involved

Spilling the Beans

Another thing (this month anyway) that will make the pregnancy seem more real is telling other people about it. By the end of the third month, I'd pretty well gotten over my fears of miscarriage or other pregnancy disaster, and we'd decided it was safe to spill the beans to our family and close friends. Somehow just saying the words "My wife's pregnant" (I switched to "We're pregnant" a while later) helped me realize it was true.

The decision about when to let other people in on your pregnancy is a big one. Some people are superstitious and opt to put off making the announcement for as long as possible. Others rush to the phone or start shooting off e-mails as soon as they get out of bed. Even if you're in the first category, sooner or later you're going to have to start spreading the word—and the end of the third month is a pretty good time.

Whom you decide to tell, and in what order, is your own business. But there are a few guidelines you might want to keep in mind.

FAMILY

Unless you have some compelling reason not to, you should probably tell your family first. Your close friends will forgive you if they hear about the pregnancy from your Aunt Ida; if it happens the other way around, Aunt Ida may take real offense. There are a few cases, however, when telling your family first might not be a great idea. One couple we know, Lawrence and Beth, kept their pregnancy a secret from their friends for five months—and from their family for longer—hoping that Lawrence's brother and sister-in-law, who had been trying to get pregnant for years, would succeed in the interim.

FRIENDS

If you do decide to tell your friends first, make sure you swear them to secrecy—good news travels a lot faster than you might think. As in the case of relatives, be considerate of friends who have been trying but who haven't been as successful as you.

THE OFFICE

You'll probably want to tell your coworkers and your boss (if you have one) at about the same time as you tell your friends. But remember that society has some pretty rigid work/family rules for men, so be prepared for a less-than-enthusiastic response from some people (see the "Work and Family" section,

pages 112–21, for a complete discussion). Whatever you do, though, don't wait until the last minute to tell the folks at work—especially if you're planning to take some time off or make any work schedule changes after the birth.

YOUR OTHER CHILDREN

If you have other children, give them plenty of time to adjust to the news. But do not tell them until after you want everyone else to know. Until they're over six, kids don't understand the concept of "keeping a secret." When she was four, one of our older daughter's big thrills in life was to gleefully whisper in people's ears things that were supposed to be secrets.

Make a special effort to include your other children as much as possible in the pregnancy experience. Our older daughter came with us to most of the doctor appointments and got to hold the Doppler (the thing you hear the fetus's heartbeats through) and help the doctor measure my wife's growing belly. Finally, keep in mind that it's perfectly normal for expectant siblings to insist that they, too, are pregnant—just like Mommy. Insisting that they're not may make them feel excluded and resentful of the new baby. This is especially true for little boys.

A FEW SPECIAL CIRCUMSTANCES

If your partner had a miscarriage and you're expecting again, the "rules" (to the extent that there are any) for telling family and friends change somewhat. You might want to tell selected people immediately—you may be craving your family's or friends' support, or you may just need someone to be happy for you. Most people, though, want to put it off as long as possible (although in another month or so it'll be pretty obvious). Here are some common reasons why:

- You may be worried that there could be another miscarriage and don't want to put yourself through the pain of calling everyone to give them bad news. This is especially true if your partner has had more than one.
- If your partner got pregnant right after a miscarriage, you may worry that other people will think you're being disrespectful by not waiting longer to grieve.
- You may want to wait until you're over the hump—past the point when the miscarriage happened last time. If you have other kids who know about the previous miscarriage, it's a good idea to wait until the pregnancy is pretty far along. They may worry about your partner or the new baby, and they might even be afraid that something they did caused the first miscarriage. If you have even the slightest inkling that this is the case, spend some time gently explaining to your other children that they are not responsible at all, that sometimes things happen that we just can't explain.

Telling friends and family that you've decided to adopt can also be surprisingly tricky. First of all, you or your partner might be ashamed at what you might consider the "inadequacy" of not being able to get pregnant. Second, although you'd think that everyone would be overjoyed at your decision to adopt, that's not always the case. Some people—especially family—might not be too happy that you're bringing an "outsider" into your family. You have every right to expect your family to respect your decision and treat you and your partner with respect. At the same time, as Patricia Irwin Johnson points out, your family has the right to expect certain things from you:

- **Information** They can't be sensitive about something they don't understand. You might want to recommend some books on adoption, such as Patricia Irwin Johnson's *Launching a Baby's Adoption* (see Selected Bibliography).

Trying to Keep the Secret

Despite your attempts to control the flow of information, if you're not careful about what you do, people—especially your close friends—are going to guess. If you're serious about not wanting anyone to know, here are a couple of things to keep in mind:

- Stay away from expressions like "in her condition" or "I think she really needs to rest." That's exactly how I inadvertently leaked the news to a friend who had asked how we liked working out on the Stairmaster machine at the gym.
- Be unobtrusive if you change your habits. If your partner used to drink or smoke before she got pregnant, you might want to think a little about how your friends and family will react to her new, vice-free lifestyle. When my wife was pregnant with our second daughter, we agreed to meet some good friends at a bar one Saturday night. No one really noticed that my wife was drinking mineral water instead of her usual beer. But when she ordered an ice cold glass of milk, the jig was up.

- **Sensitivity** You must acknowledge that your decision to adopt might cause some people some pain. Your parents, for example, might be disappointed that they're not going to become grandparents the "right" way or that a genetic family link has been broken. Like you, they may need some time to mourn the loss of their hopes and dreams.
- **Patience** Even if they do have information and a good understanding of adoption, they're still lagging behind you and your partner in terms of knowledge. So give them some time to catch up and don't expect instant support and understanding. If someone makes a dumb or insensitive remark about adoption, resist the urge to bite her head off. Instead, take her aside and point out the mistake as nicely as you can.

No matter how or when you do it, telling people you're expecting will open a floodgate of congratulations and advice; after a few weeks, you may wonder what anyone used to talk about at parties before. Just about everyone has something to say about what you should and shouldn't do now that you're pregnant. You'll hear delightful stories, horror stories, and just plain boring stories about pregnancy and childbirth. You'll probably also have to endure endless "jokes" about your masculinity, speculation about who the "real" father is, and questions about what the mailman or the milkman looks like—mostly, unfortunately, from other men.

What If You're Not Married?

Even in the twenty-first century, when it's the norm for couples to live together before getting married, having a child out of wedlock still raises a lot of eyebrows in some circles. Your most liberal-minded friends and relatives might surprise you by suggesting that you "make an honest woman of her" before the baby comes. Try to keep your sense of humor about these things. You and your partner are grown-ups and capable of making the decisions you think best. And anyway, most unmarried parents-to-be find that their relatives' joy at the prospect of a new little niece, nephew, or grandchild frequently overshadows those same relatives' disappointment over your lack of a marriage certificate.

With attitudes like these, is it any wonder that 60 percent of men have at least fleeting doubts as to the true paternity of their children?

Immediately after breaking the news to our friends and family, my wife and I began to feel some slight changes in our relationship with them. What had once been our private secret was now public knowledge, and just about everyone wanted to share it with us. People would "drop in" unannounced, usually bearing either gifts or advice—just to "see how things were going"—and the phone never stopped ringing.

After a few days, you and your partner may start to feel a little claustrophobic. If this happens, don't hesitate to establish some ground rules. For example, you might want to ask your friends and families to call before coming over, or you might set up—and let everyone know about—specific visiting hours. You should also prepare yourself for the possibility that you may feel a little left out. Most people are going to be asking how your partner is feeling, what she's going through, and so on. Few, if any, will ask the same questions of you. If you start feeling that you're being treated more like a spectator than a participant in the pregnancy, there are three basic solutions. First, you can just ignore the whole thing—no one's deliberately trying to exclude you; it just doesn't occur to most people that pregnancy, at least at this stage, affects men all that much. Second, you can sulk. This (although sometimes satisfying) will probably not get you the kind of attention you're craving. Third, you can take a proactive role and volunteer information about how the pregnancy is affecting you. Tell people about how excited you are; confide your hopes and fears to your friends—especially those who already have kids and can offer advice. If you're lucky, they'll then start asking you for updates.

"You're entirely too touchy. My saving grace is my ability to laugh at myself."

Your Relationship

WITH EACH OTHER

Pregnancy is not only a time of great joy and anticipation, it's also a time of great stress. And even though you and your partner are both pregnant at the same time, you're not experiencing the pregnancy in exactly the same way or at the same pace. This can lead to an increasing number of misunderstandings and conflicts.

As Dr. Shapiro writes, when a couple becomes a family, "generally all the things that are good get better, and all the things that are bad get worse." As your pregnancy continues, then, it's critical to learn to talk—and listen—to each other, and to find ways to help each other through this marvelous, but emotionally bumpy, experience.

As men, we've been conditioned to try to protect our partners from harm. And when our partners are pregnant, protecting them may include trying to minimize the levels of stress in their lives. One way men do this is by not talking about their own concerns. Researchers Carolyn and Philip Cowan write that men fear that mentioning their own worries may not only cause stress to their partners but also expose their own vulnerability at a time when they're expected to be strong for their wives.

The Cowans also found that this overprotective, macho attitude has some very negative side effects. First, because we never give ourselves the chance to talk about our fears, we never learn that what we're going through is normal and healthy. Second, our partners never get the chance to find out that we understand and share their feelings.

There's also some evidence that there are other benefits to talking about how you're feeling—and getting your partner's support for those feelings. Researcher Geraldine Deimer found that men who receive their partners' emotional support during pregnancy have better physical and emotional health and are better able to maintain good relationships with their spouses than men who don't get that kind of support.

DANGEROUS ASSUMPTIONS

When I was in the Marines, one of my drill instructor's favorite comments was "Never assume anything. 'Assuming' makes an ass out of u and me." The sergeant's spelling problems notwithstanding (he also thought habitual thieves were called hypochondriacs and that Italians ate bisgetti), he was right about the dangers of making assumptions.

Here are a few important things you may have assumed were no problem. Not all these issues are important to everybody, but if you haven't discussed them already, do it now.

- **Your involvement in the pregnancy** Dr. Katharyn Antle May has found that there are three basic styles of father involvement during pregnancy. The Observer Father maintains a certain emotional distance and sees himself largely as a bystander; the Expressive Father is emotionally very involved and sees himself as a full partner; the Instrumental Father sees himself as the manager of the pregnancy and may feel a need to plan every medical appointment, every meal, and every trip to the gym. Whatever your style is, make sure to talk it over with your partner. After all, she's pregnant, too.
- **Your involvement in family tasks** How much child care are you planning to do when the baby comes? How much is your partner expecting you to do? How much are you expecting her to do? Several studies have shown that to a great extent, women control their partners' involvement at home. If a woman wants her partner to take an active role in child care, he generally wants the same thing. But if she wants to keep these activities to herself, he usually expects to be less involved. In addition, the Cowans have found that men who take a more active role in running their households and rearing their children "tend to feel better about themselves and about their family relationships than men who are less involved in family work."

"Me carrying the baby and you having the cravings is not *my idea of shared responsibility!"*

- **Religion** Both you and your partner may never have given a thought to the religious education—if any—you plan to give your child. If you have thought about it, make sure you're both still thinking along the same lines. If you haven't, this might be a good time to start.
- **Discipline styles** How do you feel about spanking your children? Never? Sometimes? How does she feel about it? How you were raised and whether your parents spanked you will have a great deal to do with how you raise your own children.
- **Sleeping arrangements** It's never too early to give some thought to where you want the baby to sleep: In your bed? In a bassinet next to you? In a separate room?
- **Work and child-care expectations** Is your partner planning to take some time off after the birth before going back to work? How long? Would you like to be able to take some more time off? How long? What types of child-care arrangements do you and she envision?
- **Finances** Do you need two paychecks to pay the mortgage? If you can get by on one, whose will it be?

And throughout the pregnancy, don't forget:

- **Your feelings—good, bad, or indifferent** Talk about your excitement about having a child, your dreams, your plans for the future, your fears, worries, and ambivalence, and how satisfied you are with your level of involvement during the pregnancy. But don't forget to ask your partner what she's feeling about the same things. Have these discussions regularly—what the two of you are thinking and feeling in the third month may be completely different from what you'll be thinking and feeling in the fourth, sixth, or ninth months. As difficult as it may seem, learning to communicate with each other now will help you for years to come.

Getting Time Alone

There may be times when you find the pressures of the pregnancy so overwhelming that you need just to get away from it for a while. If so, take advantage of the fact that you don't have a baby inside you, and take some time off. Go someplace quiet where you can collect your thoughts or do something that will give you a break from the endless conversations about pregnant women and babies. Before you go, though, be sure to let your partner know where you're headed. And whatever you do, don't rub it in: she'd probably give anything to be able to take a breather from the pregnancy—even for a couple hours.

Here are a few things you might want to do with your free time:

- Hang out with some childless friends.
- See a movie or a play.
- Start a journal about what you're feeling and thinking during the pregnancy.
- Read.
- Go to the batting cages and let off a little steam.
- Go for a long drive or for a walk on the beach or in the woods.
- Be a kid for a while—blow some quarters on a video game.
- Sleep (good luck).

Notes:

THE 4TH MONTH

Money, Money, Money

What's Going On with Your Partner

Physically

- Nipples darkening; freckles and moles might get darker and more obvious (a normal side effect from her increasing skin pigmentation)
- Increasing appetite as morning sickness begins to wane
- Clumsy—dropping and spilling things
- She may be able to feel some slight movements (although she probably won't associate them with the baby unless she's already had a child)
- She may notice some strange changes in her vision; if she wears contacts they may be bothering her
- She may get gingivitis (swollen, bleeding gums)—60 to 75 percent of pregnant women do

Emotionally

- Great excitement when she sees the sonogram
- Worries about miscarriage are beginning to fade
- Concerned about what it really means to be a mother
- Continuing forgetfulness and mood swings
- Increasingly dependent on you—needs to know you'll be there for her, that you still love her
- She may get very depressed when her regular clothes stop fitting her and may become nearly obsessed with her appearance

What's Going On with the Baby

During this month, the baby will grow to about four or five inches long. His heart will finish developing and will start pounding away at 120 to 160 beats per minute—about twice as fast as yours—and his whole body is covered with smooth hair called *lanugo.* The fetus can—and often does—kick, swallow, and suck his thumb. He can also tell when your partner is eating sweet things or sour things and reacts accordingly. He can also react to light and dark—if you shine a strong light on your partner's abdomen, the baby will turn away.

What's Going On with You

Increasing Sense of the Pregnancy's Reality

By the time the fourth month rolls around, most men are still in what Katharyn May calls the "moratorium phase" of pregnancy—intellectually we know she's pregnant, but we still don't have any "real" confirmation. Oh, sure, there was the pregnancy test, the blood test, the doctor's pelvic exams, her swelling belly and breasts, the food cravings, and hearing the baby's heartbeat a month before. Even with all that, I had the lingering suspicion that the whole thing was an elaborate, *Mission: Impossible*–style fake.

But the day my wife and I went in for the ultrasound, everything began to change. Somehow, seeing the baby's tiny heart pumping and watching those bandy little arms and legs squirm convinced me that we might really be pregnant after all.

If you're expecting twins (or more), you may want to pay extra attention to the ultrasound (and you may want to see if you can schedule a couple more over the next few months), because the way the fetuses behave in utero may give you some insight into what you can expect after they're born. Each twin has its own temperament from the very early stages of development, and each set of twins establishes a characteristic pattern of behavior, according to researcher Alessandra Piontelli. Both the temperament and the way the twins interact continues for at least the first year after birth. Even odder (assuming that's possible), one group of researchers found that with triplets, two of the fetuses tend to interact with each other while ignoring the third. After the birth, that dynamic continued for a year or so, with the third baby isolated by his siblings.

Can We Really Afford This?

Besides being fun, seeing the ultrasound filled me with a wonderful sense of relief. After counting all the fingers and toes (not an easy task, considering how small they were and how fast they were moving), I felt I could finally stop worrying about whether our baby would be all right.

But my newfound sense of ease didn't last long. I suddenly became possessed by the idea that we couldn't possibly afford to have a baby—not an uncommon thought among expectant fathers. Not surprisingly, though, expectant fathers in their early and mid-twenties feel more financial pressures than dads-to-be who are over 32. These "older" fathers tend to be more settled in their careers and have greater income than the young bucks.

American society values men's financial contribution to their families much more than it does their emotional contribution. And expressing strong feelings, anxiety, or even fear is not what men are expected to do—especially when their wives are pregnant. So, as the pregnancy progresses, most expectant fathers fall back on the more traditionally masculine way of expressing their concern for the well-being of their wives and little fetuses: they worry about money.

Some men express their financial worries by becoming obsessed with their jobs, their salaries, the size of their homes, even the rise and fall of interest rates. Expectant fathers frequently work overtime or take on a second job; others may become tempted by lottery tickets or get-rich-quick schemes. Insurance agents and financial advisors sometimes try to take advantage of an expectant father's concerns about money by encouraging him to buy insurance policies he doesn't need or make investments he and his family can't afford. Clearly, a new baby (and the decrease in household income while the mother is off work) can have a significant impact on the family's finances. But as real as they are, write Libby Lee and Arthur D. Colman, authors of *Pregnancy: The Psychological Experience,* men's financial worries "often get out of proportion to the actual needs of the family. They become the focus because they are something the man can be expected to handle. The activity may hide deeper worry about competence and security." In other words, calm down.

Safety—Your Partner's and the Baby's

As if worrying about finances weren't enough, many expectant fathers find themselves preoccupied with the physical health and safety of the other members of their growing family (but not their own—studies have shown that men go to the doctor much less frequently than usual when their partners are pregnant). In some cases, men's health and safety concerns take on a rather bizarre twist. For example, psychiatrist Martin Greenberg found that "more than a few men purchase weapons during a pregnancy." Fortunately, most of them sell their weapons after the baby is born.

I'd seen the ultrasound and knew that the baby was fine. And I'd already read that at this point in the pregnancy, there was very little chance of a miscarriage. But still, I worried. I quizzed my wife about how much protein she was eating; I reminded her to go to the gym for her workouts; I even worried about the position she slept in. All in all, I was a real pain. (I was right about the sleeping position stuff, though: sleeping on the back is a bad idea; the baby-filled uterus presses a major vein—the inferior vena cava—and could cause hemorrhoids or even cut off the flow of oxygen or blood to both your partner and the fetus.)

A word of advice: If you're feeling overly concerned and protective of your partner and your baby, be gentle and try to relax a little. She's probably feeling some of the same things. If you're still worried, though, discuss your concerns with her practitioner at your next appointment. But leave your gun at home.

Ways to Show Her You Care

Here are some ideas that will make you popular around the house (and make your wife the envy of all of her friends—pregnant and otherwise):

- Offer to give her back rubs and foot massages.
- Suggest activities that might be harder to do when the baby comes, like going to movies or concerts.
- Bring home roses for no reason at all.
- Vacuum the house—even under the bed—without being asked.
- Give your wife lots of hugs; research shows that the more she is hugged, the more she'll hug the baby after he comes.
- Buy her a moisturizing bubble bath.
- If you're traveling on business, arrange to have a friend take her to dinner.
- Offer to pick up a pizza on your way home from work—and surprise her with a pint of her favorite frozen yogurt, too.
- Offer to run errands (pick up cleaning, shop, go to the drugstore, and so forth). Better yet, do them before you get asked to.
- Do the laundry before it piles up.
- Tell her you think she's going to be a great mother.
- If she arrives home after you, have a candlelight dinner on the table, complete with sparkling cider.
- Write her a love letter and send it to her in the mail.
- Go away for a romantic weekend (together, of course).
- Buy a toy or outfit for the baby, have it gift-wrapped, and let her unwrap it.
- Buy her a pretty maternity dress.
- Go on a long walk with her.
- Learn baby CPR.
- Offer to give her a back rub—again.
- If you smoke, stop.
- Tell her she's beautiful. Then tell her again a few hours later.
- Pay extra attention to making sure she has enough to eat—pack some snacks for her before the two of you go out for an evening or for a hike.
- Organize a surprise baby shower for her.

- Keep a list of your favorite names or buy her an interesting name book.
- Paint a picture for or write a letter to your unborn baby.
- Set up some interviews with potential child-care people.
- Tell her she looks good even if she's put on weight.
- Buy her a Mother's Day gift—even if it's November.
- Go to her prenatal appointments.
- Keep a journal (either written, tape-recorded, or videotaped) of what you're thinking and feeling during the pregnancy.
- Do something with her that she knows you absolutely hate to do.
- Take her to visit the nursery at your local hospital.
- Help her address envelopes for the birth announcements.
- Learn a few easy recipes (see pages 40–48).
- Smile and nod agreeably when she says, "You have no idea what it's like to be pregnant."
- If you already have children, take them to the park and let your partner have time alone to relax or run an errand she's had to put off.
- Surprise her with breakfast in bed on a lazy Sunday. Or, on a workday, get up five minutes earlier and surprise her with a power shake.
- Take the day off from work and hang around the house with her.
- Give other expectant mothers seats on trains and buses.
- Make a donation to a local children's hospital or school.
- Discuss your fears with your partner. Listen to hers, too, but don't make fun of them—no matter how insignificant they may seem to you.
- Paint or wallpaper the baby's room.
- Listen to her complain and don't tell her she's complaining.
- Help put together the changing table and crib.
- Install smoke detectors in your house.
- Make a new will that includes your baby.
- Join a health club together.
- Clean out closets to make room for baby things.
- Call her on the phone during the day—just to tell her you love her.
- Offer to carry her bags.
- Buy a few tapes of her favorite music to listen to in the labor room.
- Say "No" if she asks if she's acting crazy.

Staying Involved

Focus on Her

Although every pregnant woman will need and appreciate different things, there is a lot more common ground than you might imagine. Basically, she needs three things from you now—and for the rest of the pregnancy—more than ever before: expressions of affection, admiration, and support (both verbal and physical) for her; sensitivity to her changing physical condition (hunger, fatigue, muscle pains, and so on); and expressions of affection and excitement about the baby and your impending parenthood. Your support is absolutely critical. According to psychologist Edward Hagen, it actually has a concrete effect on your partner's emotional and physical health, as well as on the kind of mother she'll be after the baby comes.

Finances

PLANNING A COLLEGE FUND

It may seem hard to imagine now, but in eighteen years or so the baby you haven't even met yet may be graduating from high school and heading off to college. And so, at the risk of reinforcing the old stereotype that a father's role in his children's lives is primarily financial, it's time to talk about money.

Over the past twenty years or so, college tuition and expenses, such as room and board, have gone up an average of 7 percent a year—that's a lot faster than inflation—and they'll continue to rise at close to the same rate for the foreseeable future. This means that by the time your child walks off the stage with his high school diploma, a single year at a public college will probably cost around $45,000; at a private college, it could be more $80,000. No wonder the American Council on Education reports that more than 70 percent of Americans feel that "a four-year college education is not affordable." In fact, the four-year college education may not even exist eighteen years from now. Even today, costs are so high that more and more kids spend five or six years in college because they have to work so much during the school year to pay their bills.

Now don't panic. Things are not as bad as they might seem. First of all, you don't have to—and probably shouldn't—pay for your child's education in cash. You wouldn't buy a house for cash, right? So why would you pay cash for an education that costs about the same?

So how are you going to pay for it? As counterintuitive as it sounds, you start by putting as much money as you can into your *own* retirement accounts.

"I just found out what braces cost."

Doesn't make sense? It didn't to me either, until financial guru Eric Tyson gave me the following example:

If you were paying attention to the flight attendant before taking off on your last airplane trip, you'll remember that if those oxygen masks drop from the ceiling, you're supposed to put yours on first, then your child's. The idea is that if *you* can't breathe, you certainly won't be able to help anyone else. Tyson makes the same basic point about money: take care of your finances first—especially your IRA, 401(k), Keogh, or company-sponsored retirement plan—and your whole family will be better off.

But that still doesn't clear up the problem of how feathering your own retirement accounts instead of starting a college fund in your child's name will help put her through college. Well, here's how it works:

- Money you invest in your retirement accounts is often at least partially tax deductible and always grows tax free until you start withdrawing it. In contrast, investments made in your child's name are after-tax dollars, and interest and dividends may be taxable as income or capital gains at your rate.

- The more assets your child has, the less eligible she'll be for financial aid. Schools will assume that 35 percent of your child's assets will be available for educational purposes but only 6 percent of yours. Money in your retirement accounts doesn't count at all.
- Plenty of financial-aid options are available: student loans (usually available at below-market rates), grants, fellowships, work-study programs, and so forth.
- You can borrow against the equity in your home or against the equity in your retirement accounts.

Digging out of the Hole

Before you even start worrying about how you're going to finance the future, it's critical that you spend some time making sure the present is taken care of. If you have huge debts, the place to start is by paying them off. Adopting a child or conceiving one artificially, for example, can cost a ton of money—$25,000 to $50,000 is not at all uncommon, says Sharon Luker, a financial advisor in Plano, Texas. If you dipped into your retirement accounts, took out a second mortgage, or put it on your credit cards, start working on those before, or at least at the same time as, you start saving for your child's education. You have a responsibility to your child, yourself, and your family to stay in as good financial shape as you can. But big debts—particularly on high-interest-rate credit cards—can undermine your whole family's long-term financial health.

If you need to, get together with a professional who can help you put together a budget that includes servicing your debt and savings (see pages 90–91 for more on this). Get in the habit of putting something aside every month, even if it's just a few dollars. The best way to do this is through *dollar cost averaging*. This means that on a regular basis—weekly, monthly, quarterly—you contribute a fixed amount to the same mutual fund or other investment. When prices are up you're buying fewer shares; when prices are down, you're buying more.

The problem with this or any other regular savings plan is remembering to do it. If things get tight—as they have plenty of times at my house—the education checks can get "overlooked" or "rescheduled." Having it automatically taken out of your paycheck is a great—and somewhat less painful—way to go. If you can get control of your finances now, who knows, you might even be able to afford to have another kid.

- If you'll be over 59½ by the time your child starts college, you may be able to withdraw money from your IRA or other retirement account without incurring any penalties.

Of course, this approach may not work for everyone. You may have already maxed out all your retirement options or you may be wealthy enough that there's not much chance that your child will qualify for financial aid. Or maybe you just want to put some money away for your child to use later. In these cases, there are still a number of options. We can't possibly cover them all here, but we've focused on a few of the most common ones. Before you make any big decisions, I urge you to talk over your choices with a financial planner and/or an accountant to make sure that the plan you're considering fits in with your overall financial objectives.

BONDS

ZEROS Zero coupon bonds are issued by the U.S. Government and by corporations and are purchased for a fraction of their "face value," what they'll be worth when they mature. You could, for example, pay $200 today for a bond that would be worth $1,000 by the time your child enters college. How much you pay now and what the bonds will be worth at maturity depends on current interest rates (the higher they are, the less you pay now) and when they mature (the longer you hold them, the less you pay).

Because Zeros allow you to pick almost any maturity date, from next year to thirty years in the future, you'll know exactly how much you'll have when it's time to cash them in. There's an active market for Zeros, so if you have some kind of financial emergency, you can always sell them for whatever they're worth at that time—which may be more or less than you paid for them.

With government-issued Zeros there's absolutely no risk of default. And there's not a whole lot of return either. You'll have to pay taxes every year on the interest you earn, even though you don't actually receive it. Chances are you could do a lot better putting your money in the stock market instead.

SERIES EE SAVINGS BONDS Like Zeros, these bonds are issued by the U.S. Government and are purchased at a fraction of their face value. Unlike Zeros, you don't have to pay taxes on them until you cash them in. If you use them for your child's education, you won't have to pay tax at all, provided that you and your partner together earn less than about $80,000 a year (the IRS adjusts this amount every year for inflation).

PREPAID TUITION PLANS Some states have plans that allow you to prepay all or part of your child's state college tuition costs. How much you pay depends on when you expect your child to start college and on current interest rates. Some private colleges offer similar programs.

These plans usually offer pretty good value for the money, especially if you're able to prepay the tuition at today's rates, which will be lot less than eighteen years from now. But in most cases you're limited to the state or college you selected. If your child ends up not going to school at all or decides to go somewhere else, you'll usually get back only the principal you put in plus a paltry 3 to 5 percent.

Overall, you'd probably be better off investing your prepaid tuition money in the stock market, which has grown slightly faster than tuition costs—over 10 percent a year on average for at least the past fifty years. But if you just want to get this whole tuition issue out of your hair right now and not think about it again, these plans may be the way to go. Keep in mind, however, that in some states you may owe taxes on the difference between what you paid today and the cost of tuition eighteen years from now.

EDUCATION IRAS If you and your partner make less than $150,000 together, you can put away $500 each year into a special account for each of your children. Contributions to these special Education IRAs aren't deductible from your income like regular IRAs, but they grow tax free if the money is used to pay for education, room, board, books, and related expenses. When the money is taken out, it will be taxed at your child's tax rate, which will presumably be lower than yours.

Watch out, though. If you're thinking you'll need financial aid, this account will be considered an asset and will reduce the amount of aid your child is

Beware of Good-Hearted Relatives

Because the IRS rules for Education IRAs, prepaid tuition programs, state college savings accounts, custodial accounts, and life in general are often confusing and contradictory, there's way too much potential to get yourself into major tax trouble. So let your parents and any other potentially generous relatives and friends know that they should check with you *before* opening up any accounts in your child's name. And if you aren't absolutely sure what to do and how, have an accountant or financial planner take a look.

eligible for (see pages 85–86 for more on this). More important, you cannot contribute to an Education IRA and a prepaid tuition or state-sponsored savings plan in the same year without incurring some major penalties. Given that those other plans have much higher contribution limits, you might be better off putting your money there instead of here.

CUSTODIAL ACCOUNTS There are two types of custodial accounts: UGMAs (Uniform Gift to Minors Act) consist of money or stock only; UTMAs (Uniform Transfer to Minors Act) can include property too. The big advantage of these accounts is that there are no lifetime contribution limits, although more than $10,000 a year could subject the recipient to a gift tax. Unlike some of the other choices in this section, the gains are taxed every year. The first $700 is tax free, the next $700 is taxed at the child's rate, and everything after that is taxed at your rate. (After your child turns fourteen, everything will be taxed at the child's rate.) The major disadvantage of these accounts is that whatever gets put in there becomes an irrevocable gift to the child. As the custodian, you can invest it any way you want but you can't take it out unless it's to spend on something that directly benefits the child, such as education or summer camps. Spending it on yourself could land you in court. In addition, when the child turns eighteen (for UGMAs) or twenty-one (for UTMAs), the money becomes his to spend any way he wants. You have absolutely no control anymore.

STATE-SPONSORED SAVINGS PLANS Sometimes called 529s, for the IRS regulation they're named after, these plans offer what may be the best college savings plan of all. Although each state's plan varies slightly, they all have a lot in common.

Like Roth IRAs, you make contributions with after-tax dollars but the earnings are completely federally tax-exempt. Depending on the state, you may be able to contribute as much as $150,000 over the lifetime of the plan, including $50,000 in one chunk if you don't make any additional contributions for the next five years. In some states, your contributions may actually be deductible from your state tax.

These plans are especially attractive because, unlike Education IRAs, there are no income restrictions. Plus, the money can be used for nearly any post–high school educational expenses (including tuition, books, room, and board) anywhere in the country. This includes state and private colleges, community colleges, or even vocational schools. If your child doesn't go to college, you can transfer the account to another member of your family.

Picking a Financial Planner

Most financial planners are paid a commission, based on your insurance purchases, stock trades, and/or the total value of your portfolio. So whether or not your investments do well, the financial planner gets his commission. Others are paid a fee and typically charge from $50 to $250 per hour.

This doesn't mean, of course, that fee-based planners are inherently better than their commission-based colleagues (although many experts believe that you'll be happier, and possibly richer, with someone who charges a fee). Your goal is to find someone whom you like and who you believe will have your best interests at heart. Here are a few things you can do to help weed out the losers:

- Get references from friends, business associates, and other people whose opinions you trust. Alternatively, the Financial Planning Association, (800) 282-7526 or www.fpanet.org, will give you references to local Certified Financial Planners. The National Association of Personal Financial Advisors, (800) 322-4237 or www.napfa.org, makes referrals only of fee-based (as opposed to commission-based) planners.
- Select at least three potential candidates and set up initial consultations (which shouldn't cost you anything). Then conduct tough interviews. Here's what you want to know:
  - **Educational background.** Not to be snobby here, but the more formal the education—especially in financial management—the better. Certified Financial Planners (CFPs) go through a rigorous training program and the CFP certification can help you

Unlike custodial accounts, the money is in your name even though your child is the beneficiary. This means that you can withdraw it (with a penalty, of course) if you really need to. And since the 529 account is really a parental asset, it won't hurt your child's ability to get financial aid.

In each state 529 programs are managed by a different organization—Fidelity, Merrill Lynch, and the like—and money in the accounts is carefully allocated according to specific formulas that change as your child gets closer to entering college. For example, a newborn's account would be differentiate between someone who's really a planner from someone who just sells stocks and insurance.

- ◊ **Licenses.** Is he or she legally able to buy and sell financial products such as stock, bonds, mutual funds, and insurance?
- ◊ **Level of experience.** Unless you've got money to burn, let your niece break in her MBA on someone else. Stick to experienced professionals with at least three years in the business.
- ◊ **Profile of the typical client.** What you're looking for is a planner who has experience working with people whose income level and family situation are similar to yours.
- ◊ **Compensation.** If fee based, how is the fee calculated? If commission based, what are the percentages on each product offered? Any hesitation to show you a commission schedule is a red flag.
- ◊ **Get a sample financial plan.** You want to see what you're going to be getting for your money. Be careful, though: fancy graphics, incomprehensible boiler-plate language, and expensive leather binders are often used to distract you from the report's lack of substance.
- ◊ **References.** How long have customers been with the planner? Are they happy? Better off? Any complaints or weaknesses?

- ♦ Check your prospective planner's record with state and federal regulators. You can call the federal Securities and Exchange Commission, (202) 272-7450, or your state's equivalent to check on disciplinary action and to see whether your candidates have ever been sued.

70 percent in a growth stock fund, 10 percent in an international stock fund, and 20 percent in bonds. By age 16, the mix will have gradually shifted to 15 percent in growth stocks, 5 percent in international, 45 percent in bonds, and 35 percent in money markets. Some states allow you to be more aggressive if you wish, while other states take the most conservative route possible and invest everything in bonds. If you don't like your state's program, you may be able to invest through another state. You can find out more about 529s from the College Savings Plan Network at http://www.collegesavings.org.

INSURANCE

LIFE INSURANCE While you may not think that this is the time to be talking about life insurance, you couldn't be more wrong. Because there are so many different kinds of life insurance, and because each of them is right only in certain circumstances, we're not going to go into much detail here. Suffice it to say that you and your partner should get life insurance if you don't have any, or meet with your agent to discuss if and how your new baby will change your insurance needs. The point is that if, God forbid, either of you dies unexpectedly, the survivor shouldn't have to worry about having to get a better job just to keep up the mortgage or private-school tuition payments.

LIFE INSURANCE FOR CHILDREN This one is pretty simple. In most cases, taking out a life insurance policy on a child is a complete waste of money.

DISABILITY As long as you've got insurance on your mind, you really should take a long, hard look at disability coverage. If your employer offers a long-term disability policy, sign up now. If not, explore the subject of getting one of your own through your broker. In many cases, a long-term disability could be more devastating to your family's finances than death.

A FEW INSURANCE TIPS

There are two basic kinds of life insurance: *term* and *cash value*. Each is further divided into several subcategories.

TERM Comes in a variety of flavors: *renewable* (if you keep your death benefit the same, the premiums will rise, but if you develop a health problem, you may get canceled altogether); *level* (you can lock in death benefit and premium levels, sometimes for as long as thirty years); and *decreasing* (death benefit decreases every year but the premium stays the same). Term policies are, as their name indicates, in effect only for the specified period of time. They're also pretty cheap, especially in the early years.

CASH VALUE There are an increasing number of cash-value insurance products available, all of which essentially combine term insurance with some kind of investment. Part of your premium goes to buy term insurance; the rest goes into a fund. Depending on the plan, you'll have more or less control over how the fund is invested. Your investments accumulate tax free, plus, you can borrow against the fund—usually at pretty competitive rates—if you need to.

You can set your premium at virtually any level you want. But because the cost of the underlying term insurance is rising every year, you may reach a point where your payment isn't enough to cover the cost of the insurance. When that happens, the shortfall is taken out of your investment fund.

The big drawback with cash-value policies is that the commissions and fees kill you. Commissions—which are built into your costs—routinely run as much as 100 percent of the first year's premium. And management fees are often much higher than the industry average. According to *Smart Money* magazine, two-thirds of people who have life insurance have some kind of cash-value product. But half of them cancel their policies within ten years. Thanks to the early cancellation fees, this frequently results in the partial or complete loss of the cash value that's been building all that time.

So which is better? At the risk of getting death threats from some insurance salespeople, it's a fairly simple choice: get yourself a guaranteed-renewable, level-premium term policy and either invest your money on your own or get a financial planner to help you.

There is one exception to this rule: if you expect your estate to be worth more than $600,000 (or $1.2 million with your partner), a cash-value policy is a good way to leave your heirs the wherewithal to pay off federal estate taxes. Estates under those amounts pass tax free.

Whether you go with term or cash value, be sure to choose a carrier you can count on being around when the time comes to pay up. The best way to do this is to go with a company that's rated A or better by Standard & Poor, Duff & Phelps, or AM Best. You can find these ratings online or at your local library.

WHERE TO GET IT If you work for a big company or belong to a union, you probably already have at least some life and/or disability insurance. And you may even be able to get additional coverage for great rates and without having to have a physical. No matter how much coverage you get this way, though, be absolutely sure that you get some additional, independent insurance. "If you leave your job, you may suddenly find yourself without any coverage," says Dan Candura, a certified financial planner in Braintree, Massachusetts, "and that could come at a time when you most need it."

If you have an insurance broker, start there. But don't be shy about shopping around. Costs for the very same policy can vary by as much as 200 to 300 percent. Services such as QuickQuote.com and BestQuote.com can help you find the cheapest, best-rated policy.

GETTING PROFESSIONAL ADVICE

Over the course of the next twenty years or so, you're probably going to be spending a lot of your hard-earned money on health, life, and disability insurance; college investment plans; and retirement plans. The way you spend all that money will have a powerful—and long-lasting—effect on you and your family. So, unless you're a financial planner, stockbroker, or insurance agent yourself, you've probably got no business making major financial decisions without advice. See pages 90–91 for how to get the best advice.

Notes:

THE 5TH MONTH

The Lights Are On and Somebody's Home

What's Going On with Your Partner

Physically

- May feel the baby's movements—and she knows what they are
- May have occasional painless tightening of the uterus called Braxton-Hicks contractions or "false labor" (during real labor, the cervix begins to open; in false labor, it doesn't)
- Continuing darkening of nipples, appearance of dark line from belly button down the abdomen
- Breasts are getting larger and may "leak" a little when she's sexually excited—and even when she's not
- Hormones are causing all sorts of trouble: she's forgetful, her fingernails may be brittle, and her skin may be splotchy, but her hair probably never looked better (pregnant women tend to lose less hair than nonpregnant women).

Emotionally

- Very reassured by the baby's movements and less worried about miscarriage
- Developing feeling of bonding with the baby
- Sensitivity about her changing figure
- Increase in sexual desire
- Increasingly dependent on you
- Feelings of jealousy (after all, it was her private pregnancy until now)

What's Going On with the Baby

The baby's eyelids are still sealed but her eyebrows and lashes are fully grown in and you might be able to see some hair on her head. By the end of this month she'll be about nine inches long and weigh in at close to a pound. She kicks, punches, grabs at the umbilical cord, and has developed something of a regular sleep pattern—waking and dozing at regular intervals. She'll spend a lot of her awake time doing somersaults. Best of all, she can now hear what's going on outside the womb.

What's Going On with You

Oh My God, I'm Going to Be a Father

I have to admit that even after seeing the baby on the sonogram, I still found it hard to believe I was really going to be a father (the technology to fake a sonogram must exist, right?). But when my wife grabbed my hand, placed it on her belly, and I felt that first gentle kick, I knew the whole thing was true. And as usual, after the initial excitement passed, I found something to worry about.

More Interested in Fatherhood

After that first kick, I suddenly became consumed with the idea that I just wasn't ready to be a father. I still wanted children—nothing had changed there—but I suddenly realized that in only four months I would face the biggest challenge of my life, and I didn't know a thing about what I was getting into. I felt as though I were about to attempt a triple back flip from a trapeze—without ever having had any lessons, and without a safety net.

I had already done a lot of reading about pregnancy and childbirth, but I felt I still didn't know what fathers are really supposed to do. Doesn't it seem a little strange—scary, really—that you need a license to sell hot dogs on the street or to be a beautician, but there are absolutely no prerequisites for the far more important job of being a father?

Feeling the baby's first kicks may make you much more interested in reading about pregnancy, if you haven't been doing so already. You may also find yourself wanting to spend more time with friends or relatives who have small kids or just watching how other men interact with their children. You'll probably notice that younger dads (those under about twenty-five) spend a little less time with their kids—playing, teaching, reading—than older dads (those over thirty-two).

Turning Inward

You've had a lot to think about lately—your family's finances, your new role as a father, your partner's (and your baby's) safety. So don't be surprised if you find yourself preoccupied with your own thoughts—sometimes to the exclusion of just about everything else, even your partner.

Just as it was for your partner, this sort of "turning inward" is perfectly normal. The problem is that while you're focusing on everything that's going on inside your head, your partner (who has been pretty focused on *herself* until now) is now starting to focus on you too. She may be feeling insecure and may need to be reassured that you aren't going to leave her. She may also be feeling emotionally needy and crave confirmation of your love for her. Pay close attention to her subtle (or not so subtle) hints and make sure she gets the attention she needs. If she doesn't, she may think you don't care. As Arthur and Libby Colman write, "A man who ignores his partner's anxieties may find they escalate rather than abate with a condescending 'Everything is going to be all right, dear.'"

At the same time, though, don't forget about your own needs. It can be extremely tempting to try to get away from the external pressures by distancing yourself from your partner (you can't, of course, get away from your internal pressures). If you can, tell her what's on your mind; it'll probably make you feel a lot better. (If you're having a tough time opening up, you might want to review the "Your Relationship" section on pages 74–77.) If she doesn't react well, reassure her that even though you might be a little preoccupied, you still love her and you'll still be there for her.

Staying Involved

Prenatal Communication

As we've discussed elsewhere, good communication is a critical part of your pregnancy. But what about communicating with your unborn child? While the very idea may sound a little wacky, research has shown that months before they are born, fetuses are extremely responsive to what's happening "on the outside."

The big question, of course, is: What can they hear in there besides heartbeats and gas? After all, their ears are filled with amniotic fluid and any external sounds have to pass through your partner's abdomen. Well, despite what you'd think, the uterus is a pretty noisy place.

In one study, for example, an obstetrician inserted a microphone into a woman's uterus while she was in labor (after her water had broken), and recorded the external sounds that could be heard from the inside. He got clear recordings—not only of voices and the mother's internal body sounds but also of Beethoven's Ninth Symphony, which was being played in the delivery room.

The fetus's ability to hear starts long before delivery. Armed with ultrasound machines, researchers Peter Hepper and Sara Shahidullah found that fetuses first start reacting to some outside sounds as early as 14 weeks. The range is rather limited, though, with mid- and low-frequency sounds provoking a response but high-frequency sounds being completely ignored. At about 35 weeks, fetuses not only can hear both high and low frequencies, but can actually tell the difference between the two. Even more amazing, they can discriminate between two different speech sounds ("ba" and "bi").

Hearing noises is one thing, but are fetuses affected in any way by what they hear from within the womb? Absolutely. In one study, Peter Hepper found that newborns whose mothers had watched a particular soap opera while they were pregnant stopped crying when they heard the show's theme song. Babies who hadn't been exposed to the show had no reaction when they heard the music.

In another fascinating study, researcher Anthony DeCasper asked sixteen women to make a tape of themselves reading a poem called "The King, the Mice, and the Cheese," and two different tapes of Dr. Seuss's *The Cat in the Hat.* Then, during the last six and a half weeks of their pregnancies, the women were instructed to choose only one of the tapes and play it three times a day for their unborn child.

When the babies were three days old, DeCasper offered them a choice between the tape they'd heard over and over and one of the other tapes. Since three-day-old babies aren't real good about speaking up, DeCasper used a "suck-o-meter" (a specially rigged pacifier that enabled the babies to determine which tape they'd get to hear merely by changing their sucking speed) to allow the children to express their preferences. Fifteen out of the sixteen babies chose the tape they'd heard while in the womb. If nothing else, this research ought to convince you that even before they're born, babies' lights are on and there's somebody home.

Even more amazing, fetuses can tell the difference between two languages and exhibit a strong preference for their native one. French researcher Jacques Mehler and his colleagues had a completely bilingual woman record several phrases in French and Russian, then played them to several dozen brand-new French babies. Using a device similar to DeCasper's suck-o-meter, the babies adjusted their sucking so they could hear the French instead of the Russian.

So why should you try to communicate with your growing fetus? First of all, because it's a lot of fun. In the evenings, I used to place my hands on my wife's belly and tell the current resident all about what I'd done during the day. Sometimes I'd even do "counting" exercises: I'd poke once and say (loudly), "One." Most of the time, I'd get an immediate kick back. A few seconds later, I'd poke twice and say, "Two." Frequently, I'd get two kicks back.

The second reason to try some prenatal conversations is that they can help you establish a bond with your baby before the birth. It may even help make the pregnancy seem a little more "real." I have to admit that in the beginning, the idea of talking to a lump in my wife's belly seemed silly. But after a while I got used to it and began to feel a real closeness with the baby. Another father felt that by communicating extensively with his unborn daughter, he was able to establish a loving relationship with her while she was still inside. And when she finally was born, he described their first encounter as "like meeting someone face to face with whom you had only spoken on the telephone."

Communicating with your unborn child will also help him or her start developing a bond with you. Many fathers are jealous of the immediate bond newborn children have with their mothers. It seems, though, that this bond may have more to do with the mother's voice (which the baby has heard every day for nine months) than anything else. In another suck-o-meter study, Dr. DeCasper found that nine out of ten newborns selected a story recorded by their own mother over the same story recorded by another woman. And other research has shown that for their first few days newborns prefer their mother's voice to their father's; if she whispers in one ear and the father whispers in the other, the baby will most likely turn toward the mother.

But that's no reason to give up. When you speak to your baby before he's born, he "learns to recognize the tone, pitch, and speech patterns that are unique to you, and will instantly identify your voice after birth," says Dr. Sarah Brewer, author of *Superbabies*. This means that if you whisper in one of your baby's ears and an unknown man whispers in the other, the baby, who "recognizes" you, will turn toward you 80 percent of the time.

Communication with the fetus isn't limited to words, of course. Boris Brott (yes, he's a relative, but I've never met him), a famous Canadian orchestra conductor, traces his interest in music to the womb:

> As a young man, I was mystified by this ability I had to play certain pieces sight unseen. I'd be conducting a score for the first time and, suddenly, the cello line would jump out at me: I'd know the flow of the piece before I turned the page of the score. One day, I mentioned this

> to my mother, who is a professional cellist. I thought she'd be intrigued because it was always the cello line that was so distinct in my mind. She was; but when she heard what the pieces were, the mystery quickly solved itself. All the scores I knew sight unseen were ones she had played when she was pregnant with me.

In an effort to harness the power of prenatal communication, several physicians and obstetricians have developed organized communication programs. Psychiatrist Thomas Verny claims that by singing and talking to the fetus, "parents create a positive intrauterine environment, reducing the level of anxiety-producing hormones that lead to frenetic activity and even ulcers in the unborn." And Dr. F. Rene Van de Carr maintains that his "Prenatal Classroom" provides systematic stimulation that may "actually help the growing fetus' brain become more efficient and increase learning capacity after birth."

Dr. Brewer goes even further. "Your baby's brain is literally shaped by the stimuli and nutrients received from his environment," she says. "By enriching his prenatal environment with additional stimuli, you can encourage the growth and development of his brain cells (neurons) so they develop more complex 'communication antennae' (dendron trees), more 'satellite dishes' (dendritic spines), and stronger synaptic connections." Translation: it may make your baby smarter.

Perhaps the most dramatic claims, though, are made by developmental psychologist Brent Logan, whose BabyPlus technology uses what he calls the "cardiac curriculum" to pump a set of increasingly complex heartbeatlike sounds into the mother's womb. Logan may really be on to something with the heartbeat thing. It's the one sound that fetuses hear even more than their mothers' voices. And after birth, many newborns are soothed by recordings of their mothers' heartbeat (recordings of other people's hearts don't work nearly as well). Interestingly, although scientists have documented this, ordinary people seem to have known it all along. About 80 percent of mothers—whether they're right- or left-handed—naturally hold babies on the left side, where the baby's head can be nearer the heart. Even artists—a far less stodgy group than researchers and scientists—have noticed the left-side bias: studies of classical paintings and sculptures have shown that 80 percent of the people depicted carrying babies hold them on the left side. Those carrying inanimate objects, however, do so half the time on the right, half on the left.

Whether it's the heartbeats or something else, Logan says his "graduates" frequently learn to talk as early as five or six months and to read at eighteen

A Few Things to Remember about Prenatal Communication

- Respect your partner. You've got a right to speak with your child, but she's got a right to privacy. If she's not completely into the idea, you might want to tell her that Logan and others have found that women who are carrying prenatally stimulated babies seem to have shorter labors and a lower C-section rate. In addition, certain kinds of stimulation may reduce the risk of breech births (where the baby comes out feet first instead of head first). Because they like sounds so much, some fetuses will "chase" after music playing through headphones placed against the mother's abdomen. The theory is that if you move the headphones to the bottom of the abdomen during the last month or so of the pregnancy, a stubborn yet music-loving breech fetus could be convinced to shift its head downward, right where it's supposed to be.
- Try to overcome the feeling that what you are doing is absolutely ridiculous. The idea that communicating with unborn babies could actually benefit them has been around for more than a thousand years.
- Don't whisper. Speak to the fetus loudly enough so that a person standing across the room could hear you clearly.
- Don't do it when you're feeling bored. The fetus will pick up on your tone of voice.
- Don't go overboard. An hour twice a day at most, says Dr. Brewer. Fetuses need plenty of time to rest, even more than newborns or kittens.
- Set up a routine. Try to do it at the same time every day so that the baby will get used to the idea that something's going to happen. Pat your partner's belly before you start, to let the baby know you're out there. Use the baby's name (if you know it).
- Mix it up. Playing the same piece of music or reading the same poem or story every day is great, but be sure to keep the rest of the program different. When fetuses hear the same thing over and over they just block it out.
- Don't get your expectations too high. There's very little you or anyone else can do to guarantee that your child will be a genius.
- Have fun.

months (most kids don't usually talk until they're at least a year old, or read until they're five or six).

Besides that, Logan, Brewer, and other researchers have found that prenatally stimulated babies tend to:

- cry less at birth
- have longer attention spans
- hold their heads up unassisted sooner
- have remarkable (for babies, anyway) physical strength
- sleep better
- be less likely to develop dyslexia
- demonstrate advanced musical and creative talents
- have an IQ in the 125 to 150 range (average is 100)

If you're interested in finding out more about prenatal learning, take a look at the Resources section.

Sex

Pregnancy can do funny things to your libido. Some expectant fathers are more interested in sex and more easily aroused than ever before. Others are repelled by the very idea. Whether you're feeling either of these ways or something in between, rest assured that it's completely normal.

In this section, we'll talk about the sexual issues that may come up in the first six months of your pregnancy. Late-pregnancy sexual issues are covered on pages 145–146.

WHY YOU AND/OR YOUR PARTNER MIGHT BE FEELING *INCREASED* SEXUAL DESIRE

- After about the third month, her nausea and fatigue are probably gone, making sex more appealing—for both of you.
- You may find her pregnant body (with its larger breasts and fuller curves) erotic.
- Your partner may be proud of her more ample figure and may be feeling sexier.
- You may be turned on by the feeling of power and masculinity at having created life.
- Your partner may be turned on by the confirmation of her femininity and by the awe at what her body is doing. She may also be aroused by how much she's arousing you.

- Throughout pregnancy, you both may experience a newfound feeling of closeness that frequently manifests itself sexually.
- One or both of you may be having more erotic dreams.
- The increased blood flow to her pelvic area may make your partner's orgasms more powerful and easier to reach. (If that were happening to you, you'd want to have sex more often too.) It may also stimulate her to masturbate more than usual, or if she didn't before, she might start.
- If you experienced a miscarriage in an earlier pregnancy, you may have been abstaining from sex for the first trimester. Now that it's safely behind you, all that pent-up desire may have gotten you both to the point where you're about ready to explode.

WHY YOU AND/OR YOUR PARTNER MIGHT BE FEELING *DECREASED* SEXUAL DESIRE

- In the first trimester, your partner may be too nauseated or tired to be interested in sex. In the second trimester, she may feel too uncomfortable or too awkward to want to have sex (about 25 percent of pregnant women feel this way).
- She may think that you don't find her attractive and don't want to have sex with her.
- You may not, in fact, be attracted to a woman whose body has been transformed from fun to functional.
- You may think your partner isn't feeling attractive and wouldn't be interested in sex.
- You or your partner may be afraid that sex will hurt her—or the baby. In fact, there's nothing to be afraid of. The baby is safely cushioned by its amniotic fluid-filled sac, and, unless your partner has cramps or bleeds during sex or her doctor feels there are extenuating circumstances, sex during pregnancy is no more dangerous for your partner than at any other time. You (and your partner) may find this information reassuring. If you do, great; if not, now may be the time to talk about and try some different sexual positions (lying on your sides or with your partner on top, for example) and different ways of bringing each other to orgasm (oral sex, vibrators, and so on). Often simply making a few such changes can go a long way toward alleviating your fears.
- Although in most cases sex is required to become a parent, you and your partner may feel, as it gradually sinks in that you are about to become parents, that parents aren't supposed to be sexual. (Even though we are

all living proof that our parents had sex at least once, it's somehow hard to imagine the two of them, in bed, naked . . .)

- You or your partner may feel that sex serves only one purpose: creating children. And once you've done that, there's no more need for sex—until you want more kids.
- She may actually find it painful.

WHAT THE EXPERTS SAY

As you can see, the range of feelings about sex is broad. But if you still aren't convinced that you're not the only one feeling the way you do, here are a few interesting things researchers have found out about expectant couples' sexuality during pregnancy:

- According to psychologists Wendy Miller and Steven Friedman, expectant fathers generally underestimate how attractive their partners feel, and expectant mothers consistently underestimate how attractive their partners find them. (The bottom line is that most men find their pregnant partners' bodies erotic, and most pregnant women feel quite attractive. But many men and women fail to convey this to their partners.)
- According to the Cowans, expectant fathers have more psychological inhibitions about physical intimacy during pregnancy than their partners do.
- The old myth that pregnancy somehow desexualizes women is just that—a myth. In fact, Miller and Friedman found that there are no significant differences in the level of sexual desire or sexual satisfaction between expectant men and women.

When to Be Particularly Careful

If your partner is at risk for, or has a history of, premature labor, placenta previa (when the placenta covers the cervix), or an incompetent cervix (when the cervix is not strong enough to hold the fetus inside until truly ready to be born), talk to her doctor *before* you hop in the sack. Nipple stimulation and orgasm have a direct impact on the uterus and could possibly trigger some contractions. If your partner has any of these conditions or is at risk for going into labor early, use a condom when you have sex. No, it's not a birth control thing. Strange as it sounds, there's a slim chance that one of the hormones in semen (prostaglandin) may cause contractions.

WHEN YOU AND YOUR PARTNER ARE OUT OF SYNC

Of course, you and your partner may not always be on the same wavelength. She may feel like having sex just when you're feeling put off by her Rubenesque figure. Conversely, you may want to have sex at a time when she's simply not interested. Here are a few suggestions that might help:

- **Talk.** At these and so many other times during your pregnancy, communicating with your partner is essential. As Arthur and Libby Colman so wisely write, "Unless the couple can talk about their sex life, their entire relationship may suffer, and that in turn will compound their sexual problems."
- **Try some nonsexual affection,** such as snuggling, touching, or just hugging each other. And say up front that that is what you're interested in doing, because it isn't as easy as it sounds. Professors Cowan and Cowan have found that many couples need practice finding sensual ways to please each other short of intercourse. And both men and women hesitate to make affectionate overtures if they aren't sure they're ready to progress to intercourse and are worried they'll be misinterpreted.
- **Be nice to each other.** Being critical of her figure will make her feel self-conscious, less attractive, and less interested in sex.

Notes:

THE 6TH MONTH

Work and Family

What's Going On with Your Partner

Physically

- Period of greatest weight gain begins
- Increased sweating
- Increased blood supply gives her that pregnant "glow"; it may also be giving her some sciatica or even carpal tunnel syndrome as all the extra fluid compresses some of her nerves
- Swelling of the hands and feet
- Fatigue, dizziness, and a runny nose are not uncommon
- A constant, nagging backache—especially if she's carrying twins or more
- Some incredibly bizarre food cravings (see page 111 for more on this)

Emotionally

- Moodiness is decreasing
- Continued forgetfulness and even some short-term memory loss (see page 111 for more on this)
- Feeling that the pregnancy will never end
- Increased bonding with the baby
- Still very dependent on you

What's Going On with the Baby

The baby looks pretty trim—he hasn't started putting on much fat yet—and is starting to get covered with vernix, a thick, waxy, protective coating. His eyes are starting to open, he coughs and hiccups, and if you were inside the uterus you could see his unique footprints and fingerprints. The movements of your

now foot-long two-pounder are getting stronger, and he can hear, and respond to, sounds from the outside world. He may, for example, jump at the sound of a door slamming or a car backfiring.

What's Going On with You

Reexamining Your Relationship with Your Father

As the reality of your prospective fatherhood unfolds, you'll probably find yourself contemplating how you'll juggle the various roles—parent, provider, husband, employee, friend—that will make up your paternal identity. As mentioned in earlier chapters, you may be spending more time reading about parenting and watching how your male friends, family members, or even strangers, do it.

But eventually you'll realize that your own father—whether you know it or not—has already had a profound influence on the kind of father you'll be. You also may find yourself nearly overcome with forgotten images of childhood—especially ones involving your father. Just walking down the street, I'd suddenly remember the times we went camping or to the ballet, how he taught me to throw a baseball in the park, and the hot summer afternoon he, my sisters, and I stripped down to our underwear in the backyard and painted each other with watercolors. There's nothing like impending paternity to bring back all the memories and emotions of what it was like to be fathered as a child.

Not all childhood memories of fathers are positive. Many men's images of their fathers are dominated by fear, pain, loneliness, or longing. Either way, don't be surprised if you find yourself seriously reexamining your relationship with your dad. Was he the kind of man you want as your role model? Was he the perfect example of the kind of father you don't want to be? Or was he somewhere in between? Many men, particularly those who had rocky, or nonexistent, relationships with their fathers find that the prospect of becoming a father themselves enables them to let go of some of the anger they've felt for so long.

Don't be surprised if you start having a lot of dreams about your father. Researcher Luis Zayas found that an expectant father's uncertainty about his identity as father, his actual role, and the changed relationship with his wife and family are "among the psychic threads of fatherhood" that are fundamentally related to the man's relationship with his own father and are frequently present in his dreams.

So, whether you're awake or asleep, as you're thinking about your father, remember that what's really going on is that you're worried about what kind of a father you will be when your baby arrives. And remember, despite all those silly aphorisms like "the acorn never falls far from the tree," the kind of father you become is completely up to you. If you work at it, you can be the father *you* want to be, rather than the one that you might think fate planned.

A Sense of Mortality

Although I've always been more than just a little fascinated by death, it wasn't until my wife got pregnant the first time that death became more than a mere abstraction. Suddenly it occurred to me that my death could have a serious impact on other people.

This realization had some interesting and fairly immediate results. The first thing that happened was that I became a much better driver—or at least a

safer one. Overnight, yellow lights changed their meaning from "floor it" to "proceed with caution." I began to leave for appointments a few minutes earlier so I wouldn't have to hurry, I wove in and out of traffic less, and I found myself not quite so annoyed with people who cut me off in traffic. But besides becoming a better driver, I began to look back with horror at some of the risky things—parachuting, scuba diving—I'd done before I'd gotten married, and I began to reconsider some of the things I'd tentatively planned for the near future—bungee jumping, hang gliding. After all, now there were people counting on me to stay alive.

My preoccupation with my own mortality had other interesting consequences as well. I found myself strangely drawn to my family's history; I wanted to learn more about our traditions, our history, our family rituals, the wacky relatives no one ever talked about. I even bought a family-tree computer program and began bugging my relatives about their birth dates. I didn't realize it at the time, but it's quite common for expectant fathers to experience a heightened sense of attachment to their relatives—both immediate and distant—even if they weren't particularly close before.

This really isn't so unusual, especially when you consider that one of the main reasons we have kids in the first place is so that a little piece of us will live on long after we're gone. I guess the hope is that one day seventy-five years from now, when my great-grandson is expecting a child, he'll start to explore his roots and want to get to know more about me.

Feeling Trapped

As we've already discussed, you and your partner probably aren't feeling the same things at the same time. Earlier on in the pregnancy, your partner may have turned inward, preoccupied with how the pregnancy was affecting her.

You may have felt a little (or a lot) left out. By now, though, your partner may be "coming out"—concentrating less on herself and the baby, and more on you.

Meanwhile, you may have just begun the process of turning inward that we began discussing last month (page 97). You're going to be a father in less than four months, and you've got a lot of things to think about, many of which you need to work through on your own. The potential problem here is that just as you begin to focus on yourself, your partner is becoming increasingly dependent on you. She may be afraid that you don't love her anymore and that you're going to leave her. Or she may be worried—just as you are—about your physical safety. Although being doted upon is nice, it can sometimes get out of hand. And your partner's increased dependence on you may cause you to feel trapped. As the Colmans found, a pregnant woman's "sudden concern may make a man feel over-protected, as though his independence is being threatened." If you are feeling trapped, it's important to let your partner know in a gentle, nonconfrontational way. At the same time, encourage her to talk about what she's feeling and what she wants from you.

Staying Involved

Having Fun

Besides being a time of great change—physical as well as emotional—pregnancy can be a fun time, too. Here are a few ways to amuse yourselves:

- **Take lots of pictures.** I took regular shots of my wife—from the front and the side, with emphasis on the belly—holding a mug-shot-style card labeled "Pregnant Woman Number 1 (2, 3, and so on)." For another series of photos, she stood up while I lay on my back between her legs and took pictures of her soft underbelly. If you don't have a camera that marks the date right on the prints, you'll want to take note of the critical day the belly completely blocks your view of your partner's face. Take pictures at least once a month until the eighth month, then once a week after that.

A Few Positively Odd Things Your Partner Might Be Experiencing

You've probably heard all about pregnant women's strange and oddly timed food cravings—such as pickles and ice cream at two in the morning, or strawberries and garlic for breakfast. As repulsive as some of them may be, cravings like these are completely normal. Some pregnant women, though, crave laundry starch, wax, gravel, dirt, coffee grounds, paint, ashes, clay, and even the smell of gasoline. Needless to say, such cravings are anything *but* normal. They are part of a fairly rare condition called *pica,* which generally affects only kids one to six years old and pregnant women (yet another reason I'm glad I'm not a woman). Women who grew up or live in the South or in rural communities seem to be at greater risk, as are women who suffered from pica as children. Some people believe that these wacky cravings are the body's way of satisfying its nutritional needs; there is, for example, plenty of iron in clay. The problem is that there's also a lot of downright dangerous stuff in it. Other experts discount the nutrition angle completely: if she's missing some nutrients, she needs to eat better or take some vitamins. So if you catch your partner licking ashtrays, or if she wakes you up in the middle of the night asking for a handful of gravel or a candle to chew on, offer her a healthy snack, get her to sleep, and call her doctor first thing in the morning.

As if that wasn't weird enough . . . if your partner has been forgetful lately, or seems to be losing a lot of things—including her memory—it may be because her brain is shrinking. Yep. Anita Holdcroft, an English anesthesiologist, found that during pregnancy, women's brains actually get 3 to 5 percent smaller. Now that you know this, it's probably best that you keep it to yourself. After all, there's really no nice way to tell someone that her brain is shrinking. You could mention it in the hope that your partner will forget it right away, but if she doesn't, you're in big trouble. And anyway, the shrinkage seems to be attributed to the brain cells being compressed—not to an actual loss of cells. And, oh yes, it generally clears up within a few months after the birth.

- **Get some special clothes.** His-and-hers "Yes sir, that's my baby" T-shirts and "Father-to-bee" hats (featuring a picture of a bumblebee) are favorites in some circles.
- **Get some exercise—together.** Taking a water aerobics or swimming class together can be a lot of fun. You'll be amazed at how agile pregnant women can be when they're floating in water. Unless you're quite confident about your partner's sense of humor, it's best to stifle your comments about whales—beached or otherwise.
- **Start a clipping file for the baby.** Just before our older daughter was born, my wife started putting together a file with newspaper and magazine photos of the hot fashions of the day; lists of the top ten movies, books, and records of the year; articles on the pressing political and social issues; pictures of the house we live in and the baby's room—before and after we fixed it up; and ads—showing the prices, of course—for a variety of items (houses for sale in our neighborhood, computers, food, movie and theater tickets, and so on).
- **Go shopping for baby announcements.** Or, you can design your own. See pages 130–32 for more details.
- **Make a plaster belly cast.** Believe it or not, this is my all-time favorite. It's a little complicated, but well worth the trouble. Long after the baby is born, you, your partner, and your friends will be absolutely amazed that your partner was ever that big (and the baby that small). If you're interested in trying it, Francine Krause (P.O. Box 1832, Sebastopol, CA 95473, [707] 824-8357 or www.bellymask.com) sells a wonderful kit that includes all the materials you'll need. An important warning: Don't even *think* about making a cast of your partner's belly using any kind of plastic, rubber, or resin. No matter what anybody tells you, these products can be harmful to both your partner and the baby.

Work and Family

FAMILY LEAVE

Let's face it: while your partner is pregnant, it's going to be kind of tough for you to put in a lot of quality time with your unborn child—a little before work, a bit more after work, a few hours on weekends. But what about after the pregnancy? Is a few hours a day going to be enough time to spend with your child? If it were, you probably wouldn't be reading this book. Contrary to the common stereotypes, most fathers want to spend a lot of time with their families. Consider the results of a few recent studies:

- Three out of four fathers consider family to be the most important aspect of their lives.
- One major corporation found that 57 percent of men (up from 37 percent five years earlier) wanted work-schedule flexibility that would enable them to spend more time with their families.
- According to the Radcliffe Public Policy Center, more than 70 percent of men aged twenty-one to thirty-nine would give up some of their pay to be able to spend more time with their families. Men were actually more likely than young women to give up pay.
- Seventy-four percent of fathers would rather have a "daddy-track" job rather than a "fast-track" one.
- Forty-eight percent of dads actually reduced their work load or passed up promotions in order to spend more time with their children.
- A *Los Angeles Times* poll found that 39 percent of men say they would quit their jobs and stay home with the kids.
- Eighty percent of fathers want to take more of a role in parenting than their own fathers did and expect to make parenting a fifty-fifty proposition with their wives.

Despite contemporary fathers' good intentions, however, only about 1 to 3 percent of men ever take advantage of their companies' family-leave options when they have the chance. So what accounts for the contradiction between what men say and what they actually do? First of all, the vast majority of family-leave plans (including the Family and Medical Leave Act) are unpaid. Since the average working woman still makes less than the average working man, if one person is going to take time off from work, many families conclude that they can better survive the loss of the woman's salary.

But financial pressure isn't the only reason men don't take family leave. Even when their companies offer paid paternity leave, men still don't participate. Why not? A lot of men have a deep-rooted conviction that getting on the "daddy track" will hurt their careers. Tom, an attorney friend of mine who elected not to take advantage of his firm's paid family-leave plan, told me: "I wanted to take the leave, but I knew I'd never make partner if I did. All the male associates knew it would be career suicide."

Unfortunately, Tom's fears are not unfounded. Dr. Joseph Pleck, of Wellesley College, says that "because employers don't understand or accept the idea of child-care leave for anyone, they find the concept of paternity leave incomprehensible, or simply frivolous." It's not surprising, then, that many companies send their male employees mixed messages about whether or not it's okay

"Adorable, Kravitz, but from now on baby pictures will suffice."

to take family leave. A 1996 report from a bipartisan family-leave commission reported that just 58 percent of covered employees had heard of the Family and Medical Leave Act. It's pretty hard to exercise your options when you don't know what they are!

When researchers asked more than 1,500 human resources directors and CEOs how much time they thought would be reasonable for men to take as paternity leave, 63 percent said "None." Even at companies that did offer paternity leave, 41 percent said no amount of paternity leave was reasonable.

Sadly, even today, when most larger employers are required by law to grant family leave to men, the prevailing attitude hasn't changed. Some employers even go so far as to actively discourage fathers from taking time off. The Houston Oilers docked David Williams about $100,000 for missing a single game to attend the birth of his child. And when the Cleveland Indians traded Matt Williams, some speculated that it was because he'd missed a practice game for the same reason.

But it looks as though a few small cracks may be developing in the glass ceiling that keeps men away from their kids. When Maryland state trooper Kevin Kussman was denied parental leave, he sued his employer and won $350,000.

Some companies aren't waiting to get sued. In fact, they not only offer paternity leave, they actively encourage their male employees to take it. For example, the Los Angeles Department of Water and Power (over 70 percent of whose employees are men) started a complete fathering program called Doting Dads. The highly publicized program includes a four-month paternity-leave plan, a father mentorship program, child-care referral services, and even breastfeeding classes for both spouses. Before the program started, a total of only three or four men took paternity leave. But after Doting Dads came into being, the number of men taking paternity leave has grown to about thirty each year. A few other large employers have begun to notice a small increase in the number of men who take family leave. The numbers are still minuscule—especially when compared to the number of women who take additional time off after the disability portion of their maternity leave has run out—but it's progress.

Even those new dads who don't take paternity or family leave manage to take some time off from work in order to be with their newborns. They do it by cobbling together sick days, comp time, vacation days, and so on.

LONG-TERM WORK-SCHEDULE CHANGES

So far we've talked about taking a few weeks off just after the birth of your child. But what about after that?

Not long after our first daughter was born, my wife left her big, downtown law firm and found a less stressful, three-day-a-week job closer to home. Almost everyone we knew applauded. But when I made the announcement that I, too, would be cutting back to three days a week, the reaction was quite a bit different. At work, I was hassled repeatedly by my boss and coworkers, and a lot of my friends and relatives began to whisper that if I didn't go back to work full-time, my career might never recover.

For the most part, flexible schedules, job sharing, part-time work, or working-at-home options have been considered "women's issues." But they're not. As a new (or a veteran) father, you're probably going to want to spend more time with your children than your own father did with you, and just about the only way you'll get to is to make some changes in your work schedule.

I'm not suggesting that everyone should cut back their work schedules to three days a week. Clearly, that just isn't practical for most people (although it sure would be nice if you could, wouldn't it?). Frankly, you may never be able to resolve your work/family conflicts completely. But there are a few ways you can maximize your time with your family, minimize your stress, and avoid trashing your career.

Here are some rather painless flexible-scheduling options you might want to run by your employer:

- Work four ten-hour days instead of five eight-hour days.
- Work 5:00 A.M. to 1:00 P.M. (or some other schedule) instead of the usual 9:00 to 5:00.
- Consider a split shift; for example, work 8:00 A.M. to noon and 5:00 P.M. to 9:00 P.M.

WORKING LESS THAN FULL-TIME

If you can afford to, you might want to consider one of the following options:

- **Job sharing.** You and another person divide up the responsibilities of the job. You'd probably use the same office and desk. A typical job-share schedule might have you working two days one week and three days the next, while the person you're sharing with does the opposite. One warning: be very careful to negotiate a continuation of your health benefits. Many employers routinely drop them for less-than-full-time employees.
- **Switch to part-time.** This is pretty much the same as job sharing, except you probably won't have to share a desk with someone else.
- **Become a consultant to your current employer.** This can be a great way for you to get a lot of flexibility over your workday. There are also lots of tax advantages—particularly if you set up a home office. At the very least, you'll be able to deduct auto mileage and a percentage of your phone and utility bills. There are some disadvantages too. As a company employee, you split the roughly 15 percent of your check that goes to Social Security: you pay 7.5 percent, your employer pays 7.5 percent. But when you're self-employed, you pay both halves. In addition, if you become a consultant, you'll lose your company-paid benefit package. So be sure to set your daily or hourly rate high enough to recoup those extra payroll taxes, your insurance costs (health, life, disability), vacation and holiday pay, and anything else, including your employer's matching contribution to your 401(k).

WORKING AT HOME (TELECOMMUTING)

Years ago, when I was a commodities trader, I used to spend eight or nine hours a day on the phone haggling with people—most of whom I never met—about grain prices. My coworkers were similarly occupied, and my boss was two thousand miles away. Realistically, there was no reason I couldn't have been working at home.

Granted, commodities trading is not a typical job, but the fact is that many Americans do work that doesn't require their physical presence in any

The Family and Medical Leave Act

The Family and Medical Leave Act is not a simple document to understand. You can (and should) get a free copy from your senator or congressional representative. Here's a summary of what it means for fathers:

- **Who can take the leave?** Any person who works for a public agency (federal, state, or local) or a private-sector company that employs fifty or more people. You must have been employed by that company for at least twelve months, and have worked at least 1,250 hours. This covers about two-thirds of the total U.S. labor force.
- **How much leave can you take?** Eligible employees can take up to twelve work weeks of leave at any time during the twelve-month period that starts the day your child is born or adopted. If you and your wife are employed by the same company, though, you may be entitled to a *total* of twelve weeks between you. You don't have to take it all in one chunk—you may be able to arrange to take every Friday off for a year rather than twelve weeks straight.
- **Is it paid?** Employers are not required to pay you your salary while you're on leave. But say your employer pays for six weeks of family leave, you're still entitled to take another six without pay.
- **What about benefits?** Your employer must maintain your coverage under the company's health plan for the duration of your leave.
- **Is your job protected?** In most cases, yes. Your employer cannot fire or replace you while you're on leave unless he or she can prove that your being gone has caused "substantial and grievous economic injury to the operations of the employer."
- **Do you have to give notice?** Under the act, you're required to give your employer at least thirty days' notice before taking your family leave. But the more notice you give, the more time everyone will have to get used to the idea.

Check with your state's employment department to see whether it offers family-leave benefits that are more liberal than those of the federal program. In some states, for example, companies that employ as few as twenty-five people are required to offer their employees family leave. And remember: these benefits are completely separate from the (potentially more liberal) ones your company may offer. So be sure to check with your employer's Human Resources department.

Family Leave If You're an Employee

- **Take it.** Every man I interviewed who took paternity or family leave told me he'd do it again. One even told me he thought that men who didn't take family leave were "nuts."
- **Know your rights.** Find out whether you're eligible under the Family and Medical Leave Act (see page 117), your company's voluntary plan, or any other federal- or state-mandated program.
- **Start talking to your employer now.** If you're covered by a leave plan, start working out the details in a nonthreatening, nonconfrontational way. If you're not covered by a leave plan, you may be able to arrange for some time off anyway.

particular place at any particular time. If you're not a construction worker or a retail salesman, you might be a prime candidate for telecommuting.

Now before you start to panic, I'm not suggesting that you rent out your office to someone else—most telecommuters work only a day or two a week at home. The point is that by telecommuting you may be able to reduce the time you spend getting to work and spend it with your family instead. Remember, though, that telecommuting is not meant to be a substitute for child care; you're supposed to be working when you're at home.

Telecommuting is good for your employer too. As the cost of office space rises and the cost of telecommunications equipment falls, many companies are finding that they save money by having their employees work elsewhere at least part of the time. And to top it off, employees who telecommute are more productive and get more and faster promotions than their office-bound coworkers.

Chances are you won't be the first person to raise the issue of telecommuting to your employer. Ten years ago fewer than one million people worked from home at least eight hours a week during normal business hours. By 2000 it was eleven million, and by 2005 the figure will exceed seventeen million, estimates Charles Grantham, CEO of the Institute for the Study of Distributed Work.

Another major advantage to telecommuting is that you don't have to shave and you can work in your underwear. But as great as working at home is, there are still a few disadvantages. Some of my friends began to think that since I was always at home, I wasn't really doing anything, and since I wasn't doing anything, I could run errands for them. If this happens to you, you're going to have to learn to say no. Working at home can also get a little lonely—you might miss hanging out around the water cooler and schmoozing with your buddies at work. And if you have a tendency to be obsessive about your work (as I do), you'll have to train yourself to take frequent breaks.

Creating a More Family-Friendly Workplace for Dads If You're an Employer (or Supervisor)

- **Spread the word.** At the very least, let all of your employees—especially the men—know that you support their desires to spend more time with their families and that family-friendly policies aren't just for women. Then put your money where your mouth is. If you have a chance, for example, take family leave yourself. The ultimate responsibility for helping men get more involved with their families rests at the top—with male managers. If you demonstrate that it's okay for men to put their families first, everyone else will see that it's acceptable and follow your lead.
- **Encourage other men to take the leave.** Most of your male employees will be reluctant to approach you with their family-leave plan. If you know they're expecting, raise the issue with them first. Chances are, they'll be grateful. If you can afford to make the leave paid, so much the better.
- **Encourage flexible schedules.** This doesn't mean that your employees will work less, just that they'll have more control over when and where they do their jobs. You can do this by wiring your workplace so that more people can telecommute or work remotely. Research has shown that flexibility is the most important factor in a family-friendly workplace.
- **Educate your workers.** Have an occasional brown-bag lunch at which dads get together to discuss their work-family issues. You—and they—will probably be amazed that a lot of other people are facing the same issues.
- **Don't worry about the cost.** "The more support employees receive on the job—the more flexible their work arrangements and supportive their supervisors—the higher their productivity, the more willing they are to go the extra mile, and the more likely they are to stay with their current employers," according to a recent study by the Families and Work Institute.

I can't tell you how many times I've realized—at ten at night—that I hadn't eaten all day and that the only time I went outside was to take the newspaper in from the porch.

A WORK-FAMILY SOLUTION YOU MIGHT NOT HAVE THOUGHT OF

On pages 226–28 we'll discuss a number of the child-care options you and your partner will have to sift through sometime soon. But what if you'd both really prefer to have your child raised in the arms of a loving relative? Most families that make the decision to have a parent stay home automatically assume that it has to be Mom. Sometimes, though, that just won't work. She might have a more stable career than you, she might make more money, or she might simply have no interest in staying home. Well, all is not lost. If you and your partner truly want to have your children raised by a parent, the solution may be only as far away as the nearest mirror: you.

Now before you throw this book down and run out of the room screaming, take a minute to consider the idea. It may not be as crazy as it sounds, particularly if there aren't any other interested family members nearby. Let's start with some of the benefits:

- You won't have to agonize over picking the right baby-sitter or nanny or day-care center.
- You'll have a wonderful opportunity to get to know your child.
- You'll be giving your child what you think is the best possible upbringing.
- You'll be able to help your partner's career and give her some peace of mind at the same time.

Still with us? Deciding to be a stay-at-home dad is a big decision, one that will affect everyone in your family. If you're even remotely considering it, start by asking yourself the following very important questions:

- **Can you afford it?** If you're really committed to the idea, there are all sorts of ways to cut your expenses. Here are just a few: buy food in bulk, eat out less often, raise your insurance deductibles, take vacations closer to home, make presents instead of buying them, get rid of the housekeeper, move to a smaller house or a place where the cost of living is lower.
- **Can you take the career hit?** This is a big one, since earning power and masculinity are inextricably linked in so many people's minds. (If I'm not making money, I'm not a good man/father, the thinking goes.) If you can get over this one, you may still be able to keep a finger or a foot in the

work world by teaching, consulting, writing, or starting a home-based business. But don't be hasty. If you decide to reenter the workforce later, you may find that the employment gap on your résumé could cause you some problems with potential employers, many of whom are going to be a lot less enlightened and a lot more closed-minded than you.

- **Can you handle it?** Staying home with a child is a lot more work than you think. It can also be a bit lonely. According to researcher Robert Frank, about two-thirds of stay-at-home dads feel isolated, compared to only about one-third of stay-at-home moms. There's not a lot of social support for men who decide to stay home, and you won't see many other guys around who are doing it. You'll also probably find that women—moms, nannies, baby-sitters—tend not to welcome men into their groups at parks or playgrounds or malls and the other places people take their kids during the day. And you'll have to get used to the funny looks and stupid comments you'll hear from people who see you with your kids in the middle of the day. ("Hey, are you baby-sitting today?" is one that always bugs me. "No, bozo, I'm not baby-sitting, I'm taking care of my children.")

In reality, you won't be quite as alone as it might seem. At least two million stay-at-home dads are doing it every day, and the number is rising all the time, according to Peter Baylies, director of the At-Home Dad Network. There are also a lot of great resources out there. On the Web, www.slowlane.com has tons. In print, you might want to subscribe to Peter Baylies's *Stay-At-Home Dads* newsletter (for contact info, see the Resources section).

Notes:

Entering the Home Stretch

What's Going On with Your Partner

Physically

- Increasing general physical discomfort (cramps, dizziness, abdominal achiness, heartburn, gas, constipation, and so forth)
- Itchy belly
- Increasing clumsiness and decreasing stamina
- Her hip joints are expanding and she's having to learn to walk in a new, awkward way, which may explain why she's a little more susceptible to muscle pulls
- Some thick, white, vaginal discharge (it's called *leukorrhea*, and is completely normal)
- Increased Braxton-Hicks (false labor) contractions

Emotionally

- Decreased moodiness
- Dreaming/fantasizing about the baby
- Concerned about work—not sure she'll have the energy to go back, and anxious about how to balance roles of mother, wife, employee . . .
- Fear about the labor and delivery

What's Going On with the Baby

The baby's lungs are maturing, and if she were born right now, she'd have a pretty good chance of survival. She's getting a little cramped inside now—

especially if she's got a womb-mate. Her eyes are fully open and her irises react to light and dark. She can now move in rhythm to music played outside the womb. The fetus's skin has turned red and wrinkly, and she's bulked up to three pounds and measures fifteen inches long. Her brain is developing incredibly quickly, but the surface of it is still fairly smooth and she's not really capable of much rational thought (given her living situation, that's probably a good thing).

What's Going On with You

Increasing Acceptance of the Pregnancy

As we've discussed earlier, for most expectant fathers the process of completely accepting the pregnancy is a long one—with the baby becoming progressively more real over the course of the nine months. "It's like getting the measles," said one man interviewed by researcher Katharyn May. "You get exposed, but it takes a while before you realize that you've got it." Another researcher, Pamela Jordan, found that despite seeing the fetus on a sonogram many men don't really experience their children as real until they meet them face-to-face at birth.

Visualizing the Baby

The growing reality of the pregnancy is reflected in men's dreams as well. Researcher Luis Zayas has found that in expectant fathers' dreams in the early and middle stages of the pregnancy "the child is not represented as a person. Instead, symbols of the child are present." But as the pregnancy advances to the final stage, expectant fathers—consciously and unconsciously—produce clearer images of their children.

If you're discussing this with your partner, keep in mind that women typically begin visualizing their children very early in pregnancy. These visions, which occur both in daydreams and night dreams, undoubtedly have something to do with the physical link the woman has with the fetus, as well as with the fact that many women—thanks largely to socialization—have no problem seeing themselves as mothers. In addition, pregnant women generally dream and fantasize about babies, while expectant dads tend to imagine themselves with three- to five-year-old children. This was certainly true for me. In almost every dream or fantasy that I had involving children while my wife was pregnant, I was holding hands, leaving footprints on the beach, or playing catch—all things you can't do with an infant. My wife, in contrast, dreamed of a palm-sized, hairless baby who talked to her like an adult.

"I want kids. He wants children."

Speculating about Gender

In case you hadn't noticed, our society is fixated on gender. So it's not surprising that most parents (if they don't already know) eventually—or constantly—speculate about the sex of their unborn baby. Is your partner carrying the baby high? Wide? Low? Are the baby's kicks hard enough to move your hand, or are they more gentle? Is your partner's complexion clear, or does she have a little acne? There are literally hundreds of absolutely, positively surefire ways of determining what flavor your baby will be. Each has a fifty-fifty chance of being right, and before your baby is born, you'll hear every one.

A lot of the speculating people do about their unborn children is based on common stereotypes and prejudices that almost all of us have about gender long before our kids are born. Take the baby's kicks, for example. Expectant mothers who know they're carrying boys often describe the babies' movements as "vigorous," "earthquakelike," or even just "very strong." They describe girls' kicks as "very gentle," "not terribly active," or "lively but not excessively energetic." Truth is, says Carole Beal, author of *Boys and Girls: The Development of Gender Roles,* there aren't any differences between boys' and girls' fetal activity levels.

Preconceived notions (so to speak) such as these may also have an influence on expectant parents' preferences. "Parents usually say they don't care what gender their child is as long as it's healthy," says Beal. "But the truth is that couples have a definite preference for the sex of their child." That preference is usually for a boy, and it's expressed by both men and women. Generally speaking, dads prefer boys because they feel more comfortable with them or because they feel that a boy would carry on the family name. Mothers may prefer boys because they know—instinctively or otherwise—how much it means to their husbands.

Interestingly, more women than men call their unborn baby "it." However, both men and women prefer to call the baby by some kind of nickname. In our case, the nicknames we gave our in-utero daughters stuck with them long after they were born. We called our older "The Roo"—as in kanga—because she kicked so hard she could knock an open book off my wife's belly. And we called our younger "Pokey" because, unlike her sister, she preferred to jab and poke.

Some expectant fathers are actually afraid of getting a child of the "wrong" gender, feeling that if they do, they won't be able to have the parenting experience they'd imagined. For many men, their images of themselves as parents are closely linked to the gender of their children. As boys, we spent a great deal of our childhood engaging in physical activities such as running, jumping, wrestling, and playing football. So it's natural to imagine ourselves doing the same things with our own children. Yet some men feel uncomfortable with the idea of wrestling with their daughters, believing that playing physically with girls would somehow be inappropriate. The truth of the matter is that not only is it safe and appropriate to play physically with girls, it's quite beneficial for them in some unexpected ways (see pages 235–38 for more on this).

Your preferences may have a major impact on a lot of other people. According to Beal, boys tend to bring fathers into the family more: fathers of newborn boys actually visit the nursery more often and stay there longer than fathers of girls. In addition, couples who have girls first often have more children, trying to have a boy. But those who have boys first often end up with smaller families. Some experts speculate that this is at least in part due to the perception that boys are more "difficult." And two researchers in Stockholm, Sweden, recently found that men are generally more satisfied with their role as fathers when their babies—boys or girls—are the gender they'd hoped for.

At the same time, there's evidence that children who did not turn out to be the gender their parents preferred had worse relationships with their parents in childhood than preferred-gender kids. That was especially true for kids whose parents had wanted a boy but got a girl. And most interesting—and most horrifying—Beal found that divorce rates are lowest for couples who have only boys, and highest when they have only girls.

It's going to be tough, but if you find yourself preferring one gender over the other—particularly if you're hoping for a boy—try to stop. If you can't, do yourself and everyone else a favor and keep it to yourself. If your child turns out to be the "wrong" gender, chances are he or she will eventually find out about it (probably from an unthinking friend or relative whom you once told in complete confidence). Besides the problems I just raised in the previous paragraphs, the feeling of being inadequate, of "letting you down," and even of being secretly rejected or loved less, may haunt your child for many years, especially in adolescence, when self-confidence is often at a low.

Fear of Falling Apart During Her Labor

Men are supposed to be strong, right? Especially while their wives are pregnant. And any sign of weakness could be taken as an indication of, well, weakness. Perhaps it's those old societal pressures that make most men dread labor—not only because they aren't looking forward to seeing their partners in pain, but because they're afraid that they'll simply fall apart. And everybody knows that real men don't crack under pressure.

If you're worried about how you'll perform during your partner's labor, do yourself these favors:

- Read the "Classes" section on pages 132–41—especially the "What If You Feel Like You Don't Want to Be in the Delivery Room at All?" section at the end. The more you know about what to expect during the labor and delivery, the less likely you are to worry that you won't be able to handle things.

- Remember that it rarely happens. Dr. Jerrold Shapiro interviewed more than two hundred expectant fathers, none of whom fell apart during his partner's labor.
- Keep talking to your partner and let her know how you feel. The more supported and understood you feel, the less likely you'll be to feel that you need to do everything absolutely perfectly.
- Talk to some other dads who've been through it. Most fathers who have will say it was some combination of tiring, exhilarating, amazing, boring, scary, exciting, bloody, annoying, and just about any other positive or negative feeling you can come up with. And just about all of them will also tell you they wouldn't have missed it for the world.

Staying Involved

Choosing a Name

Naming a child may sound like an easy task, but it's harder than you think. And you'd better start thinking about it soon, because the second question you're going to hear after the baby comes (the first being "Boy or girl?") is "What's the baby's name?" Here are a few things you might want to keep in mind as you begin your search:

- Think about the future. That name that strikes you as unbearably cute right now might be unbearably ridiculous when your child gets nominated to the Supreme Court. Watch out for rhyming names (Jane Payne, Bill Hill), and check the initials before you make your final decision (Priscilla Isabella Grady could end up as PIG).
- According to the author of *The Best Baby Name Book in the Whole Wide World,* boys who have peculiar names (Armin, for instance) have a higher incidence of mental problems than boys with common ones, and than girls with peculiar ones.
- Do you need—or want—to honor a relative?
- Do you want a name that indicates your ethnic or religious background?
- Do you want something unique yet manageable?
- Do you want something easy to spell and/or pronounce?
- How do you feel about the nicknames that go with it?
- How does it sound with the last name? How would the nicknames sound with the last name?
- No, you can't use numbers. (There was a real-life court case a while back about a guy in Minnesota who tried to change his name to a number. He lost.)

HOW TO PICK 'EM

Start by making a list of the ten boys' and ten girls' names you like best. Exchange lists with your partner and cross off all the ones on her list you couldn't possibly live with. She'll do the same to your list. If there are any left, you're in business. If not, keep repeating the process until you come up with names acceptable to you both. Some couples who absolutely cannot agree on two names decide instead to let one partner choose the name if it's a boy and the other choose the name if it's a girl (and let the loser choose the next child's name).

Not only is this little exercise fun, but it will also give you and your partner some interesting insights into each other's minds. My wife, for example, had never really taken my interest in mythology seriously until the names Odin (the chief god in Norse legends) and Loki (the Norse god of mischief and evil) showed up on my top-ten list. I don't know what I'm more grateful for, that both those choices were vetoed or that both our children are girls.

Another approach—albeit an odd one—to picking names is offered by Albert Mehrabian in his book *The Name Game* (Signet, 1992). Mehrabian surveyed two thousand people, asking them to judge several thousand first names and rate them according to success, morality, health, warmth, cheerfulness, masculinity/femininity. Not surprisingly, Mehrabian found that certain names evoke certain stereotypes. Bunny, for example, scored high on femininity, but low on morality and success. Ann and Holly were highly rated in all categories. For boys, Grover and Aldo were big losers in all categories, while Hans (go figure) was rated highly across the board.

So what does all this mean? No one knows. Some onomasticians (people who study names) claim that a child's name has a direct and profound effect on the kind of a life, and successes, he or she will have. Some cite a study in which fifth- and sixth-grade teachers were asked to grade identical essays called "What I Did Last Sunday." The essays "written" by Michael and David were given one full grade higher than those "written" by Elmer and Hubert. Similarly, Karen and Lisa outperformed Bertha by one and a half grades. Other studies have shown that, contrary to popular opinion, unusual names may actually have a *positive* effect for college women.

If you need a little help, there are a ton of resources out there—each containing thousands of names and their meanings. Here are just a few of the most fun ones:

- For the traditional yet contemporary, try *Beyond Jennifer & Jason, Madison & Montana: What to Name Your Baby Now* by Linda

Rosenkrantz and Pamela Redmond Satran (Griffin, 1999); *The Parent Soup Baby Name Finder: Real Advice from Real Parents Who Have Named Their Babies and Lived to Tell About It* by Kate Hanley and Nancy Evans (NTC/Contemporary, 1998); or *The Greatest Baby Name Book Ever* by Carol McD. Wallace (Avon, 1998).

- Concerned about how the names you're considering will impact your child's future? Go to http://chinesefortunecalendar.com to check out her Chinese numerology or take a look at Martha Holsome's *Name Your Child for Success* (2000).
- Feeling spiritual or New Agey? Try *The New Age Baby Name Book* by Sue Browder (Workman, 1998) or *Hey Baby, What's Your Sign?: The Astrological Baby Name Book* by Nancy Burkem (Berkley, 1999).
- Are you religious? There's *Your Name Is Your Blessing: Hebrew Names and Their Mystical Meanings* by Benjamin Blech and Elaine Blech (Jason Aronson, 1999) or *A Saint for Your Name: Saints for Boys [or Girls]* by Albert J. Nevins (Our Sunday Visitor, 2000).
- Looking for something ethnic? *The African-American Baby Name Book* by Teresa Norman (Berkley, 1998) or *O'Baby: The Irish Baby Name Book* by Geoffrey Johnson (Penguin USA, 1999).
- Most of the major parenting Web sites (BabyCenter.com, ParentsPlace.com, and others) have baby name selection features.
- At http://www.childbirth.org/interactive/babynamer.html you can select names by choosing from various categories (sassy, carefree, independent, strong, sensitive, debonair, and others).
- If you're feeling lazy, you can pay the folks at Babynames.com to research and choose potential names for you after you narrow down your choices by telling them what kind of names you like: places, trendy, biblical, made-up, ethnic, and so forth).
- If you're really concerned about what other people think, epregnancy.com has polls and name-related discussion groups. You might also want to look at *The Baby Name Survey Book: What People Think of Your Baby's Name* by Bruce Lansky and Barry Sinrod (Meadowbrook, 1998), or *What Not to Name Your Baby* by Andy Meisler (10 Speed Press, 1996).

You'd think that all these resources would cover all the bases and that picking a name would be a breeze. But out of the 2,174,003 names my wife and I looked at, we came up with only four that worked for us (a first and middle for each daughter).

FAMILY PRESSURES/TRADITIONAL CUSTOMS

In many cultures (or families), your choice of names may be severely limited by tradition.

- Among the Kikuyu people of Africa, the family's first son is named after the father's father; the second son, after the father's grandfather; the first daughter, after the father's mother; and so on.
- In Myanmar, each day of the week is assigned a different letter of the alphabet and children's names must begin with the letter of the day on which they were born.
- In Thailand, the parents may ask a nearby priest—or even a fortune-teller—to give their child just the right name.
- Jews of Eastern European extraction generally don't name babies after living people because of the traditional fear that the Angel of Death might take the baby instead of the older namesake.
- If there is someone on either side of a family who absolutely has to be honored with a name for the sake of family peace, you may be able to find a reasonable compromise. Harry Truman's parents, for example, gave him the middle initial *S*—no name, no period, just the initial—to satisfy both grandfathers (whose names were Solomon and Shippe).

THE LAST-NAME GAME

If you and your partner already have the same last name, you haven't got anything to worry about; if you don't, there could be a few complications.

Perhaps we've lived in Berkeley too long, but my wife and I have various friends who have done all of the following when they had kids:

- Given the kids the man's last name (probably the most common)
- Given the kids the woman's last name (less common)
- Given the kids a hyphenated last name (but when Mary Jane O'Flaherty-Ignetowski marries Roberto Goldberg-Yamahito, what will *their* children's last name be?)
- Made up a completely new last name
- Given the boys the man's last name, and the girls the woman's

Birth Announcements

WHEN TO ORDER

Since you don't know the exact weight, height, or (unless your partner has had an amnio) gender of the baby before he or she is born, there's not much sense in having birth announcements printed until then. But running around trying

Baby Showers

Not too long ago, baby showers—like so many other baby-related activities—used to be considered "for women only." But today, if your partner's relatives or friends organize a shower for her, there's a good chance you'll be invited, too. (But don't hold your breath waiting for your friends or relatives to plan one especially for you.)

The vast majority of baby showers take place several weeks or months before the baby is born, and the idea behind them is obvious: give the new parents a selection of baby clothing, furniture, and toys so the soon-to-be newborn can come home to a well-stocked nursery. If your relatives and friends are so inclined, enjoy—a shower can be a wonderful way to share your excitement about the coming event with others. And don't forget to keep track of who gave what—after the birth, when you get around to those thank-you notes, all those yellow sleepers and *Where the Wild Things Are* dolls can look disconcertingly similar.

I've always thought, though, that having a baby shower before you've got a real baby in hand is kind of creepy—too much like tempting fate. After all, what if, God forbid, something were to happen to the baby? A friend of mine, when his wife was seven months pregnant, put a new patio in his backyard and carved the name of his yet-to-be-born son (they'd done an amnio) in the wet concrete. I could hardly bring myself to go back there until after the baby was safely home. Anyway, if you join me in the anti-shower camp, you may find that some people will be offended by your not wanting one. In such cases, try to steer them toward a post-birth shower instead (call it a "Welcome Baby" or "Baby Birthday" party if you want to stay away from the word "shower"). Be firm. Stressing how much more fun it will be for the guests to get presents for a baby whose name and gender are known may also make the no-shower news easier to swallow.

to decide on birth announcements is about the last thing you're going to want to do after the baby is born. So now is the perfect time to start shopping.

There are three basic types of birth announcements: the preprinted kind with blanks for you to fill in; the custom-made variety; and those you design yourself—either by hand or with a computer program. Fill-in-the-blank and custom-made announcements are available at most stationery and card shops. If you're ordering the custom-made kind, you can select the design you want in advance and then call in the baby's vital statistics as soon as you know them. Whatever type you choose, try to get the envelopes now and address them—or at least print up some labels—while your lives are still relatively calm.

WHAT TO INCLUDE

As medical science becomes more exact, birth announcements will probably contain your baby's IQ and future profession. But for now, all you really need to include is the baby's name, date and time of birth, weight, length (since they can't stand up, babies don't usually have "height"), and the names of the parents.

WHOM TO SEND ANNOUNCEMENTS TO

Family and friends are the obvious recipients. When it comes to more casual acquaintances and business associates, however, take it easy. Many people will feel obligated to send a gift if they receive a birth announcement, so don't send one to anyone from whom you wouldn't feel comfortable getting a gift. Exceptions include people who request an announcement as a memento, employers or employees who have already given you and/or your partner a baby gift and/or shower, and people your parents and in-laws ask you to send announcements to.

Classes

Until the late 1960s, there really was no such thing as childbirth education. Basically, all you had to know to have a baby was where the hospital was located. And all that expectant parents did to prepare for the arrival of their baby was set up a nursery. Women checked into the hospital, labored alone in stark, sterile rooms, received general anesthesia, and woke up groggy and tender, not even knowing the sex of the child they'd delivered. Meanwhile, men were left to pace anxiously in hospital waiting rooms until a nurse came to give them the happy news. Fathers who tried to buck their nonrole in the birth of their children were in for a real surprise. Dr. Robert Bradley, in *Husband-Coached Childbirth,* cites the 1965 case of a man who was arrested and fined for having "gained unauthorized admission to a hospital's delivery room in an attempt to witness the birth of his second child."

Today, however, the situation is radically different. It's hard to find a man who didn't already, or isn't planning to, attend the birth of his children (according to recent statistics, 90 percent of fathers-to-be are present at the birth) and just about everyone involved in the process—from parents to doctors—has given the word *preparation* a whole new meaning. Mothers and fathers frequently attend prenatal OB/GYN visits together, and many embark on a reading program reminiscent of cramming for college exams. In addition, an

increasing number of expectant couples are signing up for childbirth preparation classes. When my wife and I got pregnant for the first time, one of the first things we did was read everything we could get our hands on. By the time the baby was born, we'd probably read enough magazine and newspaper articles, books, and pamphlets to qualify for a degree in prenatal education. But unlike my various "real" degrees, which were fairly useless once I got out into the real world, my education in childbirth and child raising served me quite well.

SELECTING A BIRTHING CLASS

When the first childbirth preparation classes appeared in the late 1960s, the emphasis was on how to have a "natural," unmedicated childbirth. Recently, however, the focus has changed somewhat. While natural childbirth is still the goal of most classes today, the overriding principle is that the more you learn about pregnancy and the birth process—from good nutrition and exercise to the types of pain medications most frequently given to laboring women—the less you have to fear and the more in control you'll feel.

Most classes are taught in groups and give you an opportunity to ask questions about the pregnancy in a less hurried environment than your practitioner's office. They also allow you to socialize a little with other pregnant couples and

"Coach"—Don't Use That Word

Almost all of the most common childbirth methods now refer to the man as the childbirth "coach"—a term that seems to have been coined by Dr. Robert Bradley, the founder of the Bradley method. Today most expectant fathers (at least those who take childbirth classes) and their partners view themselves in those terms, but I agree with Professor Katharyn May that there are some very compelling reasons to erase the word from your nonsports vocabulary.

- The coach concept focuses attention on your role during the brief period of labor and delivery, but minimizes how important you've been throughout the pregnancy and how important you'll be to your child after the birth.
- The coach concept reinforces the sexist stereotype that you're some kind of prop, rather than a unique individual who's in the process of sharing a challenging life experience with your partner. It also places *way* too much pressure on you by implying that you should be providing direction if things don't go quite the way they're supposed to during labor and birth. Does anyone seriously expect that after maybe 20 hours of classes and absolutely no medical training you're going to know how to handle a true emergency?

So, if anyone calls you "coach," tell them you're not—you're the child's father.

compare notes. But, depending on the class and the other couples, you may not get as much out of the socializing part as your wife does. When my wife and I took our birthing classes, for example, the teacher lectured most of the time; the socializing consisted of the women discussing how much weight they'd gained, how painful their backs were, the color and consistency of their vaginal discharges, and how many times a night they had to get up to go to the bathroom. What was helpful for me was the class itself. And by the time we'd finished, I felt that whatever happened, whether we had an unmedicated birth or a medicated one, whether my wife had a C-section or an episiotomy (an incision to enlarge the vaginal opening), I'd know what was happening at every stage and what to do.

Although a lot of people use the terms "Lamaze" and "childbirth preparation class" interchangeably, there are in fact quite a few very different childbirth methods. What distinguishes one from another is the approach each takes to dealing with pain. Here's a little about the most common methods:

LAMAZE Developed by French obstetrician Ferdinand Lamaze after a trip to Russia in the early 1950s, this method is based on Ivan Pavlov's (yes, the guy with the dogs) theory that learned reflexes can be overcome by repetition and training. In this case, the learned reflex is pain and the way to overcome it is by focusing on something else—the woman's own breathing. Actually called *psychoprophylaxis,* the Lamaze method doesn't focus solely on drug-free labor and delivery. The object is to give expectant parents the knowledge they need to be able to make well-founded decisions. You can take these classes privately or at just about any hospital.

BRADLEY Like Lamaze, the Bradley method (founded by Dr. Robert Bradley) believes in educating and preparing the expectant parents for the labor and delivery experience. But instead of trying to distract the woman's attention from her pain, Bradley believes that she should just "go with it." If she feels like groaning, she's encouraged to groan; if she feels like screaming, she's encouraged to scream. The Bradley method also devotes a lot of attention to exercise and nutrition. Over 90 percent of Bradley graduates have "natural" births. Bradley was the original "husband-coached" childbirth method and does more to include the father than any of the other methods.

LEBOYER Hospital delivery rooms are usually bright, noisy places. Dr. Leboyer, a French obstetrician, contends that all the light and noise are quite stressful and upsetting for a newborn. Leboyer babies are generally born in dimmed rooms, often with the mother fully or partially submerged in warm water.

DICK-READ Grantly Dick-Read, an English obstetrician who, like most of his colleagues in the early part of the twentieth century, used chloroform to ease his patients' labor pains, developed a theory that fear is the source of pain during labor and delivery. Here's how it works: when someone's afraid,

Baby CPR

Another class you should try to fit in this month is baby CPR (if you wait until after the baby comes, you'll never get around to it). Hopefully, you'll never have to use the skills you'll learn, but learn them anyway—for your own peace of mind and for your baby's safety. You can find out where to sign up from your birth class instructor, your baby's pediatrician (if you've picked one already), the hospital you've chosen, or your local American Red Cross Community Education Center.

What Childbirth Classes *Don't* Teach You

While childbirth education classes are an important part of the birthing experience, there are a few things you probably won't learn there.

- **Ask a lot of questions.** No matter how much you've read or how thorough your class is, something you don't understand is bound to happen during the labor or delivery. When it does, don't let the hospital staff steamroller you. Have them explain everything they're doing, every step of the way. If you miss something the first time, have them explain it again.
- **Stand up for your rights.** Most couples have a tendency to step back and let the practitioners take control of the whole process, especially when something unusual happens. They feel out of place and unsure of their rights. Don't. *Your* child is about to be born—not the doctor's or the nurse's—and you have the right to have things done the way you want them done, unless you're asking for something medically unsafe. And keep in mind that there's a difference between being assertive and being annoying or confrontational, so be nice.
- **Don't be too quick to take no for an answer.** Often, the first thing out of a doctor's or nurse's mouth when you ask for something is "No"—not because it's the right answer, but because it's the easy answer. If you want the lights dimmed for the delivery and the staff refuses, do it yourself. If you want to videotape the birth and the doctor won't let you, ask why not. If you don't get a good explanation, do what you feel you should do.

the "fight or flight" instinct kicks in, drains blood away from organs that don't need it—such as the face—and pumps it to the organs that need it most, such as the legs. (Hence the expression "white as a sheet.") Fear also diverts blood away from the uterus (if you have one), leaving it unable to function correctly, which results in pain. Get rid of the fear, then—by relaxation techniques, affirmations, or even hypnosis—and the pain will follow. Dick-Read's theory—which is still very much in vogue today—was so radical at the time that it got him bounced out of the British Medical Society.

Childbirth classes usually run five to nine weeks (if you're really short on time, you may be able to find an intensive two- or three-day program) and typically cost $100 to $200 for the whole course. Your practitioner or the maternity ward of the hospital in which you're planning to deliver are good sources for information on where childbirth classes meet and how to sign up.

Whatever you do, take one as soon as you possibly can. The knowledge you'll get will help ease some of your anxieties for the rest of the pregnancy.

PREPARING YOUR OLDER KIDS

While millions of second- and third-time parents sign up every time for some kind of childbirth classes, very few of them ever consider that their older children might need some preparation as well. Here are a few things you can do to help get those big sisters- and brothers-to-be ready:

- Sign them up for a class too. A lot of hospitals offer classes for siblings.
- Try to have them spend some time with new babies.
- Give them some practice. Use a life-size doll to show them how to hold an infant and support its head. Demonstrate the proper way to touch a baby and explain the need to be gentle, but *do not* poke, or prod, or hit the doll to illustrate behavior to avoid. You'll just be showing the big kid exactly how to do what she's not supposed to do.
- Get them excited. Show them pictures of new babies, have them make a drawing for the new baby, even let them pick out some furniture or clothes or the color of the new baby's room.
- Prepare yourself for some disappointment. Most brand-new older siblings are thrilled—for a while. When the novelty wears off they're going to want to go back to being the center of the universe. See the "Helping Older Kids Adjust to Their New Sibling" section on pages 214–16 for tips on how to help the kids—and yourself—through this transition.

GETTING SOME EXTRA HELP

While you should definitely take a birthing class, don't forget that the focus is going to be exclusively on your partner: what she's going through, what she's feeling, and what you can do to help her. All these things are very important, of course, but you might still reasonably ask, "What about me?" Reading this book will help you prepare yourself for the emotional and physical experiences you'll be going through during pregnancy and birth. But while you and your partner are actually going through labor, you are both in a state of trauma. You're both under pressure and you both need support—physical as well as psychological.

Each time my wife was in labor, I tried to do everything they'd taught me in the classes we'd taken: I reassured her, held her, told her stories, massaged her back and legs, mopped her brow, encouraged her, "helped" her breathe, and fed her ice chips. It was absolutely exhausting and sometimes scary, and I sure could have used some relief and occasional comforting, but there wasn't anyone around to do it.

While You're Planning Ahead: Making an Impact

Unless you're a paramedic or an emergency room doctor, you probably don't have a lot of opportunities to save lives. But for a few minutes after your baby is born you'll have a chance to do just that. Best of all, you'll be able to do it with something you otherwise might have thrown out: your baby's umbilical cord.

The blood inside the umbilical cord is an incredibly rich source of *stem cells,* which are the essence of the body's immune system and the building blocks of every blood cell in the body. Stem cells divide and "give birth" to red blood cells (which carry oxygen from the lungs to every tissue and organ in the body), white blood cells (which protect the body against disease), and platelets (which help blood to clot).

The great thing about umbilical cord stem cells is that they can be used instead of bone marrow to help people fight cancer and other life-threatening illnesses, including various types of leukemia, anemia, and a number of other very serious diseases. So what can you do? Well, you have two basic choices: donate the cord blood so some other person can benefit, or store the cord blood for your own family's use. Donating the

Fortunately, however, there is a way to help ease the burden—both yours and your partner's—of the trauma of labor and delivery: get yourselves a *doula.*

WHAT IS A *DOULA?*

Although it sounds like it should mean "a little duel," *doula* is actually a Greek word that means "a woman caregiver of another woman." Most doulas have had children of their own, and all of them go through an intensive training period in which they are taught how to give the laboring woman *and* her partner emotional and physical support throughout labor, as well as information about the delivery.

According to Dr. Marshall Klaus, the doula concept is hardly a new one. For hundreds of years, pregnant women in more than 125 cultures have gone through labor with another woman at their side the whole time. This used to be the case here as well. But in the 1930s women began to have their children in hospitals instead of at home, and everyone but the laboring woman and her doctors was barred from the delivery room. In 1980, however, Dr. Klaus and his colleagues reintroduced the doula concept in the U.S. and gave it its name.

I've got to confess that when I met with Dr. Klaus, my first reaction was: no way. I've got too much invested in this pregnancy, and nobody is going to come between me and my wife during this critical stage. But as I continued talking to blood can be done for free; storing it will cost you from $1,200 to $1,300. (Donating cord blood isn't really necessary, unless a member of your family has or may have a high risk of needing it.)

The whole process is completely painless and noninvasive (except for the part where your partner has to give a small blood sample thirty days or so before delivery), but it has to be started within fifteen minutes after the birth. It will most likely be performed by the hospital delivery room staff and takes only a few minutes to complete.

If you're interested in either donating or storing, call one of the following:

- your partner's OB/GYN, who can tell you if your hospital offers that service
- local Red Cross chapter
- International Cord Blood Foundation: (800) 747-3319
- (888) cordblood
- Cord Blood Donor Foundation: www.cordblood.com

Whatever you do, get on it right now. You'll need to register in advance —sometimes as much as eight to ten weeks—do some paperwork, and bring a special collection and transportation kit with you to the birth.

Dr. Klaus and reading the research on doulas, I began to change my mind.

It turns out that the presence of a doula can have some rather dramatic effects on the length of a woman's labor (making it as much as 25 percent shorter), as well as on the odds of her needing pain medication (reducing them by up to 47 percent), forceps delivery (reduced by 35 to 82 percent), or a Cesarean section (reduced 34 to 67 percent). Considering my wife's history of long, painful labor, I began to feel that having a doula around the next time might be the way to go.

But would a doula do anything for me? Wouldn't she just push me out of the way? "The doula is there to help parents have the type of birthing experience they want," says Dr. Klaus. "She will never take over or attempt to control the birth. We make the mistake of thinking that a father can take a birthing class and be prepared to be the main source of support and knowledge for the entire labor. That's just unreasonable. A doula can reach out to the man, decreasing his anxiety, giving him support and encouragement, and allowing him to interact with his partner in a more caring and nurturing fashion." In one interesting study a researcher compared couples who had a doula present with others who didn't. The study found that men in each group spent about the same amount of time with their partners.

Doulas—Some Basic Q's and A's

- **What do they charge?** Most doulas charge a flat fee of about $400, although the range can be anywhere from $200 to $800, depending on where you live. This usually includes one or two prenatal visits, labor and delivery—starting whenever you feel you need the doula until one to three hours after the birth—and a few postpartum visits to answer any questions you or your partner might have and to help your partner get started breastfeeding.
- **Will my insurance company pick up the tab?** There's no hard and fast rule about this. But more and more insurers are finding that paying for a doula can significantly reduce their other birth-related costs.
- **Where can I find one?** Your practitioner, hospital, or local chapter of the LaLeche League should be able to help you locate one. The easiest way, though, might be to get a referral from Doulas of North America. You can visit their Web site at www.dona.org, or contact them the old-fashioned way: 13513 North Grove Drive, Alpine, UT 84004, tel: (801)756-7331, fax: (801)763-1847.

Many men, even after taking birthing classes, still feel unsure about how they'll "perform" during the labor. Others feel they'd like to be fully involved in the pregnancy, but that labor and delivery are experiences that women are simply better equipped to handle. If you fit into either of these categories, or if you think it might be reassuring to have someone knowledgeable and supportive at your side during labor, consider a doula.

WHAT IF YOU FEEL LIKE YOU DON'T WANT TO BE IN THE DELIVERY ROOM AT ALL?

Years ago, no one expected men to be involved in their partners' pregnancies or to be there for the births of their children. But today, men who aren't enthusiastically involved are generally regarded as insensitive Neanderthals. The problem with such a black-and-white approach is that "there's a fine line between finding options for father participation, and pressuring men to adopt levels of involvement which may be unwanted or inappropriate for them," says Katharyn May. The truth of the matter is that not all of us feel the same need to be involved, and the last place some men should be is in the delivery room.

You may be squeamish during medical procedures or worried about losing control during labor. You may not want to see your partner in pain, or you may simply be feeling ambivalent about the pregnancy. You may be downright frightened by what you saw in some of the movies you viewed during your childbirth prep class. You may even be feeling resentful about the pressure other people are putting on you to get involved. It's important to remember that these—and any other feelings you might have for just not wanting to be there—are not only completely normal, but they're shared by more men than you might think.

If you're feeling less than overjoyed about being involved in the labor and delivery, try some or all of the following:

- **Talk to other fathers.** Hearing what other men have been through may help you get over some of your concerns. You might also find that you're not alone.
- **Talk to your partner.** Let her know what you're feeling and why. At the same time, reassure her about your commitment to her and to the baby.
- **Understand what your partner is thinking.** Instead of being sympathetic, she may interpret your apprehensiveness as a sign that you don't care about her or the baby.
- **Do it for her.** No matter how well you explain it to your partner, your desire to miss the birth or to miss the classes is probably going to hurt her. If you can stomach it at all, at least try to take the class—it will help her feel more understood, and you might just learn what it is that's been bothering you.
- **Consider a doula.** See pages 138–40 for information about doulas.
- **Don't feel that you're a failure.** You're not. As many as half of all expectant fathers have at least some ambivalence about participating in the pregnancy and childbirth. Being forced into a role that isn't comfortable for you will do you—and your partner—more harm than good.
- **Don't give in to the pressure.** If, after everything is said and done, you still don't feel comfortable participating, don't. But be prepared: your family, friends, and medical practitioner will probably suggest that you just quit pouting and do what you're "supposed to."
- **Don't worry about how your child will turn out.** While there's plenty of evidence about the positive impact on children of early paternal bonding, your not being there for the actual birth—whether it's because you didn't want to or because you simply couldn't—will not cripple your children; you'll still be able to establish a strong relationship with them. Just make sure you're there right after the birth.

THE 8TH MONTH

Making a List and Checking It Twice

What's Going On with Your Partner

Physically

- Even stronger fetal activity
- Heavier vaginal discharge
- General discomfort getting more severe
- Frequent urination
- Sleeplessness—can that really be a surprise?
- Increased fatigue
- Shortness of breath as the baby takes up more room and presses against her internal organs
- Water retention, and swelling of the hands, feet, and ankles
- More frequent Braxton-Hicks contractions

Emotionally

- Feeling special—people are giving her their seats on buses or in crowded rooms, store clerks go out of their way to help her
- Feeling a bond with others, like a member of a secret club (strangers keep coming up to tell her about their own pregnancy experiences or to touch her belly); she might also be scared by all those horror stories or angry at the unsolicited touches
- Feeling exceptionally attractive—or ugly
- Worried about whether the baby will be normal, whether she'll be able to cope with the responsibilities of motherhood, and whether her body will ever get back to normal
- Afraid her water will break in public

What's Going On with the Baby

At this point, most babies will have assumed the head-down position that they'll maintain for the rest of the pregnancy. He's getting big and fat—eighteen inches long, five pounds (a little less if he's sharing his quarters with a sibling), and his body now looks a little more like it belongs with that huge head. With practically no room to maneuver around, the baby's movements are becoming a little less frequent but often so powerful that you can frequently tell which part of his body is doing the poking. His sense of hearing is getting so good that he now responds differently to your partner's and your voices. Chances of survival outside the womb are excellent.

What's Going On with You

Dealing with the "Public" Nature of Pregnancy

As intensely private as pregnancy is, it is also inescapably public. Your partner's growing belly can bring out the best—and the worst—in people. Perfect strangers will open doors for her, offer to help her carry things, give up their seats in crowded subway cars and buses. In some ways, people's interest in pregnant women and in the process of creating life is heartwarming. But there may come a point when this outpouring of interest in her status and concern for her comfort begins to feel like an invasion of privacy.

People would often come up to my wife when she was standing in the check-out line at the grocery store and start chatting. The "conversations" would usually begin fairly innocuously, with questions like, "So, when are you due?" or pronouncements about the baby's gender. But after a while the horror stories would inevitably come out—tales of debilitating morning sickness, ten-month pregnancies, thirty-hour labors, emergency C-sections, anesthesia that didn't work, and on and on. And as if that weren't enough, people would, without even asking, start touching, rubbing, or patting her belly.

Perhaps the strangest thing about the public nature of pregnancy is that many women seem to take it all in stride. I kept waiting for my wife to bite some belly-rubber's hand off, but she never did. For some men, however, this touching business can bring out feelings of anger: "Nobody touches my woman!" If this happens to you, it's best to take your cues from your partner. If she doesn't mind, try to relax.

Panic

Just about six weeks before our first daughter was born, I suddenly had a great epiphany: our childless days were about to be over. It wasn't that I was worried about becoming a father—I already felt confident and prepared for my new role: I'd read a lot of material about becoming a parent, my wife and I had been taking childbirth classes, and we'd thoroughly discussed our concerns and fears.

What had struck me was much more superficial: once the baby came, it would be a long time before we'd be able to go to movies, plays, or concerts (or just about anyplace where you might have to be quiet), or even stay out late with our friends.

As it turned out, my wife was feeling the same thing at about the same time, so during the last two months of the first pregnancy, we ate out more often, went to more movies, saw more plays, and spent more late evenings with friends than in the next three years combined. A lot of expectant dads who are worried about the impending loss of their social lives find themselves looking up and visiting old friends they haven't seen for years.

In addition to trying to pack a lot of fun activities into the last few months of the pregnancy, you might want to consider cramming in a few practical things as well: when you (or your partner) are preparing food, try to double or even triple the recipes and freeze what's left over in two-person servings. Believe me, during that first postpartum week, defrosting a container of frozen spaghetti sauce is a lot easier than making a new batch from scratch.

Nesting

After morning sickness and 2 A.M. cravings for pickles, perhaps the most famous stereotype about pregnancy is a woman's "nesting instinct." Most women, at some point in their pregnancies, become obsessed (often

unconsciously) with preparing the house for the new arrival: closets and cupboards are cleaned, and furniture that hasn't been budged for years suddenly has to be swept under.

Although much has been made of the woman's instinct, a variety of studies have shown that almost all expectant fathers experience some sort of nesting instinct themselves. Besides worrying about finances, many men spend a lot of time assembling—or even building—cribs, changing tables, and other baby furniture; shopping for baby supplies; painting and preparing the baby's room; rearranging furniture in the rest of the house; and even trying to find a larger living space for their growing families.

For some men, these activities are a way to keep busy and to avoid feeling left out. But for others, they represent something much more fundamental. As Pamela Jordan writes, "These nesting tasks may be the first opportunity the father has to do something for the baby rather than his pregnant mate."

Sex—Again

Whereas the second trimester is frequently a time of increased sexual desire and activity, during the third trimester your sex life is bound to suffer. The most common reasons for this are:

- A mutual fear of hurting the baby or your partner.
- Fear that your partner's orgasm might trigger premature labor.
- Your partner's physical discomfort.
- Your partner's changing body makes the "usual" sexual positions uncomfortable.
- Your sense of changing roles. Soon your partner will no longer be only your partner; she's going to be a mother—someone just like your own mother. Remember that as she begins to see you as a father, your partner may have similar (subconscious) thoughts.

Unless your partner's doctor has told you otherwise, sex still poses no physical risk to the baby or to your partner. As we discussed on page 102–5, if you're both still interested in sex, now would be a good time to try out some new and different positions. Again, if you and your partner aren't in sync, sexually speaking, it's critical to talk things through.

Several researchers have noted that a small number of expectant fathers have affairs during the late stages of their partners' pregnancies. But these "late-pregnancy affairs" rarely happen for the reasons you might think. Dr. Jerrold Shapiro found that most men who have had a late-pregnancy extramarital affair share the following characteristics:

- They felt extremely attracted to their partners and were very interested in "affectionate sexual contact" with them.
- They felt particularly excluded from the pregnancy and birth process.
- The affair was with a close friend or relative of the woman. (This would indicate that the person with whom the man had the affair was also feeling excluded from the pregnant woman's life during the pregnancy.)

Expectant mothers also have affairs during their pregnancies. In fact, Dr. Shapiro suggests that women are just as likely to have affairs as men. Couples who suddenly find themselves with no sexual outlet—and are feeling pushed away or misunderstood by their partners—may be tempted to satisfy their needs elsewhere.

Birth Plans

The notion that an expectant couple has some choice in the labor, delivery, and immediate postpartum-period procedures is a fairly recent one. And while you may be tempted just to "leave things up to the professionals" at the hospital, you'll have a much better—and less stressful—birthing experience if you and your partner spend some time thinking about what you really want, and writing up a birth plan.

A birth plan is a great way for you and your partner to make decisions and set goals for the labor and delivery while you still have clear heads. Remember, though, that things rarely, if ever, go the way they're supposed to. So, be flexible. Also, be sure to discuss your plan with your practitioner and with the hospital. There may be certain policies that can't be breached. Here are some topics you may want to cover in your plan:

- **Emergencies.** Do you want the doctors or midwives to handle things on their own or do you want them to explain what's going on? If your partner is unconscious or unable to make a decision, should the practitioners get your permission before doing anything out of the ordinary?
- **Pain medication.** Do you want the hospital staff to offer it if they feel your partner could use some? Or do you want them to wait for her to ask for it?
- **Staying together.** Do you and your partner want to remain together for the entire labor and delivery?
- **Freedom of movement.** Will your partner be able to labor in the hallways (or in the shower), or will she have to stay in bed?
- **Labor.** Do you want to be able to select your own positions? If labor slows down, does she want to be offered oxytocin or other drugs to speed it up?

- **Shaving.** Does your partner want her pubic area shaved or left alone? (Unless she's having a C-section, there's no real reason to shave her if she doesn't want it done.)
- **Pictures and videos.** Do you want to take them? Do you want someone else to? Do you want to be able to take them even if there's a C-section?
- **Fetal monitoring.** Does your partner want the baby's heart rate monitored by machines throughout her labor, or would she prefer that monitoring be done only when necessary?
- **The birth.** Do you want the doctors to try forceps or suction to speed up the delivery, or do you want to hold out for a while longer? Do you want any other people (friends, relatives, midwife, other children) to attend the birth? Will a mirror be available (so your partner can get a better view of the birth)?
- **Episiotomy.** If your partner's vagina won't stretch enough to allow the baby's head through, the doctor may suggest making a small cut in the perineum—the space between the vagina and the anus. Some doctors do episiotomies as a preventative measure, others don't do them unless absolutely necessary. Some people believe that a small but natural tear in the vagina is better than a surgical cut. Others say that the cut helps control the tearing. Either way, your partner should learn as much as she

Sample Birth Plan

This birth plan outlines our desires for this labor, birth, and postpartum period. These plans can be revised for medical reasons, should some complication arise, after informed consent has been well established.

- Mother will be free to move during labor and birth to any position she prefers or finds helpful to the birthing process.
- We would prefer that no pain medication be routinely offered. If the mother wants something, she'll ask for it.
- We prefer that no episiotomy be performed unless absolutely necessary; a tear is acceptable if unavoidable.
- The baby will be given directly to the mother after birth.
- The baby will be with at least one of his or her parents at all times.
- Father would like to help "catch" the baby as he or she emerges.
- Father will cut the cord, but not until it stops pulsing.

We would like to thank everyone involved for their support and respect for our desires and preferences during this birth.

can about episiotomies and think about whether—barring emergencies, of course—she would want one, and if so, whether she would want it done with or without anesthesia.

- **Cesarean section.** In case of a C-section, can you stay with your partner, or will you have to be separated? Will you be separated only for the spinal or epidural anesthesia, or for the entire procedure? Where will you be allowed to stand?
- **The baby.** Who will cut the cord, and when? Do you want the hospital staff to take the baby away for cleaning and testing right after birth, or would you like him or her handed to you and/or your partner first?
- **After the birth.** Do you want the baby to breastfeed right away, or will you be bottle feeding? Do you want the baby with one of you all the time, or would you rather have him or her kept in the hospital's nursery? What about circumcision?
- **Going home.** Do you want to stay for as long as the hospital will let you, or do you want to go home as soon as possible?

Birth instructor Kim Kaehler suggests that you keep the following points in mind when writing your plan:

- In the opening paragraph, indicate your flexibility should a medical emergency arise. But also stress the importance of informed consent.
- Try not to make it sound like a legal document. That could make a doctor or other health-care provider very nervous and defensive. Your practitioner will not be comfortable if she or she feels his or her hands will be tied in the case of an emergency.
- Try to word your desires in a positive way. Avoid beginning every statement with "No" or "Do not."

Should Your Older Children Attend the Birth?

Having older children attend the birth of the new baby can be a tricky thing. In general, it's probably okay to have children present both during labor and immediately after the birth. But for a variety of reasons, children—especially those under five—probably shouldn't be there for the birth itself.

- They may be frightened that their mother is being hurt, and that all of the blood and moaning might mean she is dying.
- Even well-prepared children can have unpredictable reactions, and you and your partner won't want to have to be distracted by anyone else's needs but yours (and the new baby's).
- The older child might be jealous of all the attention paid to the new baby.

If you're still thinking about having an older child there for the birth of his or her new sibling, be sure to discuss the idea with your doctor first. Then, get yourselves some visual aids—books, movies, or pictures of births, for example—and plan on having some long discussions with the child. *Birth: Through Children's Eyes,* edited by Sandra Van Dam Anderson and Penny Simkin (P. T. Pennypress, 1981), is a good resource. Encourage the child to ask questions, answer them, tell him what's going to happen, talk about acceptable and unacceptable behavior, plan on spending some private time with him—older children can get really jealous.

And finally, make sure there's an adult around to help each child who will be at the birth. This person should be prepared to talk to the child about what's happening and to take the child out of the room if necessary. Your place—and your focus—is with your partner.

- Refrain from including things in your plan that are not part of your birthplace's normal procedures. (If your hospital doesn't routinely do fetal monitoring, there's no need to mention it.)
- Be sure to thank everyone for their respect and support.
- After you and your partner have hammered out a draft of your birth plan, show it to your doctor. Let him or her go over it and make suggestions.
- Remember that a birth plan is not a contract. it is a way for you to communicate your preferences to your partner's practitioners. If you don't trust them to respect your desires to have your baby's best interests at heart, try to find a new team.

Making Final Plans

REGISTERING AT THE HOSPITAL

Despite what you've seen on TV and in the movies, getting to the hospital doesn't have to be a frantic exercise at breakneck speed. Fortunately for men (but not nearly as fortunately for our partners), the onset of labor and the delivery itself are usually hours (if not days) apart, so if you plan carefully, there should be plenty of time to get everything done. And once you've got your bags packed and ready to go (see pages 154–55 for details), the next most pressing concern is registering at the hospital.

Most hospitals will allow—or may even require—you to register up to sixty days before the anticipated birth of the child. This doesn't mean that you're making a reservation for a particular day. All it means is that when you do show up at the hospital, you won't have to waste time signing papers while your partner is screaming and having contractions. So check with your hospital's or clinic's administrative offices as soon as you can. Doing so is particularly important because besides making you fill out 785 forms, the hospital will have to get a verification of coverage and eligibility from your insurance company. And that can take some time.

Finding a Pediatrician

I know, you don't actually have a baby yet, but you will soon, so you'd better start putting some real thought into picking a doctor for her. Most people take their kids to pediatricians, but plenty of family practitioners see babies too. During their first year, both my daughters saw their pediatrician nine times—and they were both as healthy as horses. A typical first-year schedule includes visits every two weeks for the first month, monthly or every other month until six months, once in the ninth month, and again in the twelfth month. Clearly, since you're going to be spending a lot of time with your child's doctor, you should select someone you think you can get along with at least until your child turns sixteen or so. Given the state of health coverage in this country, your options may be limited. But if your plan gives you some flexibility, try to interview several prospective pediatricians. Here are some questions you should ask (you might want to write some of them down and bring them along to the interview):

- **What insurance plans do you participate in?**
- **What is your philosophy about vaccinations?** Although the vast majority of pediatricians advocate routine vaccination, there is a vocal minority that doesn't. The debate is interesting but beyond the scope of this book.
- **Where do you stand on breastfeeding?** Current thinking is that babies should be breastfed for a *minimum* of one year, but you want a doctor who's flexible enough not to make your partner feel bad if she can't breastfeed for some reason or simply doesn't want to.
- **How long are routine office visits?** For at least the first few visits you're going to have a ton of questions. Some doctors, though—particularly those in HMOs—often see six patients per hour, meaning that appointments can be as short as ten minutes. Other doctors are more relaxed and can spend twenty minutes or more with you and your baby.
- **How many doctors are in your practice?** You may think that male and female doctors are the same, but your child may not agree. When she was about two, my older daughter absolutely refused to see her regular (male) pediatrician, and insisted on seeing a "girl doctor." Don't worry about offending your pediatrician—about 75 percent of kids prefer to see a doctor of their own gender.
- **What about emergencies?**
- **What about nighttime and weekend hours?**
- **What about non-life-threatening emergencies?** Who's covering the phones and what happens of your child needs to be seen? During business hours, the practice we go to has a special, free phone line staffed by pediatric nurses who have successfully diagnosed at least 80 percent of the problems we've called about. At about $100 for an office visit, I can't tell you how much money this saved us.

GETTING TO THE HOSPITAL

Sooner or later—unless you're planning to have a home birth—you and your partner are going to have to get to the hospital. There are several ways of getting there, each with its own advantages and disadvantages:

- **Walking** If you live close enough to the hospital, walking may be the best option. You won't have to worry about any of the disadvantages of driving yourself or getting a ride (see below). You will, however, have to deal with the possible embarrassment of having people stare at you as your partner leans up against the side of a building every three minutes and bellows. But your partner may actually like this option, since walking can help make the contractions of early labor easier to cope with.

  If you're walking, be sure to bring enough cash to take a cab—just in case things don't go the way they should.
- **Driving yourself** No matter how much you've prepared, when labor really starts, you're going to be a little nervous, and that could be a little dangerous when you're behind the wheel of a car. You could get lost, get caught speeding, or even cause an accident. Worst of all, while your eyes and mind are on the road, they can't be where they really ought to be—on your partner. And when you finally get to the hospital, you'll have to deal with parking—and later retrieving—the car.

If you're driving, make sure you have a full tank of gas, that you know the route (and several alternatives) well, and that you allow enough time to get there. Don't worry: if you get there a little early they probably won't throw you out. Also, check with the hospital parking lot (if they have one) to find out their rates and hours of operation.

- **Getting a ride—taxi, friend, or relative** If you're in the back seat of someone else's car, you'll at least be able to tend to your partner. Problems might arise, however, if your partner goes into labor at 2 A.M. and your friends or in-laws take more than a minute or two to roll out of bed. In addition, since most people have never driven a pregnant woman to the hospital, they'll be at least as nervous (probably more) than you would have been. And watch out for potholes; my wife assures me they're hell for a laboring woman.

  If you're taking a taxi, have the phone numbers of at least three companies that can get a cab to your door within minutes, at any hour of the day or night. Also, be sure to have enough money for the fare. If you're planning on having someone else do the driving, make sure you have a few backups.

WHAT IF YOU HAVE OTHER KIDS?

If you have other kids—especially young ones—getting to the hospital can be doubly stressful and requires extra planning.

Toward the end of my wife's second pregnancy, we decided that we'd take a cab to the hospital. We also decided that if my wife went into serious labor in the middle of the night, we'd signal our friends who had agreed to take care of our older daughter by calling them, letting their phone ring once, hanging up, calling again, and letting it ring three times.

So, at one in the morning, we made the phone calls, got into the cab, and arrived at our friends' house, where, holding thirty-five pounds of sleeping deadweight, I pounded on the door for five minutes before giving up (our friends had apparently slept through the secret signals). Fortunately, we'd made a backup plan, and when we got to the hospital, we called my parents and had them take their grandchild to their house.

AND FINALLY, SOME LAST-MINUTE DETAILS

- Keep your doctor's number by the phone.
- Keep your gas tank full. Have an extra set of keys stashed someplace, or cash for a cab ready.

- Make sure you've checked to see whether there are any road closures or construction projects along your route to the hospital.
- Get ready at work. Labor usually starts without warning and can last a long time—sometimes more than a day. Be sure you've delegated urgent matters to a coworker or supervisor, and that your time-off plans are in order. (See pages 112–21 for more on work/family concerns.)

Packing Your Bags

FOR HER

- A favorite picture and/or anything else she might need or want to help her through labor and the birth.
- CD or tape player and some favorite music to help you both relax during labor.
- A bathrobe, a nightgown, or even one of your old T-shirts that she won't mind getting a little blood on.
- A large gym bottle (you know, the kind with the built-in straw) for sipping clear liquids.
- Warm socks and/or old slippers (again, ones she won't mind getting bloody).
- Change of clothes to go home in—not what she was wearing before she got pregnant. Sweats or maternity pants are particularly good.
- Nursing bra.
- Her toiletries bag. Don't forget things like mouthwash, toothbrush and toothpaste, contact lens paraphernalia, hairbrush or comb, and a hair ribbon or two.
- Box of heavy-duty maxi-pads (unless your partner doesn't mind the kind with the belt, which is what she'll get at most hospitals).

FOR YOU

- Comfortable clothes.
- Some magazines or a collection of your partner's favorite short stories to read to her.
- A swimsuit (you might want to get into the shower with your partner, and the nursing staff might be surprised at the sight of a naked man).
- Camera and film.
- This book.
- A cooler filled with snacks. This is *not* for your partner. (She shouldn't be eating while she's in labor but you'll need to keep your energy up.) You're not going to want to leave your partner, midcontraction, to run down to the

hospital cafeteria. If you have some extra room, bring along a small birthday cake and maybe even some champagne for afterward.

- Cash. Depending on the hospital, you may have to leave a cash deposit for phone or television rental. You'll probably need to pay for parking your car or for the taxi ride. You might also need a supply of quarters if you have to use a pay phone.
- Phone numbers of the people you'll want to tell the news to right away.
- Phone company credit card or your cell-phone charger—you may be making and receiving more calls that you ever though possible.
- Tennis balls for back rubs.
- Toothbrush, extra underwear, shaving kit, and the like. You'll probably end up staying at least one night.

FOR THE BABY

- An infant car seat (if you don't have one, the hospital won't let you leave).
- A little outfit to go home in—a sleeper or sleep sac is fine. (It's a good idea to wash all new clothes before putting them on the baby.)
- Diapers (and pins or diaper wraps if you're using cloth).
- Several receiving blankets, weather-appropriate.

Preterm Labor/Premature Birth

In the vast majority of pregnancies, labor doesn't start until about the fortieth week. However, a small but significant number of babies (8 to 10 percent) are born prematurely—meaning sometime before the thirty-seventh week. More than half of twins and about 90 percent of triplets, however, are born prematurely. Interestingly, identical twin boys are more likely to be born prematurely than identical twin girls. This gender distinction doesn't seem to hold for fraternal twins.

The symptoms of premature labor are exactly the same as those of real labor (see page 175 for more)—they just happen before they're supposed to. If your partner has any of the following symptoms, she may be considered high risk for giving birth early.

- An "incompetent cervix"—meaning that the cervix is too weak and may open, allowing the baby to be born too soon. Diagnosed early enough, an incompetent cervix can be "corrected" (and premature births prevented) by sewing the opening of the cervix shut.
- "Placenta previa" (when the placenta is covering up the cervix) or "placental abruption" (when the placenta has prematurely separated from the wall of the uterus).

While You're Waiting

If your partner is at risk for giving birth prematurely, try to carve out a few minutes to do a little research or make a few calls on the following topics. You're going to be plenty busy with other things, but the time you spend now will be well worth it.

- **Call Social Security and the Motor Vehicle Department.** Since premature babies sometimes need extra (and expensive) medical care, Social Security may help you out. You may also be able to get a handicapped parking pass, which should cut down on the time you have to spend looking for parking. Phone numbers are in the Government Listings section of your local phone book.
- **Find a doctor who has a lot of experience with premature babies.** Check with the pediatrician you've already selected, your insurance carrier, or the hospital where the baby will be born.
- **Find out about infant massage.** Researcher Tiffany Field found that preemies who got three fifteen-minute periods of gentle massage a day grew 50 percent faster than preemies who didn't. Hospital stays for the massaged babies were also a week shorter (and a week cheaper).

- Any kind of surgery during pregnancy.
- She's carrying twins (or more). See below.
- There's too much or too little amniotic fluid.
- She didn't eat well during the pregnancy or is (or has recently been) smoking, drinking, or using drugs.
- She's been spending a lot of time on her feet. Several recent studies have found that pregnant women who spend five hours or more standing or walking every day are as much as three times more likely to deliver prematurely than women who are on their feet less than two hours a day. So if your partner is a waitress or a nurse or runway model, she might want to switch to a desk job until after the baby's born.
- Exposure to Diethylstilbestrol (DES) while her mother was pregnant with her (many of the daughters of women who took DES to prevent miscarriage were born with abnormalities of the reproductive tract).
- She's had a previous premature labor.
- She's carrying an unusually small fetus.

When Premature Labor Really Isn't

If you're expecting twins (or more) and your partner goes into labor, chances are it's not premature at all. Although single babies spend an average of forty weeks under construction, most twins are born at about thirty-seven weeks. Triplets usually arrive at thirty-five weeks, and quads make their entrance a week earlier. Even if it turns out that you're going to be skipping the traditional ninth month, read the next chapter—especially the "What's Going On with You" section to make sure you aren't missing out on anything important.

The bad news about premature babies is that if they're born too soon they really aren't ripe yet. The fetus's lungs aren't fully developed until it's at least 28 weeks old. Babies born before that time have a far higher risk of developing serious respiratory problems, including chronic lung disease, as well as neurological and cognitive problems. Babies born at 28 to 32 weeks are far better off, but still at risk for vision and gastrointestinal difficulties.

The good news is that medical technology has advanced so much in recent years that the chances of survival are excellent. Ninety percent of 30-week babies do quite well. And by 35 weeks, it's up to 99 percent.

Obviously, it's to the fetus's benefit to spend as many days as possible right where it's supposed to be: in its mother's uterus. Therefore, if your partner shows signs of being in real labor (see page 175), call your doctor immediately. If caught early, premature labor can sometimes be arrested (usually with the help of intravenous drugs), and the fetus will be able to stay where it belongs for a few more weeks.

After an arrested premature labor, your doctor will most likely order your partner to stay in bed for the rest of the pregnancy. She may even be put on a home fetal monitor to keep an eye on the baby. If this happens, be prepared to step in and take over all of the household responsibilities, as well as responsibility for other children if you have them. If you aren't in a position to do this, you may have to hire someone or ask friends or relatives to help out. Your involvement, though, is actually a lot more important than you might think. Researcher Michael Yogman tracked a group of preemies and found that at three years old, for example, the IQ scores of the kids with highly involved dads were six points higher than the ones with less involved dads.

The Nursery: Everything You Need and What It Costs

There are literally hundreds of things you *could* buy for your newborn's nursery, but you'll go broke buying every single one of them. You could, for example, buy a special machine that warms up the wipes you use to clean your baby's bottom. But believe me, your baby's bottom will get just as clean with room-temperature wipes. Here are some of the items you'll truly need or at least have a pretty good chance of using. The prices listed are retail; you can probably save up to 80 percent by buying these things at garage sales, from friends, or at used-furniture stores.

Essentials to Have Waiting at Home

FOR THE BABY

Note: You'll have to increase the quantities somewhat if you have twins or more

- Enough diapers to last for at least a week (you're not going to want to go shopping)
- Baby soap and shampoo
- Thermometer (You may want to invest in the electronic kind that takes the temperature via the ear almost instantly. Preventing your baby from squirming for three minutes while trying to keep a thermometer in her mouth or bottom is going to be an unpleasant experience for everyone concerned.)
- An ear bulb (these are usually used for rinsing adults' ears, but for babies, they're used for suctioning mucous from their noses. Well, what do you expect? They can't do it themselves!)
- Nail scissors (essential: a baby's nails are like tiny razors and grow like Jack's beanstalk)
- Cotton swabs and alcohol for umbilical cord dressing
- Some formula, just in case. But keep in mind that some breastfeeding experts think this is a bad idea, because it might be too big a temptation to give up brestfeeding.
- Bottles and a breast pump
- 5 or 6 onesies (those cute little one-piece suits)
- 5 or 6 pairs of booties (those stretchy socks)
- 3 or 4 undershirts
- 3 or 4 outfits with separate top and bottom (that way you can wash only the part that gets dirty). Try to get the kind that have snaps.

Please remember that when acquiring *anything* for your baby, safety should be your primary concern. So before you spend a fortune on Queen Victoria's original bassinet or drag out the crib that you (or your parents or grandparents) slept in as a kid, consider this: your baby will do just about everything possible to jeopardize his or her own life, from sticking his head between the bars of the crib and throwing himself off tall changing tables to burying herself under a pile of blankets left in the corner.

Before you buy anything for your baby—whether it's new or used—make sure it complies with the most recent safety standards. Some of them are listed

- 3 or 4 nightgowns or sleep sacs
- 1 or 2 coveralls with snaps
- 4 or 5 baby blankets
- 1 or 2 hooded bath towels
- 1 or 2 sun or snow hats
- 1 or 2 sweaters
- Snowsuit (as needed)
- 0 shoes (people who don't walk shouldn't wear shoes—it can hurt their feet)

A word of advice: Your baby will poop or vomit on his clothes every single day. So skip the silk T-shirts and the lamb's wool sweaters and stick with good-quality *washable* materials.

FOR YOUR PARTNER

- Nursing pads
- More maxi-pads (she may need these for weeks)
- Any medication or dressing materials needed in the event of a C-section or episiotomy
- Milk and vitamins, especially if she is nursing
- Flowers, and favorite chocolates or other foods she might have avoided during pregnancy
- A good book about your baby's first year of life. Modesty aside, my books *The New Father: A Dad's Guide to the First Year* and *A Dad's Guide to the Toddler Years* are the best resources out there for dads. And for your partner, and you too, Julie Tilsner's *Planet Parenthood* is wonderful.

in the sections that follow. For additional guidance on the safest—and best-quality—deals, consult the latest *Consumer Reports Guide to Baby Products.* The U.S. Consumer Product Safety Commission posts a list of product recalls on its Web site, www.cpsc.gov, or you can get them by calling (800) 638-2772. And you can find out the latest standards and requirements for car seats and other travel-related equipment from the National Highway Traffic Safety Administration (www.nhtsa.dot.gov or 800-424-9393).

BABY FURNISHINGS

CRIB: $150 to over $1,000. There's nothing that says *baby* quite like a crib. And so it's no surprise that this is one of the first pieces of baby furniture an expectant couple thinks about. Here are some safety tips:

- Get rid of corner posts. Babies can accidentally strangle themselves if their clothes become caught on a post. New cribs are constructed without them, but if you have your heart set on using a vintage model, you should unscrew or saw off the posts.
- Slats or bars should be spaced no more than 2 3/8 inches apart, and none should be broken or missing.
- Never place your crib near draperies, blinds, or anything else that has long, wall-mounted cords. Babies can tear these down or become entangled in them.
- Keep the crib away from radiators, heaters, and area rugs. The last thing you want to do while holding your baby is burn yourself or slip.
- Crib sides should slide up and down easily and lock solidly at the top. Any teething rails (the hard plastic caps over the top rails of the crib side) should be firmly attached. They're going to get chewed on a lot and you don't want them to come off.

Green Babies

People generally select the products they buy based on price, quality, availability, and brand. In recent years, though, consumers are paying more attention to how products impact the environment, whether it's their home environment or the one we all live in. One recent national poll found that 61 percent of American consumers say that, given the choice, they would rather buy environmentally friendly products. And 42 percent of adults aged eighteen to thirty-four actually tried a new product because they felt the product, its packaging, or the manufacturer benefited the environment. So what does this have to do with you and your baby? Plenty.

You might be concerned that the paint you used in the nursery could emit toxic fumes. Or maybe you're worried about the bleaches in your laundry and you'd prefer that your baby wear nothing but organic fabrics. Or perhaps you're concerned about how disposable diapers are impacting the environment. Whatever your concern, there are environmentally friendly alternatives to just about any product you're currently using.

You can find some of these products at places like Walgreens and Sears (which recently opened up special green sections) or at your local natural grocer. But the widest selection and the most resources are going to be online at places like Green Home (www.greenhome.com).

CRIB MATTRESS: $100 to $150. Couples are often surprised that mattresses are usually sold separately from the crib. The theory is that some babies prefer firm mattresses while others prefer softer ones. Don't skimp on mattresses—there's no reason why the one you buy now shouldn't last you through several kids. Just make sure you get a plastic mattress protector. A few safety tips:

- The firmer the better. Studies have shown that there is an increased risk of SIDS (Sudden Infant Death Syndrome) if the mattress is too soft. For the same reason, pillows should never be placed in cribs.
- The mattress must fit tightly into the crib (no more than two fingers' width between the edge of the mattress and the side of the crib).

CRIB ACCESSORIES

- Sheets: $20 to $60. Get the fitted kind.
- Bumper: $100 (optional). Even though they can't move very well, babies somehow manage to ram their heads against the sides of the crib—hard

enough to leave an impression of the slats or bars on their foreheads. It supposedly reminds them of the feeling of having their heads smashed up against your partner's pubic bone for the last month or two of pregnancy.

- Dust ruffle: $80 (extremely optional).
- Light blankets: $80. You do *not* need a heavy comforter now. It's a choking or smothering hazard.
- Mobile: $35 to $90 (optional). Some of the most beautiful (and most expensive) ones are made to be looked at from the side—where the person who bought it is standing. But remember whom the mobile is really for, and think about whether your baby is really going to be interested in looking at the bottom of a bunch of cars or the underside of a group of jungle animals. Your baby won't be able to make out specific shapes for a while yet. Experts believe, however, that they can distinguish bold, contrasting colors, and that is why black-and-white mobiles seem to please them the most.

BASSINET: $80 to $150. For the first few months of your baby's life, you may want him or her to sleep in the bedroom with you. If nothing else, this arrangement will make breastfeeding a lot more convenient. Bassinets come in a variety of styles (wheels, no wheels, handles, no handles, rocking, nonrocking). But because they generally accommodate a baby for only three months or so, you'll be better off borrowing a safe one from someone and passing it on to the next new parents.

CAR SEAT: $40 to $100. A car seat may be the most indispensable baby item. (Again, you won't be able to take your baby home from the hospital without one.) This is a critical purchase, so don't skimp. Stay away from hand-me-downs unless they're practically new and conform to the very latest standards. You may want to consider getting two—a small one (perhaps with handles so you can carry the baby around with you) that can be used until the baby reaches twenty pounds, and a larger one for later. There are also some car seat/stroller combinations out there. They run from about $100 to $300.

CHANGING TABLE: $70 to $200. Changing tables come in an unbelievable variety of sizes and configurations. Some have drawers so that they can be used as a dresser when your child no longer needs to be changed. The problem with drawers, however, is that you have to remember to take out what you need before you get started; when you're in the middle of changing the baby, the last thing you want to be doing is fumbling around blindly for a clean outfit. Be sure to get a foam pad for the top of the table and a couple of washable pad covers. You also should stock your changing table with a good supply of the following:

- Diapers
- Baby wipes
- Diaper rash ointment, such as A&D or Desitin
- Cotton swabs and alcohol for cleaning the umbilical cord stump
- Baby shampoo and soap (a mild one like Neutrogena or Dove is best)

Note: Stay away from baby powder. Most pediatricians believe that the dust could be harmful to babies.

PORTABLE PLAYPEN: $80 to $150. Perfect for children less than thirty-four inches tall and lighter than about thirty pounds. Not only does it fold up compactly enough to check as luggage when you're traveling, but it can also be used at home, to keep your baby from crawling under your feet while you're cooking, for example. Some of our friends' children essentially lived in their playpens for the first eighteen months of their lives.

STROLLER: $100 to $600. A good stroller can make life worth living, so don't waste your time or money on one that won't last. We took our older daughter and her stroller all over the world, and the stroller is still in perfect condition. Getting a quality stroller doesn't mean you have to buy the one with every available option. Stick to the basics, such as weight, ease of folding, brakes, and balance (you don't want the thing tipping over backward with your baby in it). Finally, make sure the handles are long enough for you to push the stroller when you're standing up straight. Most strollers are made to be used by women, which means that if you're over 5'7" or so, you'll have to stoop a little to push. You might not notice it at first, but after a while, your back may give you trouble. Handle extenders cost about $20 and are a great investment. City dwellers who do a lot of traveling on subways or buses will want a sturdy but collapsible stroller—preferably one that you can fold with one hand while holding the baby with the other. Otherwise, it's next to impossible to get onto public transportation (at least without annoying everyone behind you). The stroller/car seat combos are especially bulky and hard to fold.

BATHTUB: $20. A small plastic washbasin is best for newborns because a sink is too big and can be dangerous. When the baby outgrows the basin, you can soak his or her little formula-stained clothes in it.

Watch out for Triboluminescence

Never heard of it? Well maybe it's time you should. In 1999 English housewife Jill Furlough got a fright late one night when she saw green sparks shooting out of her sleeping eleven-month-old son's disposable diaper. She called the diaper manufacturers, who assured her that the sparks were the result of triboluminescence, an extremely rare—and perfectly harmless—buildup of energy probably caused by the friction of the baby's bottom rubbing against the inside of the diaper. (It's actually exactly the same chemical reaction that produces the sparks you see when you bite down on a Wint-O-Green LifeSaver in a dark room. Unlike static electricity, it doesn't generate any heat.) The boy apparently slept through the entire episode, and there's no record of any injury to anyone. Just something to think about.

MONITOR: $15 to $75. These handy devices let you listen to your baby wherever you are. If you look in traditional toy or baby-gear stores, where they call them "baby monitors," you'll pay more than in large hardware or home supply stores, where they're called "room monitors."

BABY CARRIER: $20 to $100. Whether it's a sling, a frontpack, or a backpack, you'll want to get something that you can use to carry your baby around in. Make sure it's comfortable and, if you're planning to share it with your partner, adjustable.

DIAPERS: A few years ago, no one would have thought that diapers would become a political issue or that something so ordinary could make or break friendships, but they have. Here are the basic arguments:

Some 18 billion disposable diapers account for more than 1 percent of the nation's landfill. They're made of plastic and will stay in their present form for thousands of years. "Biodegradable" diapers, which break down after only five hundred years, are available in many cities.

Cloth diapers, in contrast, are all natural. The problem is that they're made of cotton, which is taxing on farmland. And in order to sterilize them properly, diaper services wash them seven times (it's true) in near-boiling water, thereby consuming a tremendous amount of power, water, and chemical detergents. The clean diapers are then driven all over town in trucks that fill the air with toxic pollutants.

Assuming five to eight changes a day, plan on going through a minimum of about 4,000 diapers in the first two years alone—double that if you have twins. The choice is yours.

My wife and I started out by using cloth diapers for our older daughter. But every time she filled one up, the diaper had a nasty tendency to siphon the contents away from my daughter and onto my pants—not pleasant—and that meant even more laundry! It's possible that this phenomenon was the fault of my poor diapering technique. But I'm convinced that disposables, which have elastic around the leg openings, do a better job of keeping what belongs in a diaper actually in the diaper.

- **Disposable diapers:** $8 to $9 for about 50; more for the natural or organic ones. Assuming 4,000 diapers a year, this option can get pretty pricy. But if you keep your eyes out for coupons (most parenting magazines have a bunch of them in every issue), you can save a lot. In addition, places like Toys "Я" Us have generic or house brands that are a lot cheaper and usually just as good.

  Some people say that kids who grow up with disposable diapers tend to become potty trained later than those who use cloth. Apparently, the disposable kind keep so much moisture away from the baby's bottom that the baby stays comfortable for a longer time.
- **Cloth diapers:** $12 to $15 a week for a typical diaper service, although prices vary greatly around the country. This will cover door-to-door delivery and pickup of about eighty diapers each week. If you go this route you'll also need at least three or four diaper wraps, which cost about $10 each, to help hold the diaper in place and minimize leaks. You can, of course, cut your costs a bit by buying diapers (about $10 to $14 for a package of six). If you're doing your own laundry, you'll need about forty.

  Even if you don't end up using cloth diapers for the baby, pick up a dozen anyway—they're great for drying baby bottoms on changing tables and for draping over your shoulder to protect your clothes when your baby spits up.

FORMULA: Prices vary. You can use powdered, full-strength liquid, or liquid concentrate. But when you start checking prices, your partner may decide to keep breastfeeding a while longer. When we weaned our daughters, we put them on the powdered formula—I made a pitcher of it every morning and kept it in the refrigerator.

"Dear, It's Time..."

What's Going On with Your Partner

Physically

- Some change in fetal activity—the baby is so cramped that instead of kicking and punching, all she can do is squirm
- Increased sleeplessness and fatigue
- A renewed sense of energy when the baby's head "drops" into the pelvis and takes some of the pressure off the stomach and lungs
- She may have stopped gaining weight but she's still just plain miserable, with increased cramping, constipation, backache, water retention, and swelling of the feet, ankles, and face
- If her belly button was an innie before, it may have become an outie (the change isn't permanent, though)
- Absolutely no interest in sex (although some women's interest actually increases)

Emotionally

- More dependent on you than ever—afraid you won't love her after the baby is born (after all, she's not the same woman you married)
- Impatient: can't wait for pregnancy to be over
- Short-tempered: tired of answering "So when's the baby coming?" questions—especially if she's overdue
- May be afraid she won't have enough love to go around—what with loving you, and all
- Fear she won't be ready for labor when it comes
- Increasing preoccupation with the baby and, perhaps, a sudden and unexplained interest in Martha Stewart and interior decorating

What's Going On with the Baby

Over the course of this last month of pregnancy, your baby will be growing at a tremendous clip, putting on about a quarter to a half pound a week. Before she finally decides to leave the warm uterus, she'll weigh six to nine pounds (less if she's a twin or triplet) and be about twenty inches long—so big that there will be hardly any room for her to kick or prod your partner anymore. Her fingernails and toenails are frequently so long they have to be trimmed right after birth and the lanugo and vernix that have been covering and protecting her little body are starting to sluff off. And despite the widespread myth that babies are born blind, her sight is coming along just fine. If you shine a bright light at her mother's abdomen (which you shouldn't do), she'll blink.

What's Going On with You

Confusion

Well, it's almost over. In just a few weeks, you're finally going to meet the child you've talked to and dreamed about, and whose college education you've planned. But be prepared; the last month of pregnancy is often the most

confusing for expectant fathers. At times you may be almost overcome with excitement and anticipation. At other times you may be feeling so scared and trapped that you want to run away. In short, all the feelings—good and bad—that you've experienced over the last eight months are back. But now, because of the impending birth, they're more intense than before. Here are a few of the contradictory emotional states you may find yourself going through during the final stages of the pregnancy:

- On the one hand, you may be feeling confident about your readiness to be a father. On the other, you may be worried and unsure about whether you'll be able to handle your dual roles as husband and father.
- You may really be looking forward to spending some time with your baby while your partner is recuperating. But you may be worried that you won't know how to do all the things that she usually does for the family. (If this last part is true, you'd better learn how to do the laundry and run the dishwasher in a hurry.)
- If you've taken on a second job or increased responsibilities at work, all you'll probably want to do at the end of the day is go home and relax. But with your partner less and less able to handle physical tasks, you may be greeted at the door with a list of chores that need to be done.
- You and your partner may be feeling an exceptionally strong emotional bond with each other. At the same time, your sex life may have completely disappeared.
- As your partner gets more and more uncomfortable, she may feel less and less like going out with friends, so the two of you may be spending a lot more time together. This may be the last chance you have to enjoy some quiet, private time before the baby comes. But it may also be an unwelcome opportunity to get on each other's nerves.
- You may find yourself spending a lot more time with friends and family members who have small children, or you may find yourself avoiding families with kids.

Increased Dependency on Your Partner

By this time your attention—and that of your friends and family—is focused squarely on your partner and the baby. Since you're the person she's closest to and sees most often, your partner is going to be increasingly dependent on you—not only to help her physically, but to get her through the last-month emotional ups and downs. At the same time, though, you are going to be increasingly dependent on her as you get onto the last-month roller coaster.

Your partner's increased dependency is considered a "normal" part of pregnancy. But thanks to the ridiculous, gender-specific way we socialize people in this country, men are supposed to be independent, strong, supportive, and impervious to emotional needs—especially while their partners are pregnant. So, just when you are feeling most vulnerable and least in control, your needs are swept under the rug. And what's worse, the one person you most depend on for sympathy and understanding may be too absorbed in what's going on with herself and the baby to do much for you.

This results in what Dr. Luis Zayas calls an "imbalance in interdependence," which leaves the father to satisfy his own emotional needs and those of his partner. In addition, in many cases this imbalance essentially becomes a kind of vicious circle that "accentuates the stress, intensifies feelings of separation, and heightens dependency needs." In other words, the less response you get to your dependency needs, the more dependent you feel.

Feeling Guilty

Especially in the last month or so of the pregnancy, many men begin to feel guilty about what they think they've been putting their partners through. Yes, you're the one who got her pregnant, and yes, she's uncomfortable as hell. But strange as it might seem to you, your partner does not blame you for what she's going through. She understands and accepts—as you should—that this was her idea, too, and that (at least short of surrogate motherhood or adoption) there's simply no way to have a baby without going through this. So quit torturing yourself—there are a lot more productive things you can be doing with your time during these last few weeks.

Staying Involved

Sensitivity

The bottom line is that during the last few weeks of her pregnancy, your partner is likely to be miserable and uncomfortable. And although there's not a whole lot you can do to ease her burden, here are a few suggestions that might make the final stretch a little more bearable—for both of you:

- Answer the phone. If you have an answering machine, you might consider changing the recording to something like: "Hi. No, we don't have a baby yet, and yes, Jane's fine. If you're calling about anything else, please leave a message and we'll call you back." That may sound a little snotty, but believe me, it's a lot less snotty than you would be if you were really answering the same questions twenty times a day.
- Stay nearby whenever you can. Come home a little earlier from work, give away those basketball tickets, and postpone that long business trip.
- Stay in touch. A couple of quick calls or e-mails to her every day can make her feel loved and important. They'll also reassure her that you are all right. If you need to be away from the phone, consider getting a pager or a cell phone, if you don't already have one.
- Stay as calm as you can. She'll be nervous enough for both of you.
- Be patient. She may do some pretty bizarre things, and the best thing you can do is bear with her. If the house has already passed the white-glove test and the car has been waxed twice, and she wants it all done over again, do it—she needs the rest.
- Review the breathing, relaxation, and any other techniques you plan to use during labor.
- If she wants it, give her some time to herself. And if she wants time with you, make sure you're there for her.

If you're running out of ideas, reread the "Ways to Show Her You Care" section on pages 82–83 and try the ones you didn't get to then or those that got you the most mileage the first time around.

What If She's Overdue?

There's nothing more frustrating than starting the tenth month of a nine-month pregnancy. You've already given up answering the phone, afraid it's another one of those "What are you doing at home? I was sure you'd be at the hospital by now" calls. And you're sick of ending every conversation at the office with, "Now if I'm not in tomorrow, don't forget to . . ." The empty bassinet looks forlorn, and you're just dying to meet the baby face to little wrinkled face.

In most cases, however, couples who think they're late really aren't. When doctors tell a pregnant woman her due date, they often neglect to add that it's only a ballpark figure based on an assumed twenty-eight-day menstrual cycle, and there's always a window of plus or minus two weeks. If your partner's cycle is long, short, or irregular, her "official" due date could be off by as much as three weeks. And even if her cycle is like clockwork, it's nearly impossible to tell exactly when you conceived. The bottom line is that "70 percent of post-term [late] pregnancies are due to miscalculations of the time of conception," according to the authors of *What to Expect When You're Expecting.*

While going past the due date by a week or so is usually not a problem, being truly overdue can have serious consequences:

- The baby can grow so large that he or she will have problems passing through the birth canal, thus increasing the chances of a difficult delivery or a C-section.
- After a certain point the placenta gets so old that it can no longer provide adequate nourishment for the baby. This can result in the baby's losing weight in the uterus, increasing the risk of fetal distress.
- There may no longer be enough amniotic fluid to support the baby.
- There may be inadequate room for the umbilical cord to perform properly.

If your doctor feels the baby is overdue, he or she will most likely prescribe some tests to make sure the baby is still okay. The most common are an ultrasound (to determine the level of amniotic fluid as well as to get a general idea of how the baby is doing) and a nonstress test, which monitors changes in the baby's heart rate and movement in reaction to certain stimuli.

If the baby "passes" these tests, the doctor will probably send you home, telling you to repeat the test in three to seven days if the baby hasn't come by then. Otherwise, he or she may suggest that you schedule a date for labor to be induced.

If all of this starts getting you down, remember the words of obstetrician J. Milton Huston of New York Hospital: "In all of my years of practice, I've never seen a baby stay in there."

What If It's a Boy?

Sadly, most people don't think about—and, consequently, never discuss—circumcising their sons until the thing is staring them in the face, so to speak. So if you and your partner haven't made up your minds about circumcision yet, now's the time to do so. Of course, if you know you're having a girl or if you and your partner have already decided what you're going to do, feel free to skip this section. But if either of you is still undecided, the pros and cons of circumcision are summarized below. If you and your partner aren't on exactly the same page, be careful: in recent years the whole circumcision debate has become extremely political and tempers run pretty hot on both sides.

WHY YOU MIGHT WANT TO CONSIDER CIRCUMCISION

- **Religious reasons.** Circumcision is a traditional, ritual practice for Jews and Muslims. A few years ago, the wife of a local rabbi went to court to get an injunction preventing her husband from circumcising their newborn son. Needless to say, their marriage didn't last much longer.
- **Health.** Recent studies have shown that circumcision reduces boys' (and, later, men's) chances of getting HIV and some other sexually transmitted diseases, developing urinary tract infections or cancer of the penis, and may reduce his future partner's chance of developing cancer of the cervix. In addition, circumcision completely prevents *phimosis,* a condition in which the foreskin can't be retracted. Phimosis, which affects about 1 to 2 percent of uncircumcised males, can also be cured later on by circumcision, a procedure that gets a lot more painful with age. Short of that, the foreskin may be able to be loosened by gentle stretching *(do not do this without proper medical supervision)* or by using a topical steroid cream prescribed by your pediatrician to soften it.
- **Hygiene.** A circumcised penis is a lot easier to clean—both for the parents and for the boy himself.
- **Conformity.** If you've been circumcised, your son will probably want to look like you. Worldwide, only about 25 percent of boys are circumcised. But in the United States, it's a lot more popular, and having it done will probably make him look more like the other boys in the locker room.

WHY YOU MIGHT WANT TO CONSIDER *NOT* CIRCUMCISING YOUR SON

- **Pain.** No matter how you look at it, getting circumcised is painful. The circumcision cut will take about three days to heal fully. A recent study published in *Pediatrics* found that among the physicians who perform circumcisions on a regular basis, only about 45 percent use anesthesia, with pediatricians a lot more likely to use it (71 percent) than family practitioners (56 percent) or obstetricians (25 percent). Younger doctors and those practicing in the western states are more likely to use pain blocks than older doctors or those anywhere else in the country. Whether the circumcision is done by the baby's doctor or the mother's depends on the doctor's medical training and where he or she is practicing.

- **Other risks.** Complications, while extremely rare, can occur. There is about a 1 in 500 chance of bleeding, penile injury, or local infection due to circumcision, but death is almost never a risk. In 1979, for example, there was only one circumcision-related death in the entire United States. A recent comprehensive study comparing the risks and benefits of circumcision found that the procedure prevents six urinary tract infections for every complication endured and that about two complications can be expected for every case of penile cancer prevented. "Circumcision remains a relatively safe procedure," write doctors Christakis, Harvey, Zerr, and their colleagues who conducted the study. "However, for some parents, the risks we report may outweigh the potential benefits."
- **Conformity.** As above, if you haven't been circumcised, your son will probably want to look like you.
- **Pleasure.** Some people believe that the foreskin is there for a purpose: to protect the tip of the penis, and that removing it can cause the penis to be less sensitive, which will reduce sexual pleasure later in life. A number of the more politically oriented anticircumcision groups claim that penile circumcision has the same impact on boys that "female circumcision" has on girls. There is absolutely no evidence that this is true. Female circumcision (more accurately called genital mutilation) is practiced in some parts of the world and involves completely or partially removing a girl's clitoris or sewing the labia minora together. The specific purpose is to reduce the girl's sexual pleasure or ability to have intercourse before marriage, which, supposedly, will make her less likely to stray later. There is simply no comparison between the two procedures. Billions of circumcised men around the world have perfectly delightful sex lives, and doctors have found little, if any, conclusive proof that circumcision has any negative effects on boys' or men's sexual, psychological, or emotional health.
- **Is it necessary at all?** Some claim that many of the health risks thought to be reduced by circumcision may in fact be reduced simply by better hygiene—something that can be taught. The American Academy of Pediatrics has taken a fairly noncommittal position, saying that although

scientific evidence shows the potential medical benefits of circumcising newborn boys, the benefits aren't sufficient for the academy to recommend that all infant boys be circumcised. Bottom line? It's a personal decision that's totally up to you and your partner.

CARE OF THE CIRCUMCISED PENIS

Your son's penis will be red and sore for a few days after the circumcision. And until it's fully healed—which will take a week to ten days—you'll need to protect the newly exposed tip and keep it from sticking to the inside of his diaper. A few tiny spots of blood on his diapers for a few days is perfectly normal, but call your doctor if there's more blood that that, if the redness gets worse after three or four days, or if your son hasn't urinated within six to eight hours after the circumcision. Ordinarily, you'll need to keep the penis dry and the tip lubricated with petroleum jelly and wrapped in gauze. The person who performed the circumcision or the hospital nursing staff will be able to tell you how long you'll need to keep the penis covered and how often to change the bandages.

CARE OF THE UNCIRCUMCISED PENIS

Even if you elect not to circumcise your son, you'll still have to spend some time taking care of his penis. Eighty-five percent of boys under six months have foreskins that don't retract (pull back to reveal the head of the penis), so don't try to force it. Fortunately, as boys get older, their foreskins retract on their own; by age one, 50 percent retract, and by age three, 80 to 90 percent do. The standard way to clean an uncircumcised penis is to retract the foreskin as far as it will comfortably go, and gently wash the head with mild soap and water. There is absolutely no need to use antiseptics, cotton swabs, or any other special cleaning measures.

Dealing with Contingencies

LABOR: REAL OR FALSE

By now, your partner has probably experienced plenty of Braxton-Hicks contractions ("false labor"), which have been warming up her uterus for the real thing. Sometimes, however, these practice contractions may be so strong that your partner may feel that labor has begun. The bottom line is that when real labor starts, your partner will probably know it. (This may sound strange, especially if she is carrying her first child. Nevertheless, the majority of mothers I've spoken to have told me it's true.) But until then, you—and she—may not be sure whether the contractions and other things she's feeling are the real thing or not. So before you go rushing off to the hospital, take a few seconds to try to figure things out.

FALSE LABOR

- Contractions are not regular, or don't stay regular
- Contractions don't get stronger or more severe
- If your partner changes position (from sitting to walking, or from standing to lying down), the contractions usually stop altogether or change in frequency or intensity
- Generally, there is little or no vaginal discharge of any kind
- There may be additional pain in the abdomen

REAL LABOR

- Contractions are regular
- Contractions get stronger, longer, and closer together with time
- There may be some blood-tinged vaginal discharge
- Your partner's membranes may rupture (the famous "water" that "breaks" is really the amniotic fluid that the baby has been floating in throughout the pregnancy)
- There may be additional pain in the lower back

PLANES, TRAINS, AND AUTOMOBILES

It seems like half the births you see in the movies take place on the back seat of a speeding taxi, in a snow-bound cave, in an airplane bathroom, or at the end of a bungee cord. While those sorts of images may sell movie tickets, the reality is that about 99 percent of babies are born in hospitals, according to the American College of Obstetricians and Gynecologists (ACOG). (And many of the nonhospital births were *planned* that way.) Nevertheless, at some point, just about every pregnant couple—okay, it's really more of a guy thing—starts worrying about giving birth unexpectedly.

EMERGENCY BIRTHS

Emergency births fall into two general categories: either you have a lot of time before the actual birth (you're snowed in, trapped in your basement because of an earthquake, or shipwrecked—you know you're not going to get to a hospital for a while), or you have little or no time before the birth (you're caught in traffic, you're parachuting to safety, or your partner's labor was extremely short). Either way, there's not a whole lot you can do to prepare.

If you have some time, try to make sure that your partner is in the most sheltered area of wherever you happen to be, and that she's as comfortable as possible. If you have facilities available, get yourself some clean towels or sheets and boil a piece of string or a shoelace and a pair of scissors or a knife. Then, just sit tight and let nature take its course.

If you don't have time, try to stay cool. Handling a birth is not as difficult as you might think. Doctors who do it for a living, in fact, usually show up just a few minutes before the birth and are there primarily in case any complications arise. The truth is that most of the time babies pretty much deliver themselves when they're ready. The ones who seem to be in a hurry usually come out without any complications.

Whether you have time to prepare or not, once the baby starts to come, the procedure for performing a delivery is the same. And you'll know the process has started when:

- Your partner can't resist pushing.
- The baby's head—or any other body part—is visible.

For the rest of this chapter, we'll describe what you should do if there's no way to avoid delivering the baby yourself. The information isn't intended to

An Emergency Kit

It's extremely unlikely that your partner will give birth anywhere but in the hospital. However, if you want to make sure all the bases are covered, here's a list of supplies to keep at home, in the car, or anyplace else you and your partner are likely to be spending a lot of time during the last month or so of the pregnancy. Please keep in mind, though, that this list is for emergencies only. If you're planning a home birth you'll need a lot more supplies.

- Chux pads (large, sterile pads) for absorbing blood, amniotic fluid, and so forth. They're available at medical supply stores. If you can't find Chux pads, newspapers are fine—don't worry, a little ink won't hurt anything.
- Clean string or shoelaces for tying the umbilical cord, if necessary (see page 177).
- Clean scissors or knife for cutting the cord, if necessary (see page 177).
- Some towels to warm the baby and mother after the birth.

replace the years of training your doctor or midwife has. So don't try this at home—unless you absolutely have to.

STEP ONE: PREPARATION. Call for help if a phone is available. Try to keep your partner focused on the breathing and relaxation techniques. Put a pillow or some clothing under her buttocks in order to keep the baby's head and shoulders from hitting a hard surface.

STEP TWO: THE HEAD. When the head begins to appear, do *not* pull it. Instead, support it and let it come out by itself. If the umbilical cord is wrapped around the baby's neck, *slowly* and *gently* glide it over the head. Once the head is out, try to remove any mucus from the baby's nose and mouth (although the baby's passage through the birth canal is usually enough to do the trick).

STEP THREE: THE REST OF THE BODY. Holding the baby's head, encourage your partner to push as the baby's shoulders appear. After the head has emerged, the rest of the baby's body should slide out pretty easily. Support the body as well as the head as it slides out. Despite what you may have seen or heard, you don't have to slap the baby's bottom to make him cry: he'll take care of that—and the associated breathing—all by himself. Of course, if he's blue or not breathing at all, you'll need to make use of those baby CPR skills you hopefully learned a month or two ago.

Place the baby on your partner's chest and encourage her to begin breastfeeding right away. (Breastfeeding makes the uterus contract, which helps expel the placenta and reduces the chances of excessive bleeding.) And don't worry—the umbilical cord is generally long enough to allow the baby to nurse while still attached. Dry the baby off immediately and cover mom and baby to keep them as warm as possible.

STEP FOUR: CUTTING THE CORD. Using that shoelace or piece of string you boiled a while ago, tie a tight knot around the cord three or four inches away from the baby. If you know you can get to a hospital within two hours, don't cut the cord yet. If you're not going to make it by then, tie a second tight knot in the cord about two inches farther away from the baby and cut the cord *between* the knots with your knife or scissors. Don't worry about the cord stump that's still attached to the baby: it will fall off by itself in a week or so.

STEP FIVE: THE PLACENTA. Don't think your delivery job is over as soon as the baby's out. Anywhere from five minutes to half an hour after the

Things to Remember During an Emergency Birth

- Try to relax. Do everything carefully, thoughtfully, and slowly.
- Call for help as soon as possible.
- Keep the area where the baby will be delivered as clean as possible.
- Baby CPR. If you haven't taken a baby CPR class already, you should really consider it—just in case.

baby is born the placenta will arrive. Do not pull on the cord to "help" things along; in most cases the placenta, which is surprisingly large and meaty (it kind of reminds me of a hefty chunk of liver), will slip out on its own with a soft "plop." When it does, wrap it up in something clean—but do not throw it away; your doctor will want to take a look at it as soon as possible.

After the placenta is out, gently massage your partner's lower abdomen every few minutes. This causes contractions, which limit blood loss and start the process of returning her uterus back to its original shape.

Notes:

Labor and Delivery

What's Going On with Your Partner

The entire labor process typically lasts twelve to twenty hours—toward the high end for first babies and the low end for subsequent ones—but there are no hard and fast rules. Labor is generally divided into three stages. The first stage consists of three phases.

STAGE 1

PHASE 1 (EARLY LABOR) is the longest part of labor, lasting anywhere from a few hours to a few days. At the beginning of this phase, your partner may not even be able to feel the contractions. Even if she can, she'll probably tell you that they're fairly manageable. Contractions will generally last 30 to 60 seconds and be as much as 20 minutes apart. Over the next few hours they'll gradually get longer (60 to 90 seconds) and closer together (perhaps as little as 5 minutes). Every woman will have a slightly different early labor experience. My wife, for example, had from 6 to 12 hours of fairly long, fairly regular (3 to 5 minutes apart) contractions almost every day for a week before our second daughter was born. Your partner may have "bloody show" (a blood-tinged vaginal discharge), backaches, and diarrhea.

PHASE 2 (ACTIVE LABOR) is generally shorter—three to four hours—but far more intense than the first phase. It is likely to last as much as 10 minutes longer if you're having a boy than if you're having a girl. In the early part of this phase, your partner will still be able to talk through the contractions. They'll keep getting closer together (2 to 3 minutes apart) and longer. As this stage progresses she'll start feeling some real pain. The bloody show will increase and get redder and your partner will become less and less chatty as she begins to focus on the contractions. If you aren't already there, it's time to head off to the hospital.

PHASE 3 (TRANSITION) usually lasts a few hours. You can stop wondering why they call it "labor." Your partner's contractions may be almost relentless—often two or three in a row without a break. The pain is intense and if your partner is going to ask for some drugs, this is probably when she'll do it. She's tired, sweating, her muscles may be so exhausted that they're trembling, and she may be vomiting.

STAGE 2 (PUSHING AND BIRTH)
This is the shortest—usually less than two hours—and most intense part of the process. Your partner's contractions are still long (more than 60 seconds) but are farther apart. The difference is that during the contractions, she'll be overcome with a desire to push—similar to the feeling of having to make a bowel movement. She may feel some unpleasant pressure and stinging as the baby's head "crowns" (starts coming through the vagina), but this will be followed by a huge sense of relief when the baby finally pops out.

STAGE 3 (AFTER THE BIRTH)
This stage lasts only about half an hour. Your partner will continue to have contractions as her uterus tries to eject the placenta and stop the bleeding. She'll probably be incredibly hungry.

What's Going On with You

Starting labor is no picnic, for her or for you. She, of course, is experiencing—or soon will be—a lot of physical pain. You, in the meantime, are very likely to feel a heavy dose of psychological pain.

I couldn't possibly count the number of times—only in my dreams, thankfully—I've heroically defended my home and family from armies of murderers and thieves. But even when I'm awake, I know I wouldn't hesitate before diving in front of a speeding car if it meant being able to save my wife or my children. And I know I would submit to the most painful ordeal to keep any one of them from suffering. This instinct perhaps explains the adrenaline rush you'll probably feel. A team of Scandinavian researchers took fathers' pulses during the birth of their children and found that they went from an average of 72 beats/minute to 115 beats/minute just before the birth. But helping your partner through labor is not the same as deciding to rescue a child from a burning building.

The most important thing to remember about this final stage of pregnancy is that the pain—yours and hers—is finite. After a while it ends, and you get to hold your new baby. Ironically, however, her pain will probably end sooner than yours. She'll be sore for a few weeks or so, but by the time the baby is six months old, your partner will hardly remember it. If women could remember the pain, I can't imagine that any of them would have more than one child. But for six months, a year, even two years after our first daughter was born, my wife's pain remained fresh in my mind. And when we began planning our second pregnancy, the thought of her having to go through even a remotely similar experience frightened me.

Staying Involved

Being There—Mentally and Physically

Despite your fears and worries, this is one time when your partner's needs—and they aren't all physical—come first. But before we get into how you can best help her through labor and delivery, it's helpful to get a firm idea of how to tell when she's actually gone into labor, and what stage she's in once she's there.

STAGE 1

PHASE 1 (EARLY LABOR) Although the contractions are fairly mild at this point, you should do everything you can to make your partner as comfortable as possible (back rubs, massages, and so forth). Some women may tell you exactly what they want you to do, others may feel a little shy about making any demands—especially things that might seem trivial. Either way, ask her regularly what you can do to help. And when she tells you, do it. If taking a walk makes her feel better, go with her. If doing headstands in the living room is what she wants to do (fairly unlikely at this point), give her a hand. You also need to trust her instincts about what's going on with her body. At some point during every day of my wife's week-long first-stage labor marathon, I became convinced that *this* time it was real and that *this* time she should let me call the doctor. Wisely and firmly, she refused.

Once labor has started, your partner should not eat anything unless her doctor specifically says that it's okay. If she ends up needing any medication or even a Cesarean, food in her stomach could complicate matters. Drinking water during early labor, however, is crucial. No matter what your partner does, you should eat—and drink—something. You need to keep your energy level up and you're not going to want to try to make a dash to the snack bar between contractions. Finally, try to get some rest. Don't be fooled by the adrenaline rush that will hit you when your partner finally goes into labor. You'll be so excited that you'll feel you can last forever, but you can't. She's got some hormones (and pain) to keep her going; you don't.

PHASE 2 (ACTIVE LABOR) One of the symptoms of second-phase labor is that your partner may seem to be losing interest in just about everything—including arguing with you about when to call the doctor. After my wife's contractions had been 2 to 3 minutes apart for a few hours (and so strong that she couldn't talk through them), I was encouraging her to call. She refused. Many women, it seems, "just know" when it's time to go. So, chances are if she tells you "it's time," grab your car keys. If you're still not sure whether the second phase has started, here's a pretty typical scenario that may help you decide:

YOU: Honey, these contractions have been going on like this for three hours. I think we should head off to the hospital.

SHE: Okay.

YOU: Great. Let's get dressed, okay?

SHE: I don't want to get dressed.

YOU: But you're only wearing a nightgown. How about at least putting on some shoes and socks?

SHE: I don't want any shoes and socks.

YOU: But it's cold out there. How about a jacket?

SHE: I don't want a jacket.

Get the point?

Another typical symptom of second-phase labor is (in most people anyway) an uncharacteristic loss of modesty. Birth-class instructor Kim Kaehler says she can always tell what stage of labor a woman is in just by looking at the sheet on her bed (when she's in it and naked). If she's in first phase, she'll be covered up to her neck; in second phase, the sheet is halfway down; by the third phase (see below), the sheet's all the way off.

PHASE 3 (TRANSITION) Whenever laboring women are shown in TV shows, they almost always seem to be snapping at their husband or boyfriend, yelling things like "Don't touch me!" or "Leave me alone, you're the one who did this to me." I think I'd internalized those stereotypes, and by the time we got to the hospital I was really afraid that my wife would behave the same way when she got to the transition stage, blame me for the pain, and push me away. Fortunately, it never happened. The closest we ever came was when we were in labor with our second daughter. The only place my wife could be comfortable was in the shower, and for a while I was in there with her, trying to talk her through the contractions as I massaged her aching back. Then she asked me to leave the bathroom for a while. Sure, I felt hurt for a minute—I felt I should be there with her—but it was clear that she had no intention of hurting me.

Unfortunately, not every laboring woman manages to be as graceful under pressure. If your partner happens to say something nasty to you or throws you unceremoniously out of the room for a while, you need to imagine that while she's in labor her mind is being taken over by an angry rush-hour mob, all trying to push and shove their way onto an overcrowded subway train. Quite often, the pain she's experiencing is so intense and overwhelming that the only way she can make it through the contractions is to concentrate completely on them. Something as simple and well-meaning as a word or a loving caress can be terribly distracting.

So what *can* you do? Whatever she wants. Fast. If she doesn't want you to touch her, don't insist. Offer to feed her some ice chips instead. If she wants you to get out of the room, go. But tell her that you'll be right outside in case she needs you. If the room is pitch black and she tells you it's too bright, agree with her and find something to turn off. If she wants to listen to the twenty-four-hour Elvis station, turn it on. But whatever you do, don't argue with her, don't reason with her, and above all, don't pout if she swears at you or calls you names. She really doesn't mean to, and the last thing she needs to deal with at this moment of crisis is your wounded pride.

STAGE 2: PUSHING

Up until the pushing stage, I thought I was completely prepared for dealing with my wife's labor and delivery. I was calm, and, despite my feelings of inadequacy, I knew what to expect almost every step of the way. The hospital staff was supportive of my wanting to be with my wife through every contraction. But when

The Three Stages of Labor and Delivery

STAGE	WHAT'S HAPPENING
Stage 1/Phase 1 (early labor)	♦ Her cervix is effacing (thinning out) and dilating (opening up) to about 5 centimeters ♦ Her water may break
Stage 1/Phase 2 (active labor)	♦ She's increasingly uncomfortable ♦ Her cervix continues to efface and will dilate to about 8 centimeters ♦ Water may break (if it hasn't already) or may have to be broken
Stage 1/Phase 3 (transition)	♦ Her cervix is now fully dilated ♦ She may feel the urge to push
Stage 2 (pushing and birth)	♦ Increase in bloody discharge ♦ The baby is moving through the birth canal ♦ Doctor may have to do an episiotomy
Stage 3 (after the birth)	♦ The placenta is separating from the wall of the uterus ♦ Episiotomy or tearing (if any) will be repaired

WHAT SHE'S FEELING	WHAT YOU CAN DO
♦ She may be excited but not totally sure that "this is really it" ♦ She may be anxious and restless ♦ She may not feel like doing much of anything	♦ Reassure her ♦ Tell jokes, take a walk, or rent a movie—anything to distract her ♦ If it's nighttime, encourage her to try sleep; active labor will wake her up, but any rest she can get now will really pay off later on
♦ She's getting serious and impatient about the pain ♦ She's beginning to concentrate fully on the contractions	♦ Call the doctor and get her to the hospital ♦ Reassure and encourage her ♦ Help her take one contraction at a time ♦ Feed her ice chips ♦ Praise her for her progress ♦ Massage, massage, massage
♦ She may be confused, frustrated, and scared ♦ She may announce that she can't take it anymore and is going home	♦ Do whatever she wants you to do ♦ Try to help her resist pushing until the doctor tells her she should ♦ Mop her brow with a wet cloth ♦ Feed her ice chips ♦ Massage her (if she wants it)
♦ She's feeling confident that she can finish the job ♦ She may have gotten a second wind	♦ Continue to reassure and comfort her ♦ Encourage her to push when she's supposed to and tell her how great she's doing ♦ Encourage her to watch the baby come out (if she wants to and if there's a mirror around) ♦ Let the professionals do their job
♦ RELIEF ♦ Euphoria ♦ Talkative ♦ Strong, heroic ♦ Hungry, thirsty ♦ Empty (of the baby) ♦ Desire to cuddle with her baby (and her partner)	♦ Praise her ♦ Put the baby on her stomach ♦ Encourage her to relax ♦ Encourage her to start nursing the baby, if she feels ready ♦ Bond with her and the baby

the time came to start pushing, they changed. All of a sudden, they were in control. The doctor was called, extra nurses magically appeared, and the room began to fill up with equipment—a scale, a bassinet, a tray of sterilized medical instruments, a washbasin, diapers, towels. (We happened to be in a combination labor/birthing room; if, in the middle of pushing, you find yourself chasing after your wife, who's being rushed down the hall to a separate delivery room, don't be alarmed. It may feel like an emergency, but it isn't really.)

The nurses told my wife what to do, how to do it, and when to do it. All I could do was watch—and I must admit that at first I felt a little cheated. After all, *I* was the one who had been there through almost every contraction. *My* baby was about to be born. But when the most important part finally arrived, I wasn't going to be anything more than a spectator. And unless you're a professional birthing coach or a trained labor and delivery nurse, chances are you're going to feel like a spectator, too.

The truth of the matter is that although I was feeling left out and would have liked to have been more involved in this stage, it was probably a lot better for my wife that I wasn't. As I watched the nurses do their stuff, I quickly realized that simply holding your partner's legs and saying, "Push, honey: that's great" isn't always enough. Recognizing a good, productive push, and, more important, being able to explain how to do one—"raise your butt . . . lower your legs . . . keep your head back . . ."—are skills that come from years of experience.

STAGE 2: BIRTH

Intellectually, I knew my wife was pregnant. I'd been to all the appointments and I'd heard the heartbeat, seen the ultrasound, and felt the baby kicking. Still, there was something intangible about the whole process. And it wasn't until our baby started "crowning" (peeking her hairy little head out of my wife's vagina) that all the pieces finally came together.

At just about the same moment, I also realized that there was one major advantage to my having been displaced during the pushing stage: I had both hands free to "catch" the baby as she came out—and believe me, holding my daughter's hot, slimy, bloody little body and placing her gently at my wife's breast was easily the highlight of the whole occasion.

If you think you might want to do this, make sure you've worked out the choreography with your doctor and the nurses before the baby starts crowning. (See "Birth Plans" on pages 146–50 for more information.)

Your partner, unfortunately, is in the worst possible position to see the baby being born. Most hospitals, however, have tried to remedy this situation by making mirrors available. Still, many women are concentrating so hard on the pushing that they may not be interested in looking in the mirror.

If you were expecting your newborn to look like the Gerber baby, you may be in for a bit of a shock. Babies are generally born covered with a whitish coating called *vernix.* They're sometimes blue and frequently covered with blood and mucus. Their eyes may be puffy, their genitals swollen, and their backs and shoulders may be covered with fine hair. In addition, the trip through the birth canal has probably left your baby with a cone-shaped head. All in all, it's the most beautiful sight in the world.

After the Birth

THE BABY

Your baby's first few minutes outside the womb are a time of intense physical and emotional release for you and your partner. At long last you get to meet the unique little person you created together. Your partner may want to try nursing the baby (although most newborns aren't hungry for the first twelve hours or so), and you will probably want to stroke his or her brand-new skin and marvel at his or her tiny fingernails. But depending on the hospital, the conditions of the birth, and whether or not you've been perfectly clear about your desires, your baby's first few minutes could be spent being poked and prodded by doctors and nurses instead of being held and cuddled by you.

One minute after birth, your baby will be given an APGAR test to give the medical staff a quick take on your baby's overall condition. Created in 1953 by Dr. Virginia Apgar, the test measures your baby's Appearance (skin color), Pulse, Grimace (reflexes), Activity, and Respiration. A nurse or midwife will score each category on a scale of 0 to 2. (A bluish or pale baby might get a 0 for color while a very pink one would get 2; a baby who didn't cry too much might get a 0 for respiration while one who really screamed would get a 2.) Most babies score in the 7 to 10 range. The test will be repeated at five minutes after birth.

Shortly after the birth, your baby will need to be weighed, measured, given an ID bracelet, bathed, diapered, footprinted, and wrapped in a blanket. Some hospitals also photograph each newborn. After that, most hospitals (frequently required by law) apply silver nitrate drops or an antibiotic ointment to your baby's eyes as a protection against gonorrhea. Although these procedures should be done within one hour of birth, ask the staff if they can hold off for a few minutes while you and your partner get acquainted with your baby.

Seeing the Baby

Many hospitals have very rigid rules regarding parent/infant contact—feeding may be highly regulated and the hours you can visit your child may be limited. The nursing staff may also bottle-feed the baby—either with sugar-water or with formula. If this isn't what you want, let them know.

Some hospitals, however, are more flexible. The hospital where both our children were born now no longer has a nursery (except for babies with serious health problems). Healthy babies are expected to stay in the mother's room for their entire hospital stay. There are even hospitals that permit the new father to spend the night with his partner and baby. Check with the staff of your hospital to find out their policy.

If, however, your baby was delivered by C-section, or if there were any other complications, the baby will be rushed off to have his or her little lungs suctioned before returning for the rest of the cleanup routine (see page 200 for more on this).

THE PLACENTA

Before our first child was born it had simply never occurred to me (or to my wife, for that matter) that labor and delivery wouldn't end when the baby was born. While you and your partner are admiring your new family member, the placenta—which has been your baby's life support system for the past five months or so—still must be delivered. Your partner may continue to have mild contractions for anywhere from five minutes to about an hour until this happens. The strange thing about this stage of the delivery is that neither you nor your partner will probably even know it's happening—you'll be much too involved with your new baby.

Once the placenta is out, however, you need to decide what to do with it. In this country most people never even see it, and those who do just leave it at the hospital (where it will either be destroyed or, more likely, sold to a cosmetics company—honest). But in many other cultures, the placenta is considered to have a permanent, almost magical bond with the child it nourished in the womb, and disposal is handled with a great deal more reverence. In fact, most cultures that have placenta rituals believe that if it is not properly buried, the child—or the parents, or even the entire village—will suffer some terrible consequences.

In rural Peru, for example, immediately after the birth of a child, the father is required to go to a far-off location and bury the placenta deep enough so that no animals or people will accidentally discover it. Otherwise, the placenta may become "jealous" of the attention paid to the baby and may take revenge by causing an epidemic.

In some South American Indian cultures, people believe that a child's life can be influenced by objects that are buried with its placenta. According to researcher J. R. Davidson, parents in the Qolla tribe "bury miniature implements copied after the ones used in adult life with the placenta, in the hopes of assuring that the infant will be a good worker. Boys' placentas are frequently buried with a shovel or a pick, and girls' are buried with a loom or a hoe." In the Philippines some mothers bury the placenta with books as a way of ensuring intelligence.

But placentas are not always buried. In ancient Egypt, pharaohs' placentas were wrapped in special containers to keep them from harm. And a wealthy Inca in Ecuador built a solid-gold statue of his mother—complete with his placenta in "her" womb.

Even today, the people of many cultures believe that placentas have special powers. In other parts of Peru placentas are burned, the ashes are mixed with water, and the mixture is then drunk by the babies as a remedy for a variety of childhood illnesses. Traditional Vietnamese medicine uses placentas to combat sterility and senility, and in India, touching a placenta is supposed to help a childless woman conceive a healthy baby of her own. In China, some believe that breastfeeding mothers can improve the quality of their milk by drinking a broth made of boiled placenta. This sort of placenta usage isn't limited to non-Western cultures. In medieval Europe, if a child was born with a caul (with the amniotic membranes over his head), the placenta would be saved, dried, and fed to the child on his tenth birthday. If it wasn't done, it was believed that the child might become a vampire after death. Even today, in France and other countries, placentas are found in a variety of products, including cosmetics and medicines.

Whatever you and your partner decide to do, it's probably best to keep it a secret—at least from the hospital staff. Some states try to regulate what you can do with a placenta and may even prohibit you from taking it home (although if you really want to, you can probably find a sympathetic nurse who will pack it up for you). We deliberately left our first daughter's placenta at the hospital. But we stored the second one's in our freezer for a year before burying it, along with the placentas of some of our friends' children, and planting a tree above them.

Dealing with Contingencies

Unfortunately, not all labors and deliveries proceed exactly as planned. In fact, most of them don't. The American Association of Obstetricians and Gynecologists estimates that more than 30 percent of babies are born by Cesarean section. And a good number of mothers who deliver vaginally are medicated in some way. As with so many other aspects of your pregnancy experience, having good, clear information about what's really going on and what the options are during labor and delivery will help you make informed, intelligent decisions about how to handle the unexpected or the unplanned. The key to getting the information you need is to ask questions—and to keep on asking until you're completely satisfied. Find out about the risks, the benefits, the effects on your partner, the effects on the baby. The only exception to this rule is when there is a clear medical emergency. In such a case, you might want to save your questions for later.

Here are a few of the contingencies that can come up during the birth and how they might affect you—and your partner.

PAIN MEDICATION

If you've taken a childbirth class (and even if you haven't), you and your partner may have planned to have a "natural" (medication-free) childbirth. Unfortunately, natural childbirth often sounds better—and less painful—than it actually turns out to be. Because your partner is the one who is experiencing the physical pain, defer to her judgment when considering medication. This doesn't mean, however, that you don't have anything to say about the issue. What you may want to do is discuss her attitude toward medication thoroughly before she's in labor, so you know whether she'd want you to suggest it when you get concerned or wait until she requests it. You might also want to come up with a code word that means "I really want drugs NOW." A lot of women may scream for the doctor (or you) to "do something about the pain" but not really want drugs.

And remember, if you do end up having a discussion about medication sometime during labor, make sure you do it in the most supportive possible way. It's painful to have to watch the one you love suffer, but starting an argument when she's in labor isn't a smart idea (and you're not going to resolve anything anyway).

Many women feel that taking pain medication is a sign of weakness, or that they've failed—as women and as mothers. In addition, some childbirth preparation methods view medication as the first step along a path that ultimately leads to Cesarean section. Neither of these scenarios is, by any stretch of the imagination, the rule.

I'm not suggesting that you should use—or that you'll even need—pain medication. But whatever you do, knowing a little about your options is always a good idea.

EXHAUSTION

Pain isn't the only reason your partner might need some chemical intervention. In some cases, labor may be progressing so slowly (or be stalled for so long) that your practitioner may become concerned that your partner will be too exhausted by the time she needs to push. This was exactly what happened during our second labor. After twenty hours of labor and only four centimeters of dilation, our doctor suggested pitocin (a drug that stimulates contractions) together with an epidural (see page 192). This chemical cocktail removed the pain of labor while allowing my wife's cervix to dilate fully and quickly. I'm convinced that this approach not only did not increase the risk of a C-section but actually prevented one by allowing my wife a well-deserved breather before she started pushing.

INDUCED LABOR

Any time after forty weeks of pregnancy, your baby is officially "done." They don't always get this piece of news, though, and are sometimes reluctant to come out. There are all sorts of supposedly surefire ways to bring on labor and you'll start hearing every one of them as soon as you mention that the baby is late: eat certain kinds of salad dressings or vinegars, eat spicy food, go on long walks, drink cod-liver oil, and more. There is actually some research that sex may help: nipple stimulation and your partner's orgasm may trigger some contractions, plus semen has prostaglandin it it, which is similar to the gel or pill that's used to induce labor. But before you try any kind of home remedy, check with your practitioner to make sure it's safe.

If your partner's due date is long past, your practitioner may decide that things have gone on long enough (this will happen about two months after your partner reached the same conclusion) and he'll suggest jump-starting the labor with pitocin (a chemical version of oxytocin), Cytotec, or Cervadil (these last two are types of prostaglandin). Some people claim that pitocin results in more painful labors and an increase in the Cesarean rate but just as many disagree, saying that all pitocin does is produce normal labor.

Pain Relief

Despite all the emphasis on natural (unmedicated) childbirth these days, more and more women seem to be opting for some kind of chemical pain relief during labor and childbirth. Actually, there's evidence that women have been searching for alternatives to natural birth ever since they were first introduced in the 1840s, says obstetric anesthesiologist Donald Caton, author of *What a Blessing She Had Chloroform: The Medical and Social Response to the Pain of Childbirth from 1800 to the Present.*

Women today have literally dozens of options that fall into to two basic categories: *regional,* which reduce or eliminate pain only in certain parts of her body, and *systemic,* which will relax her whole body.

REGIONALS

One recent survey found that the number of women in labor who had regional anesthesia (see below) tripled from 1981 to 1997 from 22 to 66 percent) according to the American Society of Anesthesiologists.

The most common of all regionals (and of all childbirth-related pain medication in general) is the epidural, which is usually administered during active labor (the second phase of the first stage), when the pain is greatest. Your partner will have to lean over or curl up on her side while an anesthesiologist numbs her lower back, inserts a medication-carrying catheter into the space between the spinal cord and the membrane that surrounds it, and tapes it to her back.

Epidurals are widely considered the safest and most effective labor painkiller available. It kicks in almost immediately and, properly administered (and it usually is), it will block the pain of your partner's contractions while still leaving her awake and alert. Perhaps most important, it doesn't "cross the placenta" (affect the baby).

Until just a few years ago, epidurals carried the risk of decreasing maternal blood pressure or reducing ability to feel when to push (which could slow down the course of labor), as well as causing headaches and nausea. But thanks to recent developments, anesthesiologists are now better able to fine-tune the dose, which has all but eliminated these risks. Another problem was that, since epidurals numb the lower body, women were confined to their beds for the duration. But a new "walking epidural" is being introduced that will offer the same pain relief and allow at least some mobility, so ask your partner's practitioner whether it's available at your hospital.

Other regional options include the pudental block (an injection given into each side of the vagina that deadens the vaginal opening), the paracervical block (an injection into the area around the cervix that relieves pain from dilation and contractions), the spinal block (injections into the fluid around the spinal cord in the lower back—it's similar to an epidural but doesn't last as long and carries a slightly greater risk of complications), and general anesthesia (which knocks the recipient out completely and is rarely used, except when performing an emergency Cesarean).

SYSTEMIC

This type of pain relief includes sedatives, tranquilizers, and narcotics such as Demerol and Valium, which are usually given as injections or added to existing intravenous (IV) lines.

Besides taking effect almost immediately, one of the major advantages to systemic medications is that your partner can use them from the very beginning of labor. They may relieve a lot of her anxiety and won't usually have much of an impact on her ability to push or sense her contractions.

On the downside, though, these medications affect your partner's entire body and can cause a wide variety of side effects, including drowsiness, dizziness, and nausea. In some ways, these drugs do less to remove the pain than to make your partner simply stop caring about it. Even worse, since they go right into your partner's bloodstream, they also "cross the placenta," meaning that at birth, the baby could be drowsy, unable to suck properly for a short while, or, in rare cases, unable to breathe without assistance.

Interestingly, your partner's use—or nonuse—of pain medication may have an impact on you as well. For most expectant dads, anything that makes our partners more comfortable and hurt less is great. But besides that, medication can also reduce the stress and make the whole experience more pleasant for *us*. For other guys, though, reducing her pain may be a source of disappointment—in a twisted, yet understandable, sort of way. We're supposed to be there to help her through the pain, the thinking goes, but if she doesn't need us to do that, maybe she doesn't need us at all. In other words, reducing the pain may also reduce the father's sense of usefulness and importance. A word of advice: if your partner wants some pain medication, support her. There are plenty of other ways to be helpful.

Other Common Birth Contingencies

FORCEPS OR VACUUM

If your partner's cervix is completely dilated and she's been pushing for a while, but the baby refuses to budge, her practitioner may suggest using forceps—long tongs with scoops on the end—to help things along. It used to be that the very word *forceps* struck fear into every expectant parent's heart. But today they're used only to gently grasp the baby's head to guide it through the birth canal. Most forceps deliveries will leave the baby with bruises in the temple area for a few days or a week. In rare instances, permanent scarring or other damage can occur. In addition, your partner will need additional medication and may require a larger-than-normal episiotomy (see below).

In some cases, instead of forceps, doctors may be able to use a vacuum-type suction device to move the baby around in the same way.

The doctor may also suggest using forceps or vacuum if the baby is in distress and a vaginal birth needs to be speeded up, or if your partner is too exhausted (or medicated) to push effectively. Used appropriately, forceps can sometimes prevent the need for a C-section.

EPISIOTOMY

An episiotomy involves making a small cut in the perineum (the area immediately below the vagina) to enlarge the vaginal opening and allow for easier passage of the baby's head. About 90 percent of women delivering for the first time under an obstetrician's care have an episiotomy. Many women, however, feel that a small amount of tearing is preferable (and less painful) than a routine episiotomy. But the procedure may be legitimately indicated if:

- The baby is extremely large, and squeezing through the vagina might harm the baby or your partner.
- Forceps are used.
- The baby is breech (see below).
- The practitioner can see that numerous tears are going to happen.

BREECH PRESENTATION

If a baby is breech it means that the feet will be delivered first (only 3 to 4 percent of single babies are born this way, but about a third of all twins are). Actually, there are several different types of breech births: frank breech means that the baby's feet are straight up next to his head and the baby will come out butt first. Incomplete breech means that one foot comes out first. There's little you can do to prevent your baby from coming out any way he or she wants to (see page 101 for one possible solution). But most doctors in the U.S. will not deliver breech babies vaginally. This means that if the baby can't be turned, it's going to be delivered by C-section.

ELECTRONIC FETAL MONITORING (EFM)

EFMs come in two flavors: external and internal. The external variety is a rather complicated machine—complete with graphs, digital outputs, and high-tech beeping—that gets strapped to your partner's abdomen. It's used to monitor your baby's heartbeat and your partner's contractions.

Fetal monitors are really pretty cool. Properly hooked up, they are so accurate that by watching the digital display, you'll be able to tell when your partner's contractions are starting—even before *she* feels them—and how intense they will be. In one fascinating study, researchers Kristi Williams and Debra Umberson found that most expectant fathers like fetal monitors—partly because by giving us information we feel like we're really involved. "By observing and communicating the changing intensity of the contractions, these men believed that they were able to provide valuable information to their wives," they wrote. "This creates a role for husbands to play in labor and delivery that is, from their perspective, more important than merely providing support and encouragement." Notice the use of the phrases "these men believed" and "from their perspective." Williams and Umberson also found that women often perceived the monitors as a nuisance and the information they provided not particularly helpful. After all, they're getting the same information anyway, but in a slightly different way: it hurts like hell. And the monitors don't always reflect reality. The contraction may look like it's over on the screen, but it can be far from over for her.

So be careful. These monitors may help you coach your partner through the contraction. But think long and hard before saying something like "Ready, honey? Here it comes—looks like a big one."

In many hospitals, laboring women are routinely hooked up to external fetal monitors. Internal fetal monitors (which include an electrode attached to the baby's scalp and a tube that lies next to the baby and measures contraction strength) are also frequently used. But unless there's some compelling reason why you need one (if there have been signs of fetal distress, for example), you and your partner will be a lot better off without either kind of monitor. Here's why:

- Once the fetal monitor is on, your partner is virtually confined to her bed. No more showers, no more walks to the nursery, no more creative labor positions.
- It can scare the hell out of you. When my wife was hooked up to a fetal monitor during her first labor, we were comforted by the sound of the

> baby's steady, 140-beats-per-minute heartbeat. But at one point the heart rate dropped to 120, then 100, then 80, then 60. Nothing was wrong—the doctor was just trying to change the baby's position—but hearing her little heart slow down that much nearly gave my wife and me heart attacks.

Interestingly, several recent studies have shown that intermittently listening to the baby's heartbeat is just as effective as continuous external fetal monitoring. There also tend to be fewer C-sections for fetal distress. (The moral of the story is that the doctor might see something happen to the baby on the external monitor, get worried, and operate. In a lot of cases, what looks like fetal distress actually goes away on its own).

A final word of advice about fetal monitors: if you absolutely have to have one, make sure they turn the volume down (better yet, all the way off).

Notes:

Cesarean Section

All things being equal, most parents would prefer to bring their babies into the world "normally." And most of the time that's what happens. But when things don't go exactly the way they're supposed to, the chances of having a Cesarean-section delivery increase greatly. In the U.S., in fact, more than 30 percent of all children born in hospitals are delivered by C-section.

What's Going On with Your Partner

Most childbirth preparation classes (see pages 132–37) put a great deal of emphasis on natural, unmedicated deliveries. As we discussed earlier, many women, therefore, feel a tremendous amount of pressure to deliver vaginally and may actually consider themselves "failures" if they don't—especially after they've invested many hours in a painful labor (for more on this see pages 201–2).

In addition, recovering from a Cesarean is much different from recovering from a vaginal birth (see page 201 for more details). My wife (and I) spent three nights in the hospital after the C-section delivery of our first daughter. But after our second daughter was born (vaginally), we remained in the hospital for only five hours. (We rushed it a little; most people stay twenty-four to forty-eight hours after a vaginal birth, but my wife really wanted to leave.)

What's Going On with You

Your take on the C-section is undoubtedly going to be quite different from your partner's. Researcher Katharyn May found that only 8 percent of men whose partners delivered by C-section objected to the operation; 92 percent were "greatly relieved." Although I didn't participate in this study, it accurately reflects my own experience. It simply had never occurred to me that we might somehow have "failed." On the contrary, I remember feeling incredibly thankful that my wife's suffering would finally end. And seeing how quickly and painlessly the baby was delivered made me wonder why we hadn't done it sooner.

Despite the relief a father may feel on his wife's behalf, a C-section can be a trying experience for him. As a rule, he's separated from his wife while she is being prepped for surgery, and usually isn't given any information about what's happening. I remember being left in the hall outside the operating room, trying to keep an eye on my wife through a tiny window. Besides being terribly scared, I felt completely helpless—and useless—as the doctors, nurses, and assistants scurried around, blocking my view, getting dressed, washing, opening packages of scalpels, tubes, and who knows what else. Only one person—the pediatrician who ended up attending the delivery—took a minute to pat me on the shoulder and tell me that everything would be all right. I've never felt more grateful to another person in my life.

When I was finally permitted into the operating room, I was told—no discussion allowed—to sit by my wife's head. There was a curtain across her chest that prevented me from seeing what the surgeons were doing. I was ready to put some gloves on and help out with the operation, but whenever I stood up to get a better view the anesthesiologist shoved me back down into my seat. I was too exhausted to argue, but a friend of mine whose partner had a C-section in the same hospital a few years later did argue and was able to go around to the "business end" of the operation.

Staying Involved

My friend and I may be the lucky ones; in some hospitals men aren't allowed into the operating room at all. Others permit them in only if they've taken a special C-section class. Hopefully, even before you check in you and your partner will have already told your OB exactly what your preferences are should there be a C-section, and you'll be familiar with any relevant hospital policies. (See pages 18–19 for other things to discuss with your OB.)

Don't forget that although a C-section is a fairly commonplace operation, it is still major surgery. And after the operation, your partner will need some extra special care.

Common Medical Reasons for a Cesarean Section

- **Fetopelvic (or cephalopelvic) disproportion.** The mother's pelvis is too small to allow the baby's head to pass through the birth canal.
- **Failure of the labor to progress.** Exhausted by an excessively long labor, the mother is unable to push the baby out, or the cervix stops opening after active labor has begun.
- **The baby is distressed in some way.** Her heartbeat has dropped too far, the heartbeat pattern is worrisome, or other problems.
- **You're about to have more than one baby.**
- **Maternal herpes (active).** If the mother has an outbreak of herpes at the time of labor, there isn't much choice.
- **Placenta problems.** *Abrupto placenta* (separation of the placenta from the uterine wall before labor begins) causes bleeding and can threaten the lives of both mother and baby. *Placenta previa* (the placenta is fully or partially blocking the opening of the cervix) causes hemorrhaging and prevents the baby from leaving the uterus.
- **Position of baby.** Under certain circumstances, if the baby is breech (coming out feet first) or transverse (lying sideways instead of head down), a C-section may be more likely.
- **Previous C-section birth(s).** Contrary to popular belief, having had one C-section only slightly increases the chances of subsequent C-sections. Most women with a prior C-section have V-BACs (vaginal births after Cesarean), although many decide not to. Most doctors will discuss the possibility of elective, repeat Cesarians with your partner at one of her prenatal visits.
- **The fetus weights over 4,000 grams (a little over 8½ pounds).** With babies this size there's an increaced chance of *shoulder dystocia*—where the head delivers and then the baby gets stuck.

First of all, as strange as it may sound, after having a C-section your partner may feel terribly left out. She will have been fully awake during the operation and will be anxious to meet the new baby. But whereas after a vaginal birth the mother gets to see and touch the baby immediately, after a C-section the baby is usually quickly whisked away to have his or her lungs suctioned out. Sometimes the suctioning may happen even before the baby has been fully delivered.

Some of the Most Common Nonmedical Reasons for a Cesarean Section

As cynical as it sounds, sometimes C-sections aren't really necessary.

- **Scheduling.** Doing a C-section delivery means your doctor won't have to wait around for an unpredictably long labor.
- **It's easier.** Some OBs consider C-sections safer than vaginal deliveries.
- **Your partner may want one.** Some women are afraid of labor and think vaginal delivery sounds yucky. In addition, researcher Brent Bost recently found that vaginal delivery is one of the major causes of later incontinence in women. "Cesarean section prior to advanced labor is virtually 100 percent effective at eliminating these problems," he says. Dr. Bost also found that "healthy women who undergo elective Cesarean section experience a relatively low rate of short-term complications. And long-term complications are rare."
- **It's Friday.** More operations are performed on Friday afternoons, when tired doctors are eager to get home for the weekend, than at any other time of the week.
- **Fear of lawsuits.** If something goes wrong with the birth—fetal or maternal distress, or even a birth defect—the obstetrician is likely to be blamed for having let the labor go on too long. In some cases, then, OBs perform a C-section to speed things up.

You may get to make a "ceremonial" umbilical cord cut (the surgeons will have already cut the cord during the delivery). If the baby is being cared for right in the delivery room, make sure to tell your partner exactly what's happening—she'll want to know. In some hospitals, C-section babies are removed from the delivery room immediately after the birth and taken straight to the nursery, where they're washed, examined, and put through basically the same procedures covered in the preceding chapter. This whole process can take anywhere from a few minutes to a few hours.

Although you might want to remain with your partner and comfort her immediately after the delivery, ask the doctor whether you can stay with your baby instead. It's bad enough for a newborn to be deprived of snuggling with one of his parents right away, but it would be worse if the baby couldn't be with either of you. Staying with our daughter also eased my paranoia that she might be switched in the nursery (a highly unlikely occurrence, given the rather elaborate security measures in place in most hospitals). But don't get

Facts to Remember about Recovery from a Cesarean Section

- Your partner's incision will be tender or downright painful for at least several days. Fortunately, she'll undoubtedly be receiving some intravenous pain medication.
- The nursing staff will visit quite frequently to make sure that your partner's uterus is getting firm and returning to its proper place, to see whether she's producing enough urine, and to check her bandages.
- Your partner will have an IV until her bowels start functioning again (usually one to three days after delivery). After the IV is removed, she'll start on a liquid diet, then add a few soft foods, and finally return to her normal diet.
- Your partner will need to get up and move around. Despite the fact that a C-section is major abdominal surgery, less than twenty-four hours after the delivery the nurses will probably encourage—and help—your partner to get out of bed and take a couple of rather painful-looking steps.
- Before your partner leaves the hospital the sutures or staples will be removed. Yes, staples. Until I heard the clink as the doctor dropped them into a jar, I'd just assumed that my wife had been sewn up after her C-section. If your partner is discharged a little early—two to three days after the C-section—her sutures or staples will be taken out a few days later, either in her doctor's office or by a visiting nurse in your home.

too upset if the doctor says no—a lot of C-section babies are not medically stable at birth (not in danger, just requiring a little extra attention) and the medical staff won't want you hovering around, getting in the way.

Your Partner's Emotional Recovery

Having an unplanned C-section can trigger a whole host of conflicting emotions in your partner. She, like you, may feel greatly relieved that the pain is over and the baby is safe. At the same time, it's very natural for her to second-guess herself and the decisions she made, to start wondering whether there was anything she could have done to avoid the operation, or to believe she's failed because she didn't deliver vaginally. These feelings are especially common when the C-section was performed because labor "failed to progress" (meaning that the cervix wasn't dilating as quickly as the doctors may have thought it should, or stopped dilating altogether despite adequate contractions).

If you sense that your partner is experiencing any of these negative emotions, it's important for you to counter them immediately. She really needs to know that no one could have done more, or been stronger or braver than she was; that she didn't give in to the pain too soon; that she tried everything she could have to jump start a stalled labor; that another few hours of labor wouldn't have done anyone any good; and that the decision she made (or at least agreed to) was the best one—both for the baby and for herself.

Some of these thoughts might seem obvious to you—so obvious that you might think they don't need to be said at all. But they do—especially by you. You were there with her and you know better than anyone else exactly what she went through. So, being comforted and praised by you will mean a lot more to her than hearing the same words from a well-meaning relative. Having a baby isn't some kind of competition. As author Vicki Iovene writes, "It is not designed for your personal enjoyment and fulfillment. It is not an opportunity to demonstrate your abilities or fitness. It is designed to perpetuate the species and nothing more." Not the most romantic way of looking at having a baby, but quite accurate.

An Important Warning

Never, never, never suggest to your pregnant partner that she consider a C-section—let your doctor make the first move.

When my wife was pregnant with our second daughter, the pain she had been through during her first labor and delivery was still fresh in my mind. At one point I told her that I was really upset by the thought that she might have to endure another horrible labor, and I suggested that she consider a C-section.

I had no idea that someone could get so furious so quickly. Even though I had the very best intentions and was sincerely thinking only of her and how to minimize her pain, she thought I was being completely insensitive. Clearly, I had underestimated how incredibly important giving birth vaginally—especially after already having had one C-section—was to her.

Many of the men I've talked to have had similar thoughts about making the C-section suggestion to their partners. Most of them were wise enough not to act on their impulse. And hopefully, you won't either. Telling your partner how you're feeling and what you're going through is, in most cases, the right thing to do. But when it comes to C-sections, really and truly, it's an issue that's just too hot to handle.

Gee Honey, Now What Do We Do?

What's Going On with Your Partner

Physically

- Vaginal discharge (called *lochia)* that will gradually change from bloody to pink to brown to yellow over the next six weeks or so
- Major discomfort if there is an episiotomy or C-section incision (the pain will disappear over the next six weeks)
- Constipation
- Breast discomfort starting about the third day after the birth (when her breasts become engorged with milk); if she's breastfeeding, her nipples may be sore for about two weeks
- Gradual weight loss
- Exhaustion—especially if her labor was long and difficult
- Continued contractions—especially while breastfeeding—but disappearing over the next several days
- Hair loss (most women stop losing hair while they're pregnant, but when the pregnancy's over, so are all those great hair days)

Emotionally

- Relief that it's finally over
- Excitement, depression, or both (see page 204)
- Worried about how she'll perform as a mother, and whether she'll be able to breastfeed (but over the next few weeks, her confidence will build and these worries should disappear)
- A deep need to get to know the baby
- Impatience at her lack of mobility
- Decreased sex drive, assuming she had any left before the baby came anyway

Postpartum Blues and Depression

About 70 percent of new mothers experience periods of mild sadness, weepiness, mood swings, sleep deprivation, loss of appetite, inability to make decisions, anger, or anxiety after the baby is born. These postpartum blues, which many believe are caused by hormonal shifts in a new mother's body, can last for hours or days, but in most cases they disappear within a few weeks. Researcher Edward Hagen, however, believes that postpartum blues has little, if anything, to do with hormones. Instead, he says, it's connected to low levels of social support—especially from the father. And it could be the new mother's way of "negotiating" for more involvement. If you notice that your partner is experiencing any of these symptoms, be as supportive and involved as possible. Take on more of the child-care responsibilities, encourage her to get out of the house for a while, and see to it that she's eating healthily.

In a small number of cases, postpartum blues can develop into postpartum depression. According to the American College of Obstetricians and Gynecologists, postpartum depression, if not recognized and treated, may become worse or last longer than usual. Here are some symptoms to watch out for:

- Postpartum blues that don't go away after two weeks, or feelings of depression or anger that surface a month or two after the birth
- Feelings of sadness, doubt, guilt, helplessness, or hopelessness that begin to disrupt your partner's normal functioning
- Inability to sleep when tired, or sleeping most of the time, even when the baby is awake
- Marked changes in appetite
- Extreme concern and worry about—or lack of interest in—the baby and/or other members of the family
- Worries that she'll harm the baby or herself, or threats that she'll do either one

Again, most of what your partner will go through after the birth is completely normal and nothing to worry about. So be patient, and don't expect her to bounce back immediately. If you're really concerned, however, encourage your partner to talk with you about what she's feeling and to see her doctor or a therapist. You might also want to call her doctor yourself, just to make sure.

What's Going On with the Baby

"Most people make babies out to be very complicated," says comedian Dave Barry. "But the truth is they have only three moods: Mood One: Just about to cry. Mood Two: Crying. Mood Three: Just finished crying. Your job, as a parent, is to keep the baby in Mood Three as much as possible." With just a few days of fatherhood under your belt you may be inclined to go along with Barry's summary. But the real truth is that babies' moods are a bit more subtle.

Babies actually have six clearly defined behavioral states that are apparent within just a few minutes after a baby is born. "By recognizing them and realizing when they occur and what the expected responses are in each," write Marshall and Phyllis Klaus, authors of *The Amazing Newborn,* "parents not only can get to know their infants but also can provide most sensitively for their needs."

In my first few weeks as a dad, I found that learning about these six states was a huge help in getting to know my daughter. Here's a summary of the six states, based on the Klauses' book.

Quiet Alert

Babies in the quiet alert state don't move very much—all their energy is focused on seeing and hearing. They can (and do) follow objects with their eyes and will even imitate your facial expressions.

Within the first hour of life, most infants have a period of quiet alertness that lasts an average of forty minutes. During his or her first week, the normal baby spends only about 10 percent of any twenty-four-hour period in this state. It is in this state, however, that your baby is most curious and is absorbing information about his or her new world. And while the baby is in this state you will first become aware that there's a real person inside that tiny body.

Active Alert

In this state, the baby will make small sounds and move his or her arms, head, body, face, and eyes frequently and actively.

The baby's movements usually come in short bursts—a few seconds of activity every minute or two. Some researchers say these movements are designed to give parents subtle clues about what the baby wants and needs. Others say these movements are simply interesting to watch, and therefore promote parent-infant interaction.

Crying

Crying is a perfectly natural—and for some, all-too-frequent—state (for more on this, see pages 229–33). The infant's eyes may be open or closed, the face red, and the arms and legs thrashing around.

Often, just picking up the baby and walking around with him or her will stop the crying. Interestingly, researchers used to think that babies were soothed because they liked being held upright. What really makes them stop crying, though, is actually the motion toward the upright position.

As unpleasant as it is sometimes, crying is not always a bad thing—it not only allows the baby to communicate but also provides valuable exercise. So, if your efforts to calm him or her aren't immediately successful (and the baby isn't hungry or stewing in a dirty diaper), don't worry; chances are the tears will stop by themselves in a few minutes. See pages 233–34 for more on how to handle crying.

Drowsiness

This is a transition state that occurs as the baby is waking up or falling asleep. He may move a little, but his eyes will often look dull or unfocused.

Leave the baby alone—let him drift off to sleep or move into one of the alert stages.

Quiet Sleep

The baby's face is peacefully relaxed and his eyelids remain closed and still. His body will hardly move at all, though his mouth may twitch, almost imperceptibly, from time to time.

Babies in the quiet sleep state tend to sleep very soundly—so soundly that you may be alarmed at the lack of movement and be afraid the baby has stopped breathing. If so, lean as close as you can and listen for the baby's breath. Otherwise, gently put a hand on the baby's back and feel it rise and fall. Try to resist the urge to poke the baby to make sure she's still alive—most newborns spend up to 90 percent of their first few weeks sleeping.

Active Sleep

The baby's eyes are usually closed but he may smile or frown, make sucking or chewing movements, and even whimper or twitch—just like you do in your active sleep state.

Half of a baby's sleep time is spent in quiet sleep, the other half in active sleep, with the two states alternating in thirty-minute shifts. So, if your sleeping baby starts to stir, whimper, or seems to be waking up unhappy, wait a few seconds before you pick him up to feed, change, or soothe. Left alone, the baby may very well slip back into the quiet sleep state.

For thousands of years, most people believed that newborn infants were capable only of eating, sleeping, crying, and looking around. But if you pay attention, you'll see that your new baby has an incredible arsenal of talents. Just a few hours out of the womb, your baby is already trying to communicate with you and everyone else around him. He can imitate your facial expressions, has some control over his body, can express preferences (most prefer patterned objects to plain objects and curved lines to straight ones), and has a remarkable memory. Marshall Klaus describes playing a game with an eight-hour-old girl in which he asked one colleague (who was a stranger to the baby) to hold her and slowly stick out her tongue. After a few seconds, the baby imitated the woman. Then Dr. Klaus took the baby and passed her around to twelve other doctors and nurses who were participating in the game, all of whom were told not to stick their tongues out. When the baby finally came back to the first doctor, she—without any prompting—immediately stuck out her tongue again. Even at just a few hours old, she had obviously remembered her "friend."

If you want your baby to respond to and play with you, try to establish communication during his or her active alert stage. (During the first few months infants are particularly responsive to high contrast, so black-and-white toys and patterns are often a big hit.) But be patient. Babies are incredibly bright little creatures, but they also have minds of their own. This means that despite your best efforts, your baby may not be interested in performing like a trained seal whenever you wish.

What's Going On with You

Unconditional Love

Sooner or later, almost every writer takes a crack at trying to describe love. And for the most part, they fall short. But there's a line in Maurice Sendak's classic children's book *Where the Wild Things Are* that captures the feeling of loving one's own child exactly: "Please don't go—we'll eat you up—we love you so." As crazy as it may sound, that's precisely what my love for my daughters feels like to me. Whether we're playing, reading a book, telling each other about our days, or I'm just gazing at their smooth, peaceful faces as they sleep, all of a sudden I'll be overcome with the desire to pick them up, mush them into tiny balls, and pop them in my mouth. If you don't already know what I mean, believe me, you will soon. Just you wait.

One of my biggest fears during my wife's second pregnancy was that I wouldn't be able to love our second child as much as the first—that there wouldn't be enough of the consuming, overpowering love I felt for our first daughter to share with the new baby. But I really had nothing to worry about. Three seconds after our second daughter was born, I already wanted to eat her up, too.

Feeling, Well, Paternal

Despite all the excitement, you may be filled with a sense of calm and peacefulness. You may feel less like going to work and more like hanging out with the new family. If so, you certainly aren't alone. Canadian researcher Anne Storey found that new fathers' testosterone levels often drop by as much as a third right after the birth of their children. Storey speculates that this kind of testosterone reduction would make a man feel more parental or more like "settling down."

Awe at What the Female Body Can Do

Watching your partner go through labor is truly a humbling experience; chances are, your own physical courage, strength, and resolve have rarely been put to such a test. But there's nothing like seeing a baby come out of a vagina to convince you that women are really different from men.

I know that vaginal birth has been around for millions of years and that that's the way babies are supposed to be born. Yet in a strange way, there's something almost unnatural about the whole process—the baby seems so big and the vagina so small (it kind of reminds me of the ship-in-a-bottle conundrum). Ironically, a C-section somehow seems more "normal": when the fetus is full-grown, cut an appropriately sized exit and let the baby out. You'd think that with all the technological advances we've made in other areas, we'd have invented a quicker, easier, less painful way to have children.

Jealousy

"The single emotion that can be the most destructive and disruptive to your experience of fatherhood is jealousy," writes Dr. Martin Greenberg in *The Birth of a Father.*

There's certainly plenty to be jealous about, but the real question is, "Whom are you jealous of?" Your partner for being able to breastfeed and for her close relationship with the baby, or the baby itself for taking up more than his or her "fair share" of your partner's attention, and for having full access to your partner's breasts while you aren't even supposed to touch them? The answer is, "Both."

Now that the baby's born, communication with your partner is even more important than before. Jealousy's "potential for destruction," writes Greenberg, "lies not in having the feelings but in burying them." So if you're feeling jealous, tell her about it. But if you can't bring yourself to discuss your feelings on this issue with your partner, take them up with a male friend or relative. You'll be surprised at how common these feelings are.

Feeling Pushed Away or Left Out

Another common feeling experienced by new fathers is that of being pushed away or excluded from the new parenting experience. "The mother plays a critical role," writes Pamela Jordan. "She can bring her mate into the spotlight or keep him in the wings. The most promoting mothers . . . brought their mates into the experience by frequently and openly sharing their physical sensations and emotional responses. They actively encouraged their mates to share the experience of becoming and being a father."

While it's easy to give in to your feelings, throw up your hands, and leave the parenting to your partner, don't do it. Encourage her to talk about what she's feeling and thinking, and ask her specifically to involve you as much as possible.

A good way to cut down on your potential feelings of jealousy or of being pushed away is to start getting to know your baby right away—even before you leave the hospital. Change as many diapers as you can (if you've never changed one before, get one of the nurses to show you how), give the baby a sponge bath, or take him or her out for a walk while your partner gets so me rest.

Amazement at How Being a Parent Changes Your Life

It's virtually impossible to try to explain the myriad ways becoming a parent will change your life. You already know you'll be responsible for the safety and well-being of a completely helpless person. You've heard that you'll lose a little sleep (all right, a lot) and even more privacy. And you've prepared yourself for not being able to read as many books or see as many movies as you did before. These are some of the big, obvious changes, but it's the tiny details that will make you realize just how different your new life is from your old one.

The best way I can describe it is this: sometimes one of my daughters puts some food into her mouth and after a few chews changes her mind, takes it out, and hands it to me. Most of the time I take the offering and pop it into my mouth without a second thought. You probably will too. Even more bizarre, since becoming a father, I have actually had serious discussions with my friends about the color and consistency of the contents of my children's diapers. So will you.

Bonding with the Baby

No one knows exactly where or when it started, but one of the most widespread—and most enduring—myths about child rearing is that women are somehow more nurturing than men and are therefore better suited to parenting.

In one of the earliest studies of father-infant interaction, researcher Ross Parke made a discovery that might shock the traditionalists: the fathers were just as caring about, interested in, and involved with their infants as the mothers were, and they held, touched, kissed, rocked, and cooed at their new babies with at least the same frequency as the mothers did. Several years later, Martin Greenberg coined a term, *engrossment,* to describe "a father's sense of absorption, preoccupation, and interest in his baby."

Parke and a number of other researchers have repeatedly confirmed these findings about father-infant interaction, and have concluded that what triggers engrossment in men is the same thing that prompts similar nurturing feelings in women: early infant contact. "In sum," writes Parke, "the amount of stimulatory and affectional behavior depends on the opportunity to hold the infant."

Not surprisingly, Parke and others have found that men who attended their baby's birth bonded slightly faster than those who didn't. But if you weren't able to be there for the birth, don't worry. "Early contact at birth is not a magic pill," writes Ellen Galinsky, author of *The Six Stages of Parenthood.* "It does not guarantee attachment. Neither does lack of contact prevent bonding."

But What If I Don't Bond Right Away?

Although we've spent a lot of time talking about the joys of loving your child and how important it is to bond with the infant as soon as possible, many new fathers (and mothers, for that matter) don't feel particularly close to the new baby immediately after the birth. In fact, psychiatrists Kay Robson and Ramesh Kumar have found that 25 to 40 percent of mothers *and* fathers admit that their first response to their baby was "indifference." Putting things in slightly stronger terms, researcher Katharyn May says, "This bonding business is nonsense. We've sold parents a bill of goods. They believe that if they don't have skin-to-skin contact within the first fifteen minutes, they won't bond. Science just doesn't show that."

In a way, this really makes more sense than the love-at-first-sight kind of bonding you hear so much about. After all, you don't even know this new little person. He or she may look a lot different than you expected. And, if your partner's labor and delivery were long and arduous, you may unconsciously be blaming the baby for the difficulties or may simply be too exhausted to fully appreciate the new arrival.

So, if you haven't established an instant attachment with your baby, there's absolutely nothing wrong with you. And, more important, there's no evidence whatsoever that your relationship with or feelings for your child will be any less loving than if you'd fallen head over heels in love in the first second. Just take your time, don't pressure yourself, and don't think for a second that you've failed as a father.

There's a lot of evidence that parent-child bonding comes as a result of physical closeness. So if you'd like to speed up the process, try carrying the baby every chance you get, taking him with you whenever you can, and taking care of as may of his basic needs as possible.

The whole bonding thing is probably going to be a lot tougher if you've got twins (or more). Because they tend to be born somewhat more prematurely than single babies, multiples may have to stay in the hospital nursery for a few days or even weeks, which can limit the amount of time you can spend with them—separately or together. Things can get even more complicated if one of the babies comes home with you and the other(s) stays behind. You're going to feel torn between spending time with the baby in the hospital, the other baby, and your partner. Unfortunately, there's no magic formula for how much time each of them gets. Just do the best you can and spend a lot of time talking with your partner about how you're both feeling and what each of you needs.

Gee, This Isn't at All What I Expected . . .

Despite everything you've heard about how gorgeous babies are, you may have a slightly different opinion—at least for the first week or so after your baby's born. If your baby was born vaginally, the trip through the birth canal may have flattened his nose and made him look a little cone-headed. Calm down. His nose will pop out and his head will get rounder over the next few weeks. Do those green, tarlike bowel movements make you think

Adoptive Dads Bond Too

Plenty of adoptive parents—particularly if they adopted because of infertility—feel a little insecure or inadequate. They often believe that the process of bonding and forming an attachment to the baby comes more naturally to birth parents than to them. Fortunately, this isn't true.

Studies of adoptive parents have shown that a majority feel some kind of love for their children right from the very first contact; it doesn't matter whether it's when they go to pick up the baby, when they first look at a picture that arrived months before, or right at the birth, if they're lucky enough to be there. At the same time, though, just like biological parents, a good percentage of adoptive parents don't feel anything particularly parental when meeting their child for the first time.

If you're adopting a newborn, it's going to be a little easier to establish a bond. But a lot of adoptions aren't finalized until the babies are a few months older. Realistically, this makes the bonding process a bit tougher for all concerned, as babies and parents take a little time to get used to each other. It's by no means an impossible task. "Being a first-time parent, whether by birth or adoption, evokes a variety of feelings," writes Marshall Klaus. "And although many parents feel attached to their baby at first contact, many others find it takes a week or longer to feel the baby is theirs." If you aren't consumed with paternal feelings right away, the first thing to do is take a look at the "But What If I Don't Bond Right Away" section on pages 210–11.

there's something wrong with the baby's intestines? There isn't. Those first few loads are perfectly normal and will be replaced by a much more pleasant-looking concoction as your baby starts breastfeeding. Is the baby's skin splotchy—especially on the neck and the eyelids—and does she have strange-looking birth marks or tiny pimples? Relax. Just keep her clean—no scrubbing or zit popping—and she'll be fine. Does your infant seem a little cross-eyed? It's fine. As soon as his eye muscles get a bit more developed and coordinated, he'll be able to look you straight in the eye. Do his hairy back and shoulders have you worrying about what'll happen to him when the moon is full? Don't. That fuzz is called *lanugo* and it'll fall out pretty soon.

Staying Involved

The First Few Days

In the first few days you're going to have to learn to juggle a lot of roles. You're still a lover and friend to your partner, and, of course, you're a father. But for now, your most important role is that of support person to your partner. Besides her physical recovery (which we'll talk more about below), she's going to need time to get to know the baby and to learn (if she chooses to) how to breastfeed.

When our first daughter was born (by C-section), the three of us spent four days in the hospital (which meant three uncomfortable nights on a crooked, lumpy cot for me). But when our second daughter was born (vaginally), we all checked out less than five hours after the birth. In both cases, though, my first few days at home were mighty busy—cooking, shopping, doing laundry, fixing up the baby's room, getting the word out, screening phone calls and visitors, and making sure everyone got plenty of rest.

Coming Home . . . and Beyond

Within a few minutes after we'd brought our first daughter home from the hospital, my wife and I looked at each other and almost simultaneously asked, "Well, now what are we supposed to do?" An important question, no doubt, and one that seems to come up time and time again.

A NOTE ON RECOVERY

As far as the baby is concerned, there's not much to do in the beginning besides feeding, changing, and admiring him or her. But your partner is a different story. Despite everything you've heard about women giving birth in the fields and returning to work a few minutes later, that's not the way things usually happen. Having a baby is a major shock to a woman's system. And, contrary to popular belief, the recovery period after a vaginal birth is not necessarily any shorter than the recovery period after a C-section (although most women who have had both say that vaginal birth recover is easier).

Whatever kind of delivery your partner has, she'll need some time—probably more than either of you think—to recover fully. According to a recent study, more than 40 percent of new mothers experience fatigue and breast soreness in the first month after giving birth. In addition, vaginal discomfort, hemorrhoids, poor appetite, constipation, increased perspiration, acne, hand numbness or tingling, dizziness, and hot flashes are common for a month after delivery. And between 10 and 40 percent of women feel pain during sexual intercourse, have respiratory infections, and lose hair for three to six months. Aren't you glad you can't have a baby?

Here are some things you can do to make the recovery process as easy as possible and to start parenting off on the right foot.

- Help your partner resist the urge to do too much too soon.
- Take over the household chores or ask someone else to help. And if the house is a mess, don't blame each other.
- Be flexible. Expecting to maintain your normal, prefatherhood schedule is unrealistic—especially for the first six weeks after the birth.
- Don't allow your relationship with your partner to be based solely on your child. If she's up to it, go on a date with your partner and leave the baby with a relative or friend.
- Be patient with yourself, your partner, and the baby. You're all new at this.
- Be sensitive to your partner's emotions. Recovery has an emotional component as well as a physical one.
- Make sure to get some time alone with the baby. You can do this while your partner is sleeping or while she's out for a walk.
- Control the visiting hours and the number of people who can come at any given time. Dealing with visitors takes a lot more energy than you might think. And being poked, prodded, and passed around won't make the baby very happy. Also, for the first month or so, ask anyone who wants to touch the baby to wash his or her hands first.
- Keep your sense of humor.

HELPING OLDER KIDS ADJUST TO THEIR NEW SIBLING

Handling your older children's reactions to their new baby brother or sister requires an extra touch of gentleness and sensitivity. Kids often start out wildly excited at their new status as big brother or big sister, but most will have some adjustment problems later on—as soon as they realize that the new kid is more than just a temporary visitor.

Some react with anger and jealousy. They may cry, have tantrums, and even try to hit the baby. They need to know immediately and in no uncertain terms that you understand how they feel and that it's okay to be mad and talk about how mad they are. It's even okay to draw hateful pictures or beat up a doll. But it's absolutely not okay to do anything to hurt the baby.

Others may react by regressing. My older daughter, for example, was completely potty trained before her sister was born, but began wetting her bed again a few weeks after we brought our younger daughter home. Some kids suddenly start talking baby talk again, need more bedtime stories and cuddling, or make demands for attention that you may not be able to satisfy.

Here are some ways you can help your older children cope with the big changes in their world:

- Get them involved from the very start. Our older daughter stayed at my parents' house while my wife was in labor with our younger daughter. But as soon as the baby was born, we called and gave her the chance to break the news to everyone else that she was a big sister. We also had her come to the hospital right away (even though it was past her bedtime), where she got to hold her new sister "by herself."

  If your older child comes to the hospital, keep the visit short. It won't take long for the initial excitement to wear off. And be sure to let him spend some time visiting with mom too. He may have been worried about her, and seeing her in a hospital bed, possibly with IV tubes hanging out of her arms, can be a scary sight.
- Don't push too hard. Letting the older sibling help diaper, bathe, feed, and clothe the new baby is a great idea; it helps bring him into the process by making him feel that the baby is "his." But don't force the older child to get too involved. It can make him feel as though you want him around only to wait on the more important new baby, which can make him resent the little interloper even more.
- Prepare them for reality. The first lesson is that infants aren't a whole lot of fun to have around for some time. All they do is poop and cry and eat. They can't even play any games. It might be helpful to show your big kids their own baby pictures and talk to them about how they were when they were young and how you cared for them.
- Model good behavior. Show your older kids the right ways to hold and behave with a new baby. Practicing with a doll is a great, risk-free way to get the hang of it—particularly the all-important head-supporting part. If you're bottle feeding, show the older kids the right way to hold a bottle and how to recognize when the baby's had enough. Never, ever leave the baby unattended with an older sibling (unless you've got a teenager), and make sure the older child is always sitting down when holding the baby.
- Be patient. If your older child is angry or jealous, encourage her to talk about her feelings. If she's having trouble articulating them, you might offer a few suggestions ("Are you mad that the baby is getting more attention than you are?") or encourage her to draw pictures of how she feels. If your child is regressing, resist the urge to demand that he or she

A Note on Dressing Children

Getting a baby dressed is not an easy task; their heads always seem too big to go through the appropriate openings in their shirts, and their hands regularly refuse to come out of the sleeves. There are a few things you can do to make dressing a little easier:

- Reach through the sleeve and pull your baby's hands through—it's a lot easier than trying to shove from the other side.
- Buy pants or overalls with legs that snap open. Some manufacturers make baby clothes that are absolutely beautiful but impossible to put on or take off. The snap-open legs also make diaper changing much easier—you don't have to remove the whole outfit to access the diaper. Clothing legs that don't snap all the way through the ankles are a big pain—elasticised cuffs aren't so easy to maneuver when the kid is squirming on the changing table!

Also, don't overdress your baby. For some strange reason, people tend to bundle their children up in all sorts of blankets, sweaters, hats, and gloves—even in the summer. But unless you're Eskimos, there's no reason to dress your children like one. A basic rule of thumb is to have the baby wear the same kind of clothes you do, plus a hat. Layering clothing is sometimes a good way to go—if the baby gets too hot, you can remove a layer.

Finally, remember this simple rule: "If they can't walk, they don't need shoes." It's not only a waste of money, but confining a baby's feet in a hard pair of shoes all day long can actually damage the bones.

"grow up." Kids who adopt baby behavior are usually doing so because they figure that being helpless is a good way to get people to pay attention. So instead of snapping at them, point out some of the big-kid things they get to do that babies don't, such as using a fork and knife, riding a trike, putting on their own shoes, washing their own faces, going down a slide by themselves, and so on.

- Spend some extra time with your older child. Your older child really needs to know that you still love her just as much as before. So make sure you get some private time together reading, going for walks, drawing, talking, seeing movies, or just hanging out. And make sure the big kid gets to spend some private time with mom too.

Immediate Concerns . . . with Long-term Impact

FEEDING THE BABY: BREAST VS. BOTTLE

In the 1950s and 1960s, when some of you reading this book were born, breastfeeding was out of style and most new mothers were given a wide variety of reasons (by their doctors, of course) not to breastfeed. But starting in the 1970s, breasts came back big time—so much so that it's pretty hard these days to find anyone who doesn't advocate breastfeeding. Even in the medical community, there's general agreement that breastfeeding is just about the best

A Special Note on Breastfeeding

As natural as breastfeeding is, your partner and the baby may need anywhere from a few days to a few weeks to get the hang of it. The baby may not immediately know how to latch on to the breast properly, and your partner—never having done this before—won't know exactly what to do either. This initial period, in which cracked and even bloody nipples are not uncommon, may be quite painful for your partner. And with the baby feeding six or seven times a day, it may take as long as two weeks for your partner's nipples to get sufficiently toughened up.

Surprisingly, your partner won't begin producing any real milk until two to five days after the baby is born. But there's no need to worry that the baby isn't getting enough food. Babies don't eat much the first 24 to 48 hours, and most of the sucking they do is almost purely for practice. Whatever nutritional needs your baby has will be fully satisfied by the tiny amounts of colostrum your partner produces. (Colostrum is a kind of premilk that helps the baby's immature digestive system get warmed up for the task of digesting real milk later.)

Overall, the first few weeks of breastfeeding can be very stressful for your partner. If this is the case, don't be tempted to suggest switching to bottles. Instead, be supportive, praise her for the great job she's doing, bring her something to eat or drink while she's feeding, and encourage her to keep trying. You also might want to ask your pediatrician for the name of a local lactation consultant (yes, there really is such a thing). Your support is particularly important. Research shows that women whose husbands are supportive and encouraging breastfeed longer and are happier with the decision—an outcome that's good for everyone.

A Note on Juice

If you and your partner decide not to breastfeed, or decide to supplement breastfeeding with a bottle, don't fill it with juice. A recent study found that children who drink large quantities of fruit juice—especially apple juice—suffer from frequent diarrhea and, in the worst cases, may fail to grow and develop normally. The problem is that babies love juice so much that, if you give them all they want, they'll fill up their tiny stomachs with it, leaving no room for the more nutritious foods they need. The American Dietetic Association recommends that parents refrain from giving their babies juice until they're at least six months old, and then restrict juice intake until age two.

thing you can do for your child. The American Academy of Pediatrics recently recommended that new babies be breastfed for *at least* twelve months.

If you and your partner haven't already decided to breastfeed, here are the reasons why you should (besides the fact that you'll get a lot of nasty looks from people if you don't):

FOR THE BABY

- Breast milk provides exactly the right balance of nutrients needed by your newborn. In addition, breast milk contains several essential fatty acids that are not found in baby formula.
- Breast milk adapts, as if by magic, to your baby's changing nutritional needs. Neither of our children had a single sip of anything but breast milk for the first seven or eight months of life, and they're both incredibly healthy kids.
- Breastfeeding greatly reduces the chance that your baby will develop food allergies. If your family (or your partner's) has a history of food allergies, you should withhold solid foods for at least six months.
- Breastfed babies are less prone to obesity in adulthood than formula-fed babies. This may be because with the breast, it's the baby—not the parent—who decides when to quit eating.
- Breastfed babies have a greatly reduced risk of developing respiratory and gastrointestinal illness.
- Breastfeeding is thought to transmit to the infant the mother's immunity to certain diseases. This is especially important for the first few months, until the baby's immune system matures.

FOR YOU AND YOUR PARTNER

- It's convenient—no preparation, no heating, no bottles or dishes to wash . . .
- It's free. Formula can cost a lot of money.
- It gives your partner a wonderful opportunity to bond with the baby. In addition, breastfeeding will help get your partner's uterus back into shape and may reduce her risk of ovarian and breast cancer.

Feeding Twins

Although there's no question that breastfeeding is best, nursing two infants at the same time presents some real complications. First of all, for the first weeks or so each of them is going to want to eat every two or three hours. Sometimes they'll be hungry at the same time, sometimes not. Either way, by the time the feedings are over and the diapers are changed it'll be just about time to start again, which will leave your partner feeling something like a 24-hour drive-through milk bar. In a valiant attempt to give themselves some down time, a lot of new mothers of twins opt for a mix of breast- and bottle feeding. The bottles can be filled either with breast milk (which can be pumped out faster than a baby can suck it out) or formula. Either way, if you've got twins, you're really going to have to be a lot more involved in feeding them than you otherwise might have been.

Breastfeeding and Older Kids

Despite how wonderful breastfeeding is for the new baby, your older kids may see it as little more than an attempt to displace them from the center of the universe. And seeing mom holding and cuddling and nursing often brings up all sorts of feelings—anger and jealousy being at the top of the list (see pages 214-16 for more on coping with this). Some new big brothers and sisters will want to be held the same way the baby is being held. Some will even want to nurse. If the older sibling is young enough, your partner may actually want to give in to the request. If so, it should be only on a very temporary basis. (Giving a teaspoonful or two of breastmilk might be a better solution—most older kids won't like the watery consistency or the sweet taste.) Older children need to know that your partner's milk is for the baby and that big kids get to have—and do—lots of other things that newborns can't.

- In most cases there's always as much as you need, and never any waste.
- Your baby's diapers won't stink. It's true. Breastfed babies produce stool that—at least compared to "real food" stools—doesn't smell half bad.

SLEEPING ARRANGEMENTS

Your pediatrician will probably tell you that your baby should get used to sleeping by him- or herself as soon after birth as possible. The reasoning is that in American culture we emphasize early independence, so babies should adapt quickly to being away from their parents—especially if both parents work and the children are in day care.

But there is another school of thought that maintains that babies should sleep in the same bed as their parents (an idea shared by about 80 percent of the world's population). The rationale is that human evolution simply can't keep pace with the new demands our culture is placing on its children. "Proximity to parental sounds, smells, heat, and movement during the night is precisely what the human infant's immature system expects—and needs," says James McKenna, an anthropologist and sleep researcher.

So which approach is right? Well, given the wide divergence of expert opinions out there, it's a tough call—one you'll ultimately have to make on your own. Our older daughter slept in a bassinet in our room for a month or so until we moved her into her own room. Our younger daughter, however, slept in bed with us for six months before moving to her own room. Neither of them had any trouble making the transition, or any sleep problems thereafter.

Hands-On Tips for Dads of Preemies

If your baby was born before about 35–36 weeks, he may have to spend some time in an incubator bulking up to at least four or five pounds before you can take him home.

One of the things you can do to make that happen a little sooner is to massage your baby. Tiffany Field, director of the Touch Research Institute at the University of Miami School of Medicine, found that preemies who had three fifteen-minute periods of gentle massage every day in addition to their normal treatment grew almost 50 percent more than those who didn't get the massage. Hospital stays were shortened by almost a week and the bills were correspondingly lower as well. On their first birthdays, premature babies who'd been massaged were bigger and better developed than similarly premature kids who didn't get massaged. Pretty neat, eh?

"Is There Anything We Can Do?"

One of the most common questions you'll hear from people is whether they can help out in any way. Some people are serious, others are just being polite. You can tell one group from the other by keeping a list of chores that need to be done and asking them to take their pick.

One of the nicest, and most helpful, things that was done for us both times we brought a baby home was a group effort by some of our friends. They'd gotten together and, taking turns, brought us meals every day for more than a week. Not having to cook or shop gave us a lot more time to spend together and let us get some rest. And of course, when our friends had their children, we were there with our spinach lasagna and a bottle of wine.

Here are a few of the most common questions you're likely to have if you haven't already decided where your child will be sleeping.

- **How will it affect the baby's independence?** There's absolutely no agreement on this. Richard Ferber, author of *Solve Your Child's Sleep Problems,* maintains that "sleeping alone is an important part of a child's learning to be able to separate from his parents without anxiety and to see himself as an independent individual." In contrast, Thomas F. Anders, M.D., a professor of psychiatry, contends that "every child is born with a strong need for lots of close physical contact with a caregiver, and children in whom this need isn't met early in their lives may end up trying to fill it as adults."
- **What about safety?** Most adults—even while asleep—have a highly developed sense of where they are. After all, when was the last time you fell out of bed? So, the risk of accidentally suffocating your baby is pretty slim. Nevertheless, the Federal Consumer Product Safety Commission is recommending that parents not sleep with babies under the age of two. This is based on an eight-year study that attributed the deaths of 515 children under two to sleeping in adult beds (121 of which were attributed to a parent, caregiver, or sibling rolling on top of or against the baby while sleeping). That's 64 a year. The CPSC also found that 50 babies die every year from being put into cribs that don't meet federal safety standards.
- **How will the baby sleep?** Despite what you might think, co-sleeping children tend to sleep more *lightly* than children who sleep alone

If You Decide to Share Your Bed with Your Child

Do it because you and your partner *want* to, not because you feel you have to. You're not negligent or overindulgent parents for doing it, so don't be embarrassed by your choice. But please be extremely careful: no waterbeds—a baby could roll between you and the mattress. Also, overly soft mattresses and pillows may pose a risk of suffocation.

If Family Sleeping *Isn't* for You

Don't feel guilty. You're not a bad or selfish parent for not doing it. Teaching your children to be independent does not mean that you don't have a close bond with them. But don't feel like a failure if you allow an occasional exception, such as when a child is ill or has had a frightening experience.

(blankets rustling and parents turning over in bed wake them up). But light sleeping isn't necessarily a bad thing. In fact, there seems to be a correlation between lighter sleep and a lower incidence of SIDS (Sudden Infant Death Syndrome—see below for more).

Sharing a bed with your infant not only affects your child, but it can also have a serious impact on you. You'll lose a lot of sexual spontaneity, and maybe even more sleep. Even the soundest-sleeping kids generally wake up every three or four hours; 70 percent of them just look around for a few minutes and soothe themselves back to sleep. But if your baby is in the other 30 percent, he or she may wake up, see you, and want to play.

A NOTE ON SIDS

Every year about seven thousand children die of Sudden Infant Death Syndrome. Striking one out of every thousand babies, it's the most common cause of death of children between one week and one year old.

Despite all the millions of dollars spent on researching and fighting SIDS, no one's quite sure what, exactly, causes it. And there's no medical test to determine which babies are at the greatest risk. Here's what we do know:

- It's most likely to strike infants two to four months old.
- Ninety percent of deaths happen by six months.
- It's more likely to happen to boys than girls, to preemies, multiple-birth babies, and in families in which a parent or caretaker smokes or bottle-feeds.

Do You Really Want Your Mother-in-law to Move in with You Right after the Birth?

Be careful about having people stay over to help with the newborn—especially parents (yours or hers). The new grandparents may have more traditional attitudes toward parenting and may not be supportive of your involvement with your child. They may also have very different ideas about how babies should be fed, dressed, carried, played with, and so on. If you do have someone stay with you to help out after the birth, make sure he or she understands that you and your wife are the parents and that what you say ultimately goes.

"Not so fast. I *want to be called 'Nana.'"*

- It's more common in cold weather, when respiratory infections and overheating are more prevalent.

Although two-thirds of SIDS babies don't fall into any of the above risk categories, there are a few things you can do to minimize the risk:

- Put your baby to sleep on his back. Experts used to think that babies who slept on their backs would choke on their vomit if they spit up. Turns out that it's not true—babies are smart enough to turn their heads. Since starting the Back to Sleep campaign, SIDS deaths have dropped 43 percent. One thing, though: babies who sleep on their backs don't get to exercise their arms as much and take longer to learn to push themselves up and roll over. So make sure your baby spends plenty of his awake time on his belly working out that upper body.

A Note on Middle-of-the-Night Wake-ups

If your baby wakes up in the middle of the night hungry, and your partner is breastfeeding, you might as well stay in bed and let your partner take care of things. I know that doesn't sound terribly gallant, but, really and truly, there's not much you can do to help. And your sleeping through the 2 A.M. feeding may actually benefit your partner. Whenever I was able to get a full night's sleep, I was fairly fresh for the 7 A.M. child-care shift, allowing my wife a few more precious hours in bed.

If, however, your baby is being bottle-fed (either with formula or expressed breast milk), you should do your fair share of the feedings. You might want to work out a system in which the one who does the 2 A.M. feeding gets to sleep in (or gets breakfast in bed, or whatever).

Sometimes, though, your baby might wake up at two or three in the morning for no other reason than to stay awake for a few hours and check things out. In this kind of situation, you and your partner can either split the child-entertainment duty or stay up together and see what's on late-night TV; if there were any sitcoms or detective shows you missed when you were growing up, you can probably catch the reruns at three in the morning. Thanks to my older daughter's middle-of-the-night awakenings, my wife and I once had the rare opportunity to see what may have been (hopefully) the only episode of *David Cassidy, Teen Detective.*

- Don't smoke and don't let anyone who does near your baby.
- Don't overdress the baby (see page 216).
- Put the baby to sleep on a firm mattress: no pillows, fluffy blankets, plush sofas, waterbeds, shag carpets, or beanbags. Crib mattresses should fit snugly into the crib so the baby can't slip in between it and the frame. And take out anything else, such as stuffed animals or extra blankets, that might accidentally cover the baby.
- Breastfeed.
- Don't panic. Although SIDS is a devastating, horrible experience for any parent, remember that 999 out of 1,000 babies *don't* die of it.

SEX AFTER THE BABY

Most doctors advise women to refrain from intercourse for at least six weeks after giving birth. But before you mark that date on your calendar, remember that the "six-week rule" is only a guideline. Resuming intercourse ultimately depends on the condition of your partner's vagina, and, more important, on how you're both feeling. In extremely rare cases, resuming your sex life too soon may actually be dangerous. A study published in the *Postgraduate Medical Journal* documents the cases of two new mothers who died of embolisms—air bubbles in the blood—after having sex.

It's not uncommon for couples to take quite a bit of time to fully reestablish their prepregnancy sex life. In one of the largest studies of postbaby sexuality, researcher Janet Hyde found that one month after giving birth only 17 percent of new mothers had started having sex again. By the fourth month, 89 percent had, and by their babies' first birthdays, 92 percent of women were back in the sack.

Many factors will influence when and how you and your partner decide to resume your sex life. Here are a few:

- When you had sex with your partner before, she was the woman you loved. Now, she's also a mother—a thought that reminds many men of their own mothers and can be a big turn-off. Several studies have shown that many women, too, have a tough time reconciling their roles as lover and mother, and may see themselves as unsexual.
- According to Dr. Jerrold Shapiro, some men have "emotional difficulty being sexual with the part of their wives that produced their children." While I can't say that seeing my daughter coming out of my wife's vagina was particularly erotic, I always found the sight of her feeding our babies rather arousing.
- In the first few weeks after the birth, your partner may focus more on the baby than on you.
- You may feel especially aroused at having concrete proof (the baby) of your virility.
- Your partner's vagina may be much drier than before, making intercourse painful for her. This doesn't mean she isn't aroused by you; it's simply a common postbirth occurrence—particularly if your partner is breastfeeding. According to researcher Geraldine Barrett and her colleagues, 58 percent of new mothers report pain or discomfort during sex three months after giving birth. If this happens, invest in a little K-Y jelly, Astroglide, or other similar lubricant. And be patient; the discomfort is almost always gone by the baby's first birthday.

Chances are, you were fairly abstinent during the last few weeks of the pregnancy and you can hardly wait to get your sex life back on track. But you should expect the first few times you have sex after the baby is born to be a period of tentative rediscovery for both of you. Her body has changed, and she may respond differently than she used to. She may still be worried that having sex will hurt, and you may be afraid of the same thing. Go slowly, take your cues from her, and give yourselves plenty of time to get used to each other again.

CHILD CARE

With more and more women in the work force, it's getting harder to find a traditional dad-goes-to-work-while-mom-stays-at-home kind of family anymore, and it's nearly impossible to find the mom-goes-to-work-while-dad-stays-at-home variety. And even if you or your partner wanted to be a full-time caregiver, you probably couldn't afford it anyway. (If you're considering staying at home, go back and take a look at pages 120–21.) So, sooner or later, most couples find themselves considering some form of child care. Here are some of your options.

IN-HOME CHILD CARE About a million and a half children are cared for in their homes during the day by nonrelatives, and another 500,000 are cared for by live-in help.

In-home care is convenient; you don't have to worry about day-care schedules, and your baby can stay in the environment to which he or she has become accustomed. In addition, your baby will receive individual attention, and, if you stay on top of the situation, the caregiver will keep you up to date on your child's development. Finally, by remaining at home your child will be less exposed to germs.

Every time my wife and I tried to find in-home child care, it was a traumatic experience. But the first time was the hardest. Besides being afraid that the person we chose would turn out to be an ax murderer, we were worried that no one else could love our daughter as much or care for her as well as we did. While nothing can replace your love, there are many wonderful caregivers out there who can give your baby the next best thing. You just need to know how to find them. The most common ways are:

- Agencies
- Word of mouth
- Bulletin boards (either caregivers respond to your ad, or you respond to theirs)

The first thing to do is to conduct thorough interviews over the phone—this will enable you to screen out the obviously unacceptable candidates, the ones who are only looking for a month-long job, those who don't drive if you need a driver, and those who don't like kids but want the money). Then invite the finalists over to meet with you, your partner, and the baby in person. Make sure the baby and the prospective caregiver spend a few minutes together, and pay close attention to how they interact. My wife and I ruled out a couple of people because they showed absolutely no interest in holding, cuddling, or playing with the baby. And we hired one woman largely because the moment she walked in the door she picked up our daughter and started playing with her.

One quick test you can give to any prospective caregiver is to ask her to change the baby's diaper. Does she sing or smile or try some other way to make the procedure interesting, or does she seem revolted by the whole thing? And does she wash her hands when she's done? When you've put together your short list, be sure to get—and check—references (it's awkward, but absolutely essential). Ask each one why the baby-sitter left, and what the best and worst things about him or her were. Also, make sure to ask the prospective caregiver the questions listed on pages 228–29.

When you make your final choice, have the person start a few days before you return to work so you can all get to know each other, and so you can spy.

A NOTE ABOUT LIVE-IN CHILD CARE If you're lucky enough to be able to afford it, you might consider hiring a live-in caregiver, such as an au pair. While having a live-in caregiver may sound fun (and, let's be honest, the prospect of having a cute twenty-year-old with an even cuter accent around doesn't hurt), you're essentially adding a new member to the family. The process for selecting one is similar to that for finding a non-live-in caregiver, and you can use most of the questions listed on pages 228–29 when conducting interviews. (If you're going the au pair route, though, you'll have to do it through one of only eight placement agencies that are approved by the United States Information Agency.) After you've made your choice, you might want to try out your new relationship on a non-live-in basis for a few weeks, just to make sure everything's going to work out to everyone's satisfaction. (You can't do this with an au pair, though; she'll need to stay with you.)

OUT-OF-HOME CHILD CARE Many people—even those who can afford in-home child care—feel that out-of-home centers are preferable.

For one, a good day-care center is, as a rule, much better equipped than your home and offers your child a wide range of stimulating activities. In addition, out-of-home day care gives your child the opportunity to play with other children; this, in the opinion of many experts, helps children become better socialized and more independent. The downside, of course, is that interacting with other kids usually means interacting with their germs—children in out-of-home day care get sick a lot more often than those cared for at home.

When considering out-of-home day care, keep in mind that there's no correlation between how much you pay and the quality of care. Some places charge a lot because they can. So there's no excuse for not thoroughly checking out all your alternatives.

You can find out about out-of-home child-care facilities from your friends or from ads in a local parenting newspaper. You might also want to check with Child Care Aware, a nationwide campaign created to help parents identify quality child care in their communities ([800] 424-2246).

Questions to Ask Prospective Caregivers

- What previous child-care experience have you had (including caring for younger relatives)?
- What age children have you cared for?
- Tell us a little about your own childhood.
- What would you do if . . . (give several examples of things a child might do that would require different degrees of discipline or things you might have done to discipline a child in the past)?
- When would you hit or spank a child? (If the answer is anything other than "never," find yourself another candidate.)
- How would you handle . . . (name a couple of emergency situations or ask for an example of a real emergency situation and how the candidate handled it)?
- Do you know baby CPR? (If not, you might want to consider paying for the caregiver to take a class.)
- What are your favorite things to do with kids?
- Do you have a driver's license?
- What days/hours are you available/not available? How flexible can you be if an emergency arises while we're at work?
- Are you a native speaker of any foreign language?

CRYING

Let's face it, babies cry; it's their job. The fact is that 80 to 90 percent of all babies have periods of crying that can last from twenty minutes to an hour every day. Still, there's nothing like holding an inconsolably crying child to make even the most seasoned parent feel inadequate.

I think fathers tend to feel this sense of inadequacy more acutely than mothers, perhaps because most men have been socialized to view themselves as less than fully equipped to care for children and therefore have less than complete confidence in their parenting abilities.

When (not if) your child starts to cry, resist the urge to hand him or her to your partner. She knows nothing more about crying babies than you do (or will soon enough). To start with, however, here are a few things you can do to reduce the amount of time your child will spend crying:

- **Respond immediately.** It is absolutely impossible to spoil an infant by picking her up when she's crying. At the very least you'll be teaching your baby that she's safe and that you're there for her.

- Give an example of a conflict you had with a prior employer and how it was resolved.

Other Important Topics to Cover

- Compensation and vacation. Check with other people who have caregivers for the going rate, but don't be surprised if it's way more than you were expecting. In some cities people are quitting perfectly good professional jobs to take child-care positions because they pay so much.
- Telephone privileges.
- Complete responsibilities of the job: feeding, bathing, diapering, changing clothes, reading to the baby, and so on, as well as what light housekeeping chores, if any, will be expected while the baby is sleeping.
- How much experience do you have caring for twins (if applicable)?
- English-language skills—particularly important in case of emergency (you want someone who can accurately describe to a doctor or 911 operator what's going on).
- Immigration/green card status

You might want to draw up an informal contract, listing all of the caregiver's responsibilities—just so there won't be any misunderstandings.

Taxes and Child Care

- Be sure to get your caregiver or baby-sitter's social security number; you'll need it to take advantage of the tax deduction/credit for child-care expenses.
- If you pay a baby-sitter or other household worker over a certain amount a year, you are required to deduct social security taxes. The earning floor, the amount you need to deduct, and the IRS's regulations change every year, so check with an accountant to make sure you're completely up to date.

- **Take note of what your partner eats while breastfeeding.** After one horrible, agonizing evening of inexplicable crying from our usually happy baby and a frantic call to the doctor, we discovered that the broccoli my wife had eaten for dinner was the culprit.
- **Have your partner nurse more often.** The baby could be literally crying out for more intimacy. Besides that, smaller, more frequent meals may be easier on the baby's newly operating digestive system.
- **Watch out for bottles.** Formula, cow's milk, and soy milk are frequent causes of tear-inducing allergic reactions or stomach distress. Even if your baby is being breastfed, she could still be reacting to the milk in your partner's diet, so have her cut dairy out of her diet for a few days to see what happens.
- **Know your baby.** Within just a few days after birth, your baby will develop distinct cries: "I'm tired," "Feed me now," "Change my diaper," "I'm uncomfortable as can be," "I'm bored in this car seat," and "I'm crying because I'm mad and I'm not going to stop no matter what you do." Once you learn to recognize these cries, you'll be able to respond appropriately and keep your baby happy. It's also important to know your child's routine—some babies like to thrash around and cry a little (or a lot) before going to sleep; others don't.
- **Carry your baby more.** Some studies show that the more babies are held (even when they're not crying), the less they cry.

After you've tried soothing, feeding, changing the diaper, checking for loose diaper pins or uncomfortable clothing, and rocking, the baby may still continue to howl. Sometimes there's really nothing you can do about it (see the

What to Look For in a Day-Care Center

- The level of training of the staff. Some have degrees in early childhood education; some aren't much more than warm bodies.
- Does the staff seem to like kids? And do the kids seem happy?
- Safety: windows, fences around yards, access to kitchen appliances and utensils (knives, ovens, stoves, household chemicals, and so forth).
- Overall cleanliness.
- Caregiver/child ratio. (In California, one licensed caregiver can take care of as many as four infants. I personally think that any more than two is too many.)
- Quality, condition, and number of toys. Is there enough variety to keep kids from getting bored?
- Security: what precautions are taken to ensure that kids can be picked up only by the person you select? Do strangers have access to the center?

Before you make your final choice, be sure to take a tour. Spend half an hour or so—when all the kids are there—observing. Are the children happy? Are they doing the kinds of activities you expected?

Finally, in the weeks after you pick the perfect day-care center, make a few unannounced visits—just to see what goes on when there aren't any parents around.

section on coping, pages 233–34), but sometimes all it takes is a new approach. Here are a few alternatives you might want to try:

- **Hold the baby differently.** Not all babies like to be held facing you; some want to face out so they can see the world. One of the most successful ways I've learned to soothe a crying baby—and I've tried this on many kids besides my own—is to use Dave's Magic Baby Hold. (Dave, the father of a close friend, supposedly used the Hold to calm his own three children.) Quite simply, have the baby "sit" in the palm of your hand—thumb in front, the other fingers on the baby's bottom. Then have the baby lie face down on the inside of your forearm, with his or her head resting on the inside of your elbow. Use your other hand to stroke or pat the baby's back.
- **Distraction.** Offer a toy, a story, a song. If the baby is diverted by a story or song, you'd better be prepared to repeat it over and over and over . . .

- **Give the baby something to suck on.** Just take a guess why they call them "pacifiers." If you don't approve of pacifiers, you can either help the baby suck on his or her own fingers, or loan out one of yours.
- **Give the baby a bath.** Some babies find warm water soothing. Others freak out when they get wet. If you do decide to try bathing a crying infant, don't do it alone. Holding onto a calm soapy baby is no easy chore. But keeping a grip on a squirming, screaming, soapy baby takes a team of highly trained specialists.
- **Invest in a frontpack.** A lot of crying babies just want to be held all the time, and no matter how strong you think you are, your arms—and back—won't last forever. You'll be able to use your frontpack for other purposes as well—both my daughters traveled hundreds of miles strapped to my chest, while I did my cross-country ski-machine workout. In addition, carrying the baby around in the pack might give you an inkling of what it was like for your partner to be pregnant.
- **Take the baby for a walk or a drive.** A word of caution: this doesn't work for all babies. When she was an infant, my elder daughter would fall

"I'm worried about him. He's not picking at his food."

Colic

Starting at about two weeks of age, some 20 percent of babies develop colic—crying spells that, unlike "ordinary" crying, can last for hours at a time, sometimes even all day or all night. The duration and intensity of crying spells peaks at around six weeks and usually disappears entirely within three months.

Since there's no real agreement on what causes colic or on what to do about it, your pediatrician probably won't be able to offer a quick cure. Some parents, however, have been able to relieve (partially or completely) their colicky infants with an over-the-counter gas remedy for adults. Talk to your doctor about whether he or she thinks taking this medication would benefit your child.

asleep in the stroller or the car in a heartbeat. But my younger daughter hated riding in the car, especially when she was tired, and cried even more when I put her in her car seat. If you don't feel like going out, try putting the baby on top of a running washing machine or dryer. There's also a special device called SleepTight that, when attached to the baby's crib, simulates the feel (and sounds) of a car going fifty-five miles an hour. You can reach them at www.colic.com or at 1-800-NO-COLIC.

- **Heat things up a little.** Some people believe that babies cry less when their feet are warm. So try putting an extra pair of socks on the baby. Do *not* hold the baby's feet over a fire or use some kind of electric heating device. Duh.

COPING WITH CRYING

If you've tried everything you can think of to stop the baby from crying, but to no avail, here are some things that may help you cope:

- **Tag-team crying duty.** There's no reason why both you and your partner have to suffer together through what Martin Greenberg calls "the tyranny of crying." Spelling each other in twenty-minute or half-hour shifts will do you both a world of good. Getting a little exercise during your "time off" will also calm your nerves before your next shift starts.
- **Get some help.** Dealing with a crying child for even a few minutes can provoke incredible rage and frustration. And if the screams go on for hours, it can become truly difficult to maintain your sanity, let alone control your temper. If you find yourself concerned that you might lash out

A Note on Crying in Public

Dealing with a crying child in public was particularly stressful for me. It wasn't that I didn't think I could handle things; rather, I was embarrassed by and afraid of how other people would react. Would they think I was hurting the baby? Would they call the police? If they did, how could I possibly prove that the baby was mine? Fortunately, no one ever called the police, but there was no shortage of comments, which ranged from the seemingly helpful ("Sounds like that baby is hungry") to the blatantly sexist and demeaning ("Better get that baby home to her mother").

Although my fears about my children crying in public may sound a little paranoid (okay, a lot), I know I'm not alone. Just about every father I've spoken to has had similar thoughts in similar situations. I have to admit, however, that most of the women I've mentioned this to (including my dear wife) think I'm completely nuts on this point.

(other than verbally) at your child, call someone: your partner, pediatrician, parents, baby-sitter, friends, neighbors, clergy person, or even a parental-stress hotline. If your baby is a real crier, keep these numbers handy.

- **Let the baby "cry it out."** If the crying goes on for more than twenty minutes or so, try putting the baby down in the crib and letting him or her cry. If the screaming doesn't stop after ten or fifteen minutes, pick the baby up and try a different approach from the section above for another fifteen minutes or so. Repeat as necessary. Note: don't let your baby cry it out until you've tried everything else. Ordinarily, you should respond promptly and lovingly to your baby's cries. Several studies show that babies who are responded to this way learn that someone will be there to help them if they need it. This ultimately makes them cry less and helps them grow up more confident.
- **Don't take it personally.** Your baby isn't deliberately trying to antagonize you—really. It's all too easy to let your frustration at this temporary situation permanently interfere with the way you treat your child. "Even if your powerful feelings don't lead to child abuse," write the authors of *What to Expect the First Year,* "they can start eroding your relationship with your baby and your confidence in yourself as a parent unless you get counseling quickly."

PLAYING WITH YOUR BABY

Playing with your child is one of the most important things you can do with him or her. Kids learn just about everything they need to know from playing. And to top it off, it's fun for you too.

As a rule, men and women have different play styles: women tend to stress the social and emotional type of play, while men are much more physical and high-energy. "Father-child play may be a particularly important context," writes Ross Parke, "because its range of excitement and arousal is higher than in the more modulated play of mothers and children." Neither kind of parent-child interaction is truly better than the other—each is different and indispensable, and there's no point in trying to compare or rate them.

Several researchers have done extensive studies on the impact of physical play on children and have come up with some interesting conclusions. Parke, for example, found that playful dads seem to have smarter kids than dads who don't play with their kids as much—they're better at math and score higher on intelligence tests. Physical play—particularly the dad kind—helps encourage kids' independence. Both boys and girls who are exposed to high levels of physical play are more popular among their peers and more assertive (in a good way) in their interactions later in life. They also do a better job of reading others' emotional cues and regulating their own emotions than kids who don't get as much chance to play.

In general, babies love physical play, and by the time they're just a few days old, they've already learned which of their parents will play with them which way—and they'll react accordingly. Here are some important things to keep in mind about playing:

- **Pay attention.** Even though your baby is nowhere near being able to catch a fly ball, sink a jumper, or even hold on to a rattle, you can still have fun together. Take all that wild arm and leg flailing. Surprisingly, it has a real purpose, as do many of the baby's other natural reflexes. The arm swinging, for example, may be a protective device designed to push dangerous things away. And you've probably noticed that your baby starts sucking the second anything—finger, nipple, thumb—gets in her mouth. This reflex helps ensure that they get nourishment in the days and weeks before they learn how to control their sucking muscles. We talk extensively about reflexes and how you can have fun with them in the sequel to this book, *The New Father: A Dad's Guide to the First Year.*
- **Use moderation.** It's perfectly fine to play with a baby as young as a few days old, but restrict each session to five minutes or so. Too much playing can make your child fussy or irritable.

- **Start simple.** Imitation games are a good beginning. Stick your tongue out or make an O with your mouth and see if the baby will do the same. You may have to hold the pose for a few seconds.
- **Take your cues from the baby.** If he or she cries or seems bored, stop what you're doing. This would be a great time to put on some music. Doesn't matter what kind, but try to expose the baby to a nice variety. Baby ears are pretty sensitive to noise, so keep the volume low, particularly if you have a preemie.
- **Schedule your fun.** The best time for physical play is when the baby is in the active alert state; playing with toys or books is fine during the quiet alert state (see page 205). Choose a time when your full attention can be devoted to the baby—no phone calls or other distractions. Finally, don't play too vigorously with the baby immediately after feeding. Believe me—I learned the hard way.
- **Get comfortable.** Find a place where you can get down to the baby's level—preferably on your back or stomach on the floor or bed.
- **Be patient.** As mentioned above, your baby is not a trained seal—don't expect too much too soon.
- **Be encouraging.** Use lots of facial and verbal encouragement—smiles, laughter. Although the baby can't understand the words, he or she definitely understands the feelings. Even at only a few days old, your baby will want to please you, and lots of encouragement will build his or her self-confidence.
- **Be gentle—especially with the baby's head.** Because babies' heads are relatively large (one-quarter of their body size at birth vs. one-seventh by the time they're adults) and their neck muscles are not yet well developed, their heads tend to be pretty floppy for the first few months. Be sure to support the head—from behind—at all times, and avoid sudden or jerky motions.

A COUPLE OF WARNINGS

- *Never* shake your child. This can make their little brains rattle around inside their skulls, causing bruises or permanent injuries.
- Never throw the baby up in the air. Yes, your father may have done it to you, but he shouldn't have. It looks like fun but can be extremely dangerous.

THE DIFFERENCES BETWEEN BOYS AND GIRLS

Back in the 1970s and 1980s, all the politically correct people insisted that there were no real differences between boys and girls—except for the obvious anatomical ones, of course. Any behavioral differences were supposedly the result of socialization, and were imposed on children by their parents and their environment.

But in the past few years, researchers have started questioning this theory, and their answers are confirming what most parents have always known: boys and girls are just not the same. The differences between them go far beyond mere anatomy and may even be present in our children's brains before they're born. "And these structural differences lay the foundation for behavioral differences," says brain researcher Dr. Laura Allen. Here's what we know:

- Physically, boys are a little bigger than girls—about 10 percent heavier and longer at birth. Even after taking into account this size difference, first-time mothers spend almost a hundred minutes longer in labor with a son than a daughter. This often leads to increased birth trauma and drug taking, which, in turn, may be the reason why boys tend to be a little more irritable in their first weeks outside the womb, typically crying more and sleeping less than girls.
- Within hours of birth, girls are much more interested in people and faces, while boys seem just as happy looking at an object dangled in front of them, says Ann Moir, Ph.D., author of *Brain Sex.* At only four months, girls can tell the difference between photographs of people they know from those of strangers; boys can't. Dr. Allen speculates that this difference may be the result of girls' faster-maturing brains. But other experts say it's because girls are simply more interested in interacting with people than boys are.
- Boys tend to take in less sensory data than girls, according to gender roles researcher Carole Beal. They're generally less discriminating when it comes to food, and less sensitive to touch and pain. They also hear worse in one ear than the other, meaning they don't pick up background noises as well as girls can, which may explain why your parents always thought you were ignoring them when you were little. It may also account for why girls typically learn to speak before boys do, sometimes by as much as a year.

Despite all this, the distinctions between boys and girls during the first eighteen months of life are so slight that when babies are dressed in nothing but diapers, most adults can't tell a boy from a girl. But that doesn't stop us from treating them quite differently.

In one of the first studies of its kind, two Cornell University researchers, John and Sandra Condry, showed two hundred adults a videotape of a nine-month-old baby playing with various toys. Half were told that they were watching a boy, the other half that they were watching a girl. Although everyone was actually viewing the same tape, the descriptions the two groups gave of the baby's behavior were incredibly different. The "boy" group overwhelmingly perceived the child's startled reaction to a jack-in-the-box as anger. The "girl" group saw the reaction as fear.

Parents not only perceive their boys and girls differently but often treat them differently as well. Mothers, for example, respond more quickly to crying girls than to crying boys and breastfeed them longer, according to psychologist Michael Gurian. And when girls have a difficult disposition, mothers tend to increase their level of affection, holding and comforting the child. But when a boy is similarly fussy, they generally back off. (This kind of behavior can have some serious, long-term consequences. In one study, for example, Dr. Allen found that boys who received more cuddling had higher IQs than boys who received less.)

When playing with their children, dads tend to be more rough and tumble with boys, but treat their daughters gingerly. And when babies are just starting to take their first steps, both parents tend to let their sons fall repeatedly, but will step in and pick up their daughters even before they hit the ground.

The upside of encouraging independence in boys is that it teaches them to learn to solve their own problems without adult intervention. The downside, though, is that they often end up with less supervision and, as a result, are more likely to be injured than girls. In addition, "parents who step in to rescue their daughter before she is truly 'stuck,'" writes psychologist Katherine Karraker, "not only deprive her of a chance to overcome obstacles through her own efforts, but may also be sending the message that they have no faith in her ability to do so."

So what can you do to keep from falling into these traps? Start with this:

- Don't let your own prejudices and preconceived notions get in the way.
- Make an effort. If you have a son, there's no reason why you can't cuddle with him—it's a perfectly masculine thing to do. If you have a daughter, there's no reason why—a few months from now—you can't wrestle with her. She'll love it and so will you.
- Give your child a broad range of things to play with. Most girls end up playing with dolls, but some would be just as happy with a fire truck, if they only got the chance. And while most boys will end up biting their toast into the shape of a gun, some might have a lot of fun playing with a doll.

Fathering Today

For the first weeks and months after the birth of your child, you'll be spending a lot of your time in the role of support person for your partner. But after a while, you'll settle into a more "normal" life—one and/or both of you will go back to work, and you might feel like taking in a movie or visiting some friends. And gradually, you'll figure out exactly what it means to be a father and how involved you intend to be in your child's life. Do you want to be someone he runs to when hurt or sad? Will you know her shoe size or whether she likes pants that zip up or slip on? Will you schedule his medical appointments or play dates, or will you leave all that to your partner?

Whatever you decide, it won't take long before you come face-to-face with the fact that being a father in America—especially an involved one—isn't easy. The responsibilities of the job itself are difficult and at times frustrating, but the biggest obstacles you'll face—ones you've probably never even thought about before—are societal.

It's only within the past few years that men and women have felt able to speak out against the traditional role fathers have played in the family. And it's only recently that society has finally recognized that the distant father is not the ideal father. But in the midst of this newfound freedom to lash out against yesterday's absent, neglectful fathers, today's fathers—that's you—are falling victim to old stereotypes.

According to one stereotype, men haven't taken an active role in family life because they haven't wanted to. But is this true today? Hardly. More and more of us are figuring out that the traditional measures of success are not all they're cracked up to be, and we are committed to being a major presence in our children's lives, physically and emotionally. Over 80 percent of men aged 20 to 39 in a recent Harris poll said that having a work schedule that lets them spend more time with their family is more important than doing

challenging work or even earning a high salary. And nearly three-quarters of men in their twenties and thirties said they'd give up pay for more family time. The hitch is that society (and by this I mean all of us) not only won't support us but actively discourages us. Quite simply, Americans don't value fatherhood nearly as much as motherhood. (Even the words conjure up very different images: *motherhood* is equated with caring, nurturing, and love, while *fatherhood* doesn't seem to be much more than a biological relationship.) As a result, men are rarely accepted if they assume a different role than the one they are "supposed" to assume.

The emphasis on traditional roles starts early. Even before they can walk, children of both sexes are bombarded with the message that fathers are basically superfluous. Just think of the books your parents read to you, and that you'll probably read to your own children. Have you ever noticed that there aren't any fathers in *The Cat in the Hat; Babar; Where the Wild Things Are; Are You My Mother?; Goodnight Moon; The Runaway Bunny;* and *Peter Rabbit?*

In the vast majority of children's books, a woman is the only parent, while the man—if he appears at all—comes home late after work and bounces baby around for five minutes before putting her to bed. Most libraries these days have special catalogs of children's books with positive female characters—heroines and mothers. As a father who shares the child-care responsibilities equally, I've always found it extremely annoying that there aren't any catalogs (or even many books) with positive male role models.

In recent years there's been a push to portray the important roles that women and minorities have played in shaping our history and culture. *Little Black Sambo,* for example, has all but disappeared from library and bookstore shelves, and most new children's books make a conscious effort to take female characters out of the kitchen and the nursery and give them professional jobs and responsibilities. But one group—fathers—continues to be portrayed in the same stereotypical mold as always.

One of my daughters' favorite books was *Mother Goose and the Sly Fox,* "retold" by Chris Conover. It's the story of a single mother (Mother Goose) with seven tiny goslings who is pitted against (and naturally outwits) the Sly Fox. Fox, a neglectful, and presumably unemployed, single father, lives with his filthy, hungry pups in a grimy hovel littered with the bones of their previous meals. Mother Goose, a successful entrepreneur with a thriving lace business, still finds time to serve her goslings homemade soup in pretty porcelain cups. The story is funny and the illustrations marvelous, but the unwritten message is that women take better care of their kids than men, who have nothing else to do but hunt down and kill innocent, law-abiding geese.

You'll find the same negative portrayals of fathers in the majority of children's classics. Take *Babar.* Every once in a while someone will complain about the book's colonialist slant (you know, little jungle dweller finds happiness in the big city and brings civilization—and fine clothes—to his backward elephant village). But no one seems to find it strange that after his mother is killed by the evil hunter, Babar is an "orphan." Why can he find comfort only in the arms of another female? Why do Arthur and Celeste's mothers come alone to the city to fetch their children? Don't the fathers care? Do they even have fathers?

If books were the only place children got messages about the way the world is supposed to be, you might be able to edit out the negative messages. But sooner or later your kids are going to find themselves in front of some kind of a screen. Did you know that the average six-month-old spends about ninety minutes a day in front of a television? Within just a few years it'll be up to eight hours a day! And much of that time they'll be bombarded by the same stereotypes: if dads are there at all, they're usually fairly useless. If only because of the sheer number of hours, these images have the potential to do a lot more damage than the ones they get from books.

In a recent study of sitcoms, the National Fatherhood Initiative found that fathers were eight times more likely than mothers to be portrayed negatively. In fact, if you just think of the most prominent television dads, you'll find what the NFI's study—and a lot of other research—has found: that nearly every one of them is outwitted or shown up by his wife, ridiculed by his children, and portrayed as a complete incompetent in every way. Of course these dads love their kids, but good intentions aside, they can't handle even the simplest child-related tasks.

Portrayals of fathers (and men in general) in commercials may be even worse. Frederic Hayward, the director of Men's Rights Inc., in Sacramento, California, did a survey of a thousand random TV advertisements and found that "100 percent of the jerks singled out in male-female relationships were male. There were no exceptions. . . . 100 percent of the ignorant ones were male. 100 percent of the incompetent ones were male." In the thirty-second world of the commercial, family dads—if they're part of the family at all—are not only dumber than everyone else, they're also almost completely oblivious to the needs of their children. Mothers, it seems, are the only ones who care. Here are a few examples:

- In a spot for Post Raisin Bran, a father and his daughter are oohing and aahing about their cereal. "Somebody must really love us," says Dad. "Who do you think it is?" "Mommy!!!" yelps the child.
- Another breakfast cereal, Kix, is billed as being "Kid tested, Mother approved."
- When it comes time to make lunch, advertisers insist that "Choosy mothers choose Jif."
- Robitussin cold medicines are "recommended by Dr. Mom," who sometimes has to drag herself out of her sick bed to keep an eye on her incompetent husband, who's burning dinner.
- In a nationally run magazine ad, Fisher-Price gleefully informs us that "it took Fisher-Price and 2,043 mothers to design a highchair like this."
- In a commercial for Aquafresh toothpaste, a father and child are arguing about whether fluoride or mouthwash is the toothpaste's most important ingredient. They probably would have argued all day if Mom hadn't stepped in to tell them, "You need both."
- An MCI commercial showing a bunch of kids caught in a sudden downpour tells us that a single call to mom's pager will ring her office and her cell phone and that "Mom rolls in right before the storm."

While it's possible to argue that mothers still do most of the shopping and feeding, the subtle yet critical message contained in these ads is that fathers are stupid and useless and simply don't care. Kids—and anyone else who's watching—get the clear message that dads don't feed their kids, don't clothe them, won't be there to take care of them when they're sick, and shouldn't be called in case of emergency.

It seems that we've confused men's lack of training in child care with a lack of interest in or concern about their children. A lot of today's fathers who were raised in "traditional" families simply had no role models, no one to teach them the skills they lack today.

Perhaps the most active way we have of discouraging men's involvement with children is by continually portraying men as dangerous. In an article I wrote for the *New York Times Magazine,* I described an incident that took place a few years ago. I was pushing my older daughter on the swing at our favorite park, when I heard a little girl start to scream. She was just a few feet away, teetering on the small platform at the top of a long, steep slide. As I watched, she lost her grip on the handrail and began to fall. Without thinking, I stepped over to the slide, caught the girl, and set her down on the sand. I knelt down and was about to ask her if she was all right, when a woman picked the girl up, gave me a withering look, and hustled the child away. "Didn't I tell you not to talk to strange men in the park?" the woman asked her daughter, glaring over her shoulder at me. "Did he hurt you?"

I remember standing there for a few seconds, stunned, as the woman bundled her child into the car and drove off. I wondered what she had been thinking. Hadn't she seen me playing with a happy girl who called me Daddy? As I looked around the park, I realized I was the only man there. And then it hit me: she hadn't seen *me* at all. Instead, she'd seen what years of media images had trained her to see: the stereotyped images of a man in the park, menacing and solitary.

In some twisted way, I can empathize. If I'd turned around and seen a strange man kneeling near my daughter, I might have jumped to the worst possible conclusions, too. And when my wife and I used to interview baby-sitters for our daughters, I was the one who had the most serious qualms about hiring a man for the job.

Just like the woman in the park, my "understanding" of these fears is based less on the truth about how men actually are with children than on how we've been trained to view men with children. I still remember the "safety movies" I saw in about the third or fourth grade—scary images of the sinister, mustachioed men (and they were always men) lurking behind trees in the park or trying to entice us into their cars. I'm not saying that there aren't some sick men out there, men who do horrible things to children. Men are the perpetrators in most sexual abuse cases (which constitute 11 percent of all cases of abuse and neglect). Yet there are plenty of sick women out there too; women murder more children than men do and are the perpetrators in the majority of physical and psychological abuse cases.

None of this, of course, is meant to imply that men are just hapless victims, or that all the obstacles fathers face are "someone else's" fault. In fact, some of the most significant barriers have been erected by men themselves. In the workplace, for example, where men still occupy the majority of positions of power, men who try to take time off from work to be with their families—either as paternity leave or by reducing their work schedules—find that their employers abuse them, treat them like wimps, and question how serious they are about their jobs (see pages 112–16 for more on this).

Despite the many obstacles, some of us have risked our careers and jeopardized our finances to try to break through the "glass ceiling" that keeps us at work—and away from our families. But in many cases, when we finally get home we run into another barrier—this one imposed by none other than our partners.

Here's an all-too-common scenario: When I was visiting some friends not long ago, their six-month-old son started fussing. Colin, who was holding the baby, began rocking him. Suddenly his wife, Marina, appeared and whisked the baby away. "Let me take him, honey," she said. "I think I know what he needs."

I've seen scenes of this kind played out many times before (and not only at Colin and Marina's house), but this time I began to wonder. Did Marina really know what the baby needed? And if so, did she know better than Colin did? According to a significant amount of research, the answers to my questions are "probably" and "no," respectively. In a variety of studies, researcher Ross Parke found that fathers—despite stereotypes to the contrary—are just as sensitive and responsive to their infants' needs as mothers. They know when something is wrong, and they take appropriate action. So why, then, had Colin—a man I knew wanted an active role in raising his children—simply handed his crying son over to his wife? When you factor out sheer laziness from the equation, the answer to that question is a little tougher. What it seems to boil down to is that most of us—men as well as women—simply assume that women know more about kids than men.

In some ways, that may be true. On average, women do spend more time taking care of children than men do, and their skills may be a little sharper than men's. But parenting skills are not innate—they are learned through experience and training. No first-time parents, mothers or fathers, know instinctively how to soothe a colicky baby or prevent diaper rash. In fact, when our older daughter was born, my wife was taught how to breastfeed by a male nurse.

Still, the stereotypes persist, and to a great extent women control the amount—and quality—of time men spend with their children. Although most mothers feel that fathers should play an important role in the kids' lives, research has shown that they want that role to be "not quite as important as mom's." In fact, researchers in one nationwide study found that two out of three women seem threatened by equal participation and may themselves be "subtly putting a damper on men's involvement with their children because they are so possessive of their role as primary nurturer."

It may sound as though all these obstacles are almost too numerous to overcome. Well, there may be a lot of them, and they may be quite ingrained, but if you're willing to put in the time and effort, you'll be able to have—and maintain—an active, involved relationship with your children.

Here are some things you can do:

- **Get off your butt.** If you don't start taking the initiative, you'll never be able to assume the child-rearing responsibilities you want—and that your kids deserve. So instead of letting your partner pluck a crying or smelly baby from your arms, try saying something like, "No, honey, I can handle this," or "That's okay; I really need the practice." And there's also nothing wrong with asking her for advice—you both have insights that the other could benefit from. But have her tell you instead of doing it for you.
- **Get some practice.** Don't assume that your partner magically knows more than you do. Whatever she knows about raising kids, she's learned by doing—just like anything else. And the way you're going to get better is by doing things, too. Research has shown, for example, that the lack of opportunity may be one of the biggest obstacles to fathers' being more affectionate with their children. Once they get to hold them, fathers are at least as affectionate with their children—cooing, looking at, holding, rocking, soothing—as their partners are. (So much for the stereotype about men being emotionally distant by nature.)
- **Don't devalue the things you like doing with the kids.** As discussed in the preceding chapter, men and women generally have different ways of interacting with their children; both are extremely important to your child's development. So don't let anyone tell you that wrestling, playing "monster," or other "guy things" are somehow not as important as the "girl things" your partner may do (or want you to do).
- **Get involved in the day-to-day decisions that affect your kids' lives.** This means making a special effort to share with your partner such responsibilities as meal planning, food and clothes shopping, cooking, taking the kiddies to the library or bookstore, getting to know their friends' parents, and planning play dates. Not doing these things can give the impression that you don't think they're important or that you're not interested in being an active parent. And by doing them, you make it more likely that your partner will feel comfortable and confident in sharing the nurturing role with you. But try to log some private, "quality"

time with the kids, too. Sure, somebody has to schlepp the kids all over town—to doctor appointments, ballet lessons, or soccer practice—but that shouldn't be the only contact you have with them.

- **Keep communicating.** If you don't like the status quo, let your partner know. But be gentle. If at first she seems reluctant to share the role of child nurturer with you, don't take it too personally. Men aren't the only ones whom society has done a bad job of socializing. Many women have been raised to believe that if they aren't the primary caregivers (even if they work outside the home as well), they've somehow failed as mothers. If your partner does work outside the home, you might want to remind her of what Karen DeCrow, a former president of the National Organization for Women (NOW), says: "Until men are valued as parents, the burden of childrearing will fall primarily to women and frustrate their efforts to gain equality in the workplace."
- **If you're in a position to do something for other men, do it.** All things being equal, try hiring a male baby-sitter once in a while. Or consider asking a male friend instead of the usual women friends to do some baby-sitting when you and your wife want a night out. If you need to ease yourself into it, try the responsible teenage son of some friends.

Continuing not to trust men and boys will keep men and boys thinking of themselves as untrustworthy and will make it difficult for them to be comfortable enough in their role as parent to take on as much responsibility as they—and their partners—would like.

- **Get your partner to be your publicist.** Pamela Jordan writes that "men tend not to be perceived as parents in their own right by their mates, co-workers, friends or family. They are viewed as helpmates or breadwinners." The cure? "The mother can mitigate the exclusion of the father by others by including the father in the pregnancy and parenting experiences and actively demonstrating her recognition of him as a key player," Jordan says.
- **Get some support.** Even before your baby is born, you're likely to become aware of the vast number of support groups for new mothers. It won't take you long to realize, however, that there are few, if any, groups for new fathers. And if you find one, it will probably be geared toward men whose contact with their kids is limited to five minutes before bedtime.

After having read this book, you know that men have just as many pregnancy, birth, and parenting questions as their partners. So, if you can't find a new fathers' support group in your own neighborhood, why not be a trailblazer and start one of your own?

Here are a few ways you might get going:

- Start meeting regularly with male friends who already have kids. Talk on the phone, go for walks with the kids, meet in a park for lunch.
- Encourage other expecting male friends or new fathers to join you, and ask them to contact their male friends who have or are about to have children.
- Put up signs in local children's clothing and/or toy stores.
- Check with your partner's doctor, your pediatrician, and your childbirth class instructor about helping you advertise your group.
- Contact the YMCA or some of the local family-planning agencies to see if they'll help with publicity.
- Check with the people who organize some of the new mothers' groups—maybe they'd be interested in a fathers' auxiliary.

Who knows—if you do a good enough job publicizing your new fathers' group, you might even be able to turn it into a real business. Don't laugh: plenty of people are making money on mothers' groups.

A Final Word

Throughout this book we've talked about the benefits—both to you and to your children—of your being an active, involved father, and about how fatherhood actually begins long before your first child is born. What we haven't touched upon, though, is the positive effect your fatherhood role can have on your relationship with your partner.

Sociologist Pepper Schwartz has found that couples who worked together to raise their children "seemed to create a more intimate and stable relationship. They did more together. They talked on the phone together much more and spent more child-related time together. Wives in the study said they believed that raising children together created a more intimate adult relationship." Other research confirms Schwartz's findings. For example, a 1993 study showed that fathers who were actively involved with their children had a much lower divorce rate than those who weren't.

So it's in everyone's best interests for you to do everything you possibly can to become an involved father. It's not easy, but the rewards—for you, your children, and your partner—are incalculable.

The Process Continues

Just because you've got a baby doesn't mean you can stop learning; being an involved father takes work and a lot of understanding. If you're interested in learning more, I've written two more books to help you: *The New Father: A Dad's Guide to the First Year* and *A Dad's Guide to the Toddler Years.* Both of these continue the process we started here: getting to know yourself and what you're going through, how your child is developing, and so on.

Notes:

Selected Bibliography

Books

Agnew, Connie L., Alan Klein, and Jill Ganon. *Twins: Pregnancy, Birth, and the First Year of Life.* New York: HarperPerennial, 1997.

American College of Obstetricians and Gynecologists. *The ACOG Guide to Planning for Pregnancy, Birth, and Beyond.* Washington, D.C.: ACOG, 1990.

Beail, N., and J. McGruire, eds. *Fathers: Psychological Perspectives.* London: Junction Books, 1982.

Beal, Carole. *Boys and Girls: The Development of Gender Roles.* New York: McGraw-Hill, 1994.

Bitman, S., and S. Zalk. *Expectant Fathers.* New York: Hawthorn Books, 1978.

Bradley, Robert A. *Husband Coached Childbirth.* New York: Harper and Row, 1974.

Brinley, Maryann, and Howard Berk. *The Everything Pregnancy Book.* Holbrook, Mass.: Adams Media, 1999.

Cath, H. C., A. Gurwitt, and L. Gunsberg, eds. *Fathers and Their Families.* Hilldale, N.J.: Analytic Press, 1989.

Caton, Donald. *What a Blessing She Had Chloroform: The Medical and Social Response to the Pain of Childbirth from 1800 to the Present.* New Haven, Conn.: Yale University Press, 1999.

Churchwell, Gordon. *Expecting: One Man's Uncensored Memoir of Pregnancy.* New York: HarperCollins, 2000.

Colman, L. L., and A. D. Colman. *Pregnancy: The Psychological Experience.* New York: Noonday Press, 1991.

Cowan, C. P., and P. A. Cowan. *When Partners Become Parents.* New York: Basic Books, 1992.

Eisenberg, A., H. Murkoff, and S. Hathaway. *What to Expect When You're Expecting.* New York: Workman, 1988.

Finch, Peter, and Delia Marshall. *How to Raise Kids Without Going Broke.* New York: Avon, 1999.

Grad, R., D. Bash, et al. *The Father Book.* Washington, D.C.: Acropolis Books, 1981.

Greenberg, Martin. *The Birth of a Father.* New York: Avon, 1986.

Heinowitz, Jack. *Pregnant Fathers.* San Diego: Parents as Partners Press, 1995.

Horn, Wade, and Jeffrey Rosenberg. *The New Father Book.* Des Moines: Better Homes and Gardens, 1998.

Johnson, Patricia Irwin. *Launching a Baby's Adoption: Practical Strategies for Parents and Professionals.* Indianapolis: Perspectives Press, 1997.

Keough, Carol. *New Baby Book.* Des Moines: Better Homes and Gardens, 1998.

Klaus, M., and P. Klaus. *The Amazing Newborn.* Rev. ed. Reading, Mass.: Addison-Wesley, 1999.

Klaus, M., J. Kennel, and P. Klaus. *Mothering the Mother.* Reading, Mass.: Addison-Wesley, 1993.

Kutner, Lawrence. *Pregnancy and Your Baby's First Year.* New York: William Morrow, 1993.

Lamb, Michael, ed. *The Role of the Father in Child Development.* New York: John Wiley and Sons, 1981.

Logan, Brent. "Learning Before Birth: Assuring Giftedness in Every Child." Typescript.

Minnick, M. A., K. J. Delp, and M. C. Ciotti. *A Time to Decide, a Time to Heal.* Mullett Lake, Mich.: Pineapple Press, 1990.

Osherson, S. *Finding Our Fathers: The Unfinished Business of Fatherhood.* New York: Free Press, 1986.

Parke, Ross, and Armin Brott. *Throwaway Dads: The Myths and Barriers that Keep Men from Being the Fathers They Want to Be.* Cambridge, Mass.: Houghton Mifflin, 1999.

Paulaha, Dennis. *An American Child's Portfolio.* Edina, Minn.: Patron, 1991.

Pederson, A., and P. O'Mara, eds. *Being a Father.* Santa Fe: John Muir, 1990.

Piven, Joshua, and David Borgenicht. *The Worst-Case Scenario Survival Handbook.* San Francisco: Chronicle Books, 1999.

Shapiro, Jerrold L. *The Measure of a Man.* New York: Delacorte, 1992.

———. *When Men are Pregnant.* New York: Delta, 1993.

Thevenin, Tine. *The Family Bed.* New York: Avery, 1987.

Van de Carr, F. R., and M. Lehrer. *While You Are Expecting.* Atlanta: Humanics Learning, 1997.

Verny, T., and J. Kelly. *The Secret Life of the Unborn Child.* New York: Delta, 1991.

Verny, T., and P. Weintraub. *Nurturing the Unborn Child.* New York: Delacorte Press, 1991.

Journal Articles

American Academy of Pediatrics. Task Force on Circumcision. "Circumcision Policy Statement." *Pediatrics* 103 (March 1999): 686–93.

Arabin, B., J. von Eyck, J. Wisser, H. Versmold, and H. K. Weitzel. "Fetales Verhalten bei Mehrlingsgravitat: methodische, klinische und Wissenschaftliche Aspekte" (Fetal Behavior in Multiple Pregnancy: Methodologic, Clinical and Scientific Aspects). *Geburtshilfe und Frauenheilkunde* 51 (1991): 869–75.

Barrett, Geraldine, Elizabeth Pendry, Janet Peacock, Christina Victor, Ranee Thakar, and Isaac Manyonda. "Women's Sexuality after Childbirth: A Pilot Study." *Archives of Sexual Behavior* 28 (April 1999): 179–91.

Batman, P. A., J. Thomlinson, V. C. Moore, and R. Sykes. "Death Due to Air Embolism During Sexual Intercourse in the Puerperium." *Postgraduate Medical Journal* 74 (October 1998): 612–13.

Brodzinsky, David, and Laureen Huffman. "Transition to Adoptive Parenthood." *Marriage and Family Review* 6 (1988): 267–86.

Broude, Gwen J. "Rethinking the Couvade: Cross-Cultural Evidence." *American Anthropologist* 90 (1988): 903–11.

Bryan, E. M. "Prenatal and Perinatal Influences on Twin Children: Implications for Behavioral Studies." In *Twins as a Tool of Behavioral Genetics,* edited by T. J. Bouchard, Jr., and P. Propping. New York: John Wiley and Sons, 1993.

Christakis, D. A., E. Harvey, D. M. Zerr, et al. "A Trade-off Analysis of Routine Newborn Circumcision." *Pediatrics* 105 (January 2000): 246–49.

Cummings, David. "The Effects of Miscarriage on a Man." *Emotional First Aid* 1, no. 4 (1984): 47–50.

Davidson, J. R. "The Shadow of Life: Psychosocial Explanations for Placenta Rituals." *Culture, Medicine and Psychiatry* 9 (1985): 75–92.

Diemer, Geraldine A. "Expectant Fathers: Influence of Perinatal Education on Stress, Coping, and Spousal Relations." *Research in Nursing and Health* 20 (1997): 281–93.

Goldbach, R. C., et al. "The Effects of Gestational Age and Gender on Grief after Pregnancy Loss." *American Journal of Orthopsychiatry* 61 (July 1991): 461–67.

Hagen, Edward. "Functions of Postpartum Depression." *Evolution and Human Behavior* 20 (September 1999): 325–59.

Hay, D. A., et al. "What Information Should the Multiple-Birth Family Receive Before, During and after the Birth?" *Acta Geneticae Medicae et Gemellologiae: Twin Research* 39 (1990): 259–69.

Hay, D., and P. O'Brien. "Early Influences on the School Social Adjustments of Twins." *Acta Geneticae Medicae et Gemellologiae: Twin Research* 36 (1987): 239–48.

Hepper, Peter G. "Fetal 'Soap' Addiction." *Lancet* 11 (June 1988): 1347–48.

Hepper, P. G., and Sara Shahidullah. "Development of Fetal Hearing." *Archives of Disease in Childhood* 71 (September 1994): F81–87.

Howell-White, Sandra. "Choosing a Birth Attendant: The Influence of a Woman's Childbirth Definitions." *Social Science and Medicine* 45 (1997): 925–36.

Humphrey, M., and R. Kirkwood. "Marital Relationships Among Adopters." *Adoption and Fostering* 6 (1982): 44–48.

Jordan, Pamela. "Laboring for Relevance: Expectant and New Fatherhood." *Nursing Research* 39 (January–February 1990): 11–16.

———. "The Mother's Role in Promoting Fatherhood." In *Becoming a Father: Contemporary Social Developmental and Clinical Perspectives,* edited by Jerrold Lee Shapiro, Michael J. Diamond, and Martin Greenberg, 61–71. New York: Springer, 1995.

Klein, Hillary. "Couvade Syndrome: Male Counterpart to Pregnancy." *International Journal of Psychiatry in Medicine* 21, no. 1 (1991): 57–69.

Kurki, T., L. Toivonen, and O. Ylikorkala. "Father's Heartbeat Responds to the Birth of His Child." *Acta Obstetricia et Gynecologica Scandinavica* 74 (February 1995): 127–28.

Levy-Schiff, Rachel, Ora Bar, and Dov Har-Even. "Psychological Adjustment of Adoptive Parents-to-Be." *American Journal of Orthopsychiatry* 60 (April 1990): 258–67.

Luke, B., N. Mamelle, L. Keith, et al. "The Association Between Occupational Factors and Preterm Birth: A United States Nurses' Study." Research Committee of the Association of Women's Health, Obstetric, and Neonatal Nurses. *American Journal of Obstetrics and Gynecology* 173 (September 1995): 849–62.

May, K. A. "Factors Contributing to First-Time Fathers' Readiness for Fatherhood: An Exploratory Study." *Family Relations* 31 (July 1982): 352–61.

———. "First-Time Fathers' Responses to Unanticipated Caesarean Birth: An Exploratory Study." Unpublished report to U.C.S.F., 1982.

———. "Three Phases of Father Involvement in Pregnancy." *Nursing Research* 31 (November–December 1982): 337–42.

———. "A Typology of Detachment/Involvement Styles Adopted During Pregnancy by First-Time Expectant Fathers." *Western Journal of Nursing Research* 2, no. 2 (1980): 445–61.

Mehler, Jacques, Peter Jusczyk, Ghislaine Lambertz, Nilofar Halsted, et al. "A Precursor of Language Acquisition in Young Infants." *Cognition* 29 (July 1988): 143–78.

Miller, W. E., and S. Friedman. "Male and Female Sexuality During Pregnancy: Behavior and Attitudes." *Journal of Psychology and Human Sexuality* 1, no. 2 (1988): 17–37.

Minde, Klaus, Carl Corter, Susan Goldberg, and Diane Jeffers. "Maternal Preference Between Premature Twins up to Age Four." *Journal of the American Academy of Child and Adolescent Psychiatry* 29 (1990): 367–74.

Moses, S., R. C. Bailey, and A. R. Ronald. "Male Circumcision: Assessment of Health Benefits and Risks." *Sexually Transmitted Infections* 74 (October 1998): 368–73.

Mozurkewich, E. L., B. Luke, M. Avni, and F. M. Wolf. "Working Conditions and Adverse Pregnancy Outcome: A Meta-Analysis." *Obstetrics and Gynecology* 95 (April 2000): 623–35.

Piontelli, Alessandra. " A Study on Twins before and after Birth." *International Review of Psycho-Analysis* 16, no. 4 (1989): 413–26.

Profet, Margie. "Pregnancy Sickness as Adaptation: A Deterrent to Maternal Ingestion of Teratogens," In *The Adapted Mind,* edited by Jerome Barkow, Leda Cosmides, and J. Tooby, 327–65. New York: Oxford University Press, 1992.

Ramus, Franck, Marina Nespor, and Jacques Mehler. "Correlates of Linguistic Rhythm in the Speech Signal." *Cognition* 73 (December 1999): 265–92.

Schneer, Joy A., and Frieda Reitman, "The Interrupted Managerial Career Path: A Longitudinal Study of MBAs." *Journal of Vocational Behavior* 51 (December 1997): 411–34.

———. "The Impact of Gender as Managerial Careers Unfold." *Journal of Vocational Behavior* 47 (December 1995): 290–315.

Schoen, E. J., M. Oehrli, et al. "The Highly Protective Effect of Newborn Circumcision Against Invasive Penile Cancer." *Pediatrics* 105 (March 2000): E36.

Shahidullah, Sara, and Peter G. Hepper. "Frequency Discrimination by the Fetus." *Early Human Development* 36 (January 1994): 13–26.

Stainton, M. C. "The Fetus: A Growing Member of the Family." *Family Relations* 34 (July 1985): 321–26.

Stang, H. J., and L. W. Snellman. "Circumcision Practice Patterns in the United States." *Pediatrics* 101 (June 1998): E5.

Storey, Anne E., Carolyn J. Walsh, Roma L. Quinton, and Katherine E. Wynne-Edwards. "Hormonal Correlates of Paternal Responsiveness in New and Expectant Fathers." *Evolution and Human Behavior* 21 (March 2000): 79–95.

Teichman, Y., and Y. Lahav. "Expectant Fathers: Emotional Reactions, Physical Symptoms and Coping Styles." *British Journal of Medical Psychology* 60 (1987): 225–32.

Wakefield, Melanie, Yolande Reid, Lyn Roberts, Robyn Mullins, and Pamela Gillies. "Smoking and Smoking Cessation Among Men Whose Partners Are Pregnant: A Qualitative Study." *Social Science & Medicine* 47 (September 1998): 657–64.

Williams, Kristi, and Debra Umberson. "Medical Technology and Childbirth: Experiences of Expectant Mothers and Fathers." *Sex Roles* 41, no. 3/4 (1999): 147–67.

Woodward, Joan. "The Bereaved Twin." *Acta Geneticae Medicae et Gemellologiae: Twin Research* 37, no. 2 (1988): 173–80.

Yogman, Michael W., D. Kindlon, and F. Earls, "Father Involvement and Cognitive Behavioral Outcomes of Preterm Infants." *Journal of the American Academy of Child and Adolescent Psychiatry* 34 (1995): 58–66.

Zayas, L. H. "Psychodynamic and Developmental Aspects of Expectant and New Fatherhood: Clinical Derivatives from the Literature." *Clinical Social Work Journal* 15 (Spring 1987): 8–21.

———. "Thematic Features in the Manifest Dreams of Expectant Fathers." *Clinical Social Work Journal* 16 (Fall 1988): 283–95.

Resources

Adoption

National Adoption Center offers a comprehensive list of questions to ask adoption agencies, advice on tax and legal matters, and has links to other organizations.
1500 Walnut Street, Suite 701
Philadelphia, PA 19102
Tel.: (215) 735-9988
E-mail: nac@adopt.org
http://adopt.org

Adopting.org provides information, resources, and support for adoptive families.
http://www.adopting.org/

Childbirth, Assistance

American College of Nurse-Midwives accredits midwife education programs, establishes standards, and provides information and referrals to midwives in your area.
818 Connecticut Avenue NW,
Suite 900
Washington, DC 20006
Tel.: (888) MIDWIFE
(202) 728-9860
Fax: (202) 728-9897
E-mail: info@acnm.org
http://www.midwife.org/

American College of Obstetricians and Gynecologists
409 12th St., SW
P.O. Box 96920
Washington, DC 20090-6920
http://www.acog.com/

Doulas of North America provides resources and referrals to doulas near you
13513 North Grove Drive
Alpine, UT 84004
Tel.: (801) 756-7331
Fax: (801) 763-1847
http://www.dona.com/

International Childbirth Education Association
P.O. Box 20048
Minneapolis, MN 55420
Tel.: (952) 854-8660
Fax: (952) 854-8772
http://www.icea.org/

National Association of Childbearing Centers provides information about birthing centers and resources for finding one near you.
3123 Gottschall Road
Perkiomenville, PA 18074
Tel.: (215) 234-8068
Fax: (215): 234-8829
E-mail: ReachNACC@BirthCenters.org
http://www.birthcenters.org/

Child Care and Day Care

Au Pair Search
http://www.aupairsearch.com/

Child Care Aware is a nationwide campaign to help parents identify quality child care in their communities. Great source of local referrals.
Tel.: (800) 424-2246
http://www.childcareaware.org/index.htm

International AuPair Association
Bredgade 25 H
DK - 1260
Copenhagen K
Denmark
Tel.: (+45) 3333 9600
Fax: (+45) 3393 9676
E-mail: mailbox@iapa.org
http://www.iapa.org/

International Nanny Association is a nonprofit association for nannies and those who educate, place, employ, and support professional in-home child-care providers. Provides links to placement agencies, and so forth.
900 Haddon Ave., Suite 438
Collingswood, NJ 08108
Tel.: (856) 858-0808
http://www.nanny.org/

National Association of Child Care Resource Referral Agencies will put you in touch with the local child-care resource and referral agency that serves your area.
1319 F St. NW, Suite 819
Washington, DC 20004
Tel.: (202) 393-5501
http://www.naccrra.org

National Resource Center for Health and Safety in Child Care promotes health and safety in out-of-home child-care settings throughout the nation.
UCHSC
Campus Mail Stop F541
P.O. Box 6508
Aurora, CO 80045-0508
Tel.: (800) 598-KIDS
Fax: (303) 724-0960
http://nrc.uchsc.edu/

Death and Grief

American Sudden Infant Death Syndrome (SIDS) Institute
2480 Windy Hill Road, Suite 380
Marietta, GA 30067
Tel.: (800) 232-7437
E-mail: precent@sids.org
http://www.sids.org/#bereavement

Fathers and Fatherhood, Advice and Skills

About.com offers extensive information on all sorts of father- and fathering-related issues.
http://fatherhood.about.com/parenting/fatherhood/

Dadmag.com is a great alternative to traditional parenting magazines, which routinely ignore dads and their concerns.
http://www.dadmag.com/

Edads.com
Also available in a print version, *Dads Magazine.*
http://www.edads.com/

Fathers' Forum helps guys make the transition from Man to Dad.
http://www.fathersforum.com/months.html

Fathers on Line is a site where real dads can gather on the Internet to ask questions and give advice to others. You can find—or be—a mentor.
http://www.fathersonline.com/

MrDad.com is my Web site. You can get information there about pretty much every aspect of pregnancy, childbirth, and fatherhood, find out more about my other fatherhood books, and send me questions and comments.
http://www.MrDad.com

Fathers and Fatherhood, General

The Fatherhood Project is a national research and education organization that examines the future of fatherhood and develops ways to support men's involvement in child rearing.
Tel.: (212) 465-2044
http://www.fatherhoodproject.org/

Men's Health Network is a comprehensive resource on fatherhood and other issues affecting men.
P.O. Box 75972
Washington, DC 20013
Tel.: (202) 543-6461
E-mail: info@menshealthnetwork.org
http://menshealthnetwork.org/

The National Center for Fathering offers plenty of advice on strengthening families by inspiring and equipping men to be better fathers.
P.O. Box 413888
Kansas City, MO 64141
Tel.: (800) 593-DADS
Fax: (913) 384-4665
http://www.fathers.com/

National Fatherhood Initiative provides information on the importance of involved, committed, and responsible fathers and how they can improve the well-being of their children.
600 Eden Road, Building E
Lancaster, PA 17601
Tel.: (800) 790-DADS
(717) 581-8860
Fax: (717) 581-8862
http://www.fatherhood.org/

Fathers, Stay-at-Home

At-Home Dad Newsletter
61 Brightwood Ave.
North Andover, MA 01845
Tel.: (508) 685-7931
E-mail: AtHomeDad@aol.com

Slowlane.com provides online resources and support for stay-at-home and primary caregiving dads and their families.
http://www.slowlane.com/

Finances (College Savings, Financial Planning, Insurance, and so on)

American Council of Life Insurers provides basic information on the spectrum of life insurance products and operates the National Insurance Consumer Helpline, which can give you referrals to local agents.
1001 Pennsylvania Ave. NW
Washington, DC 20004
Tel.: (800) 942-4242
http://www.acli.com/

College Savings Plans Network offers great info on all of the state-sponsored college savings plans and referrals to the one in your state.
Tel.: (877) CSPN-4-YOU
http://www.collegesavings.org/

Federal Consumer Information Center
Ask for their publication, *Preparing for College.*
P.O. Box 100
Pueblo, CO 81009
Tel.: (800) 688-9889
http://www.pueblo.gsa.gov/education.html

Financial Planning Association provides information on financial planning and referrals to certified financial planners in your area.
Tel.: (800) 322-4237
(404) 845-0011
Fax: (404) 845-3660
E-mail: membership@fpanet.org
http://www.fpanet.org/

Health and Safety

Danny Foundation educates the public about crib dangers and advises eliminating the millions of unsafe cribs currently in use or in storage.
3158 Danville Blvd.
P.O. Box 680
Alamo, CA 94507
Tel.: (800) 83-DANNY
E-mail: information@dannyfoundation.org
http://www.dannyfoundation.org/

Green Home explains everything you need to create a healthy, nontoxic home environment.
http://www.greenhome.com/

National Highway Traffic Safety Administration offers the latest info on car and car-seat safety. Includes a shopping guide for car seats, recall information, and safety literature.

Department of Transportation
400 7th Street SW
Washington, DC 20590
Tel.: (800) 424-9393
http://www.nhtsa.gov/

National Safety Council provides facts, information, and resources on environmental issues and accident prevention.
http://www.nsc.org/

U.S. Consumer Products Safety Commission provides comprehensive safety checklists, notices of recalls, and other important safety info.
http://www.cpsc.gov/

Parenting, General

There are a number of excellent Internet sites offering comprehensive parenting information, advice, resources, and products. Most have community sections where you can post questions and get advice from other parents. Most also have special sections for dads. Among the best are:

Babycenter.com
http://www.babycenter.com/

DrSpock.com
http://www.DrSpock.com/

EverythingForParents.com
http://everythingforparents.com/

Family.com
http://family.go.com/

ParentsPlace.com
http://parentsplace.com/

In addition, **100 Top Parenting Sites** maintains a constantly shifting list of, you guessed it, the top 100 parenting sites on the Internet.
http://www.100topparentingsites.com/

Pregnancy, General

All the resources in the Parenting, General section have good information on pregnancy. Here are a few more that focus specifically on pregnancy and childbirth.

BabySoon.com
http://www.babysoon.com/

BabyZone.com
http://www.babyzone.com/

E-Pregnancy Magazine
Also available in a print version, *Pregnancy Magazine.*
http://www.epregnancy.com/pregnancymagazine/

Pregnancy Today is the online journal for parents-to-be. It has a special section for dads.
http://www.pregnancytoday.com/

Pregnancy at Women.com
(formerly Storksite)
http://www.women.com/pregnancy/

Parenting, Special Concerns

CHILDREN WITH DISABILITIES

Parents Helping Parents
3041 Olcott Street
Santa Clara, CA 95054-3222
Tel.: (408) 727-5775
Fax: (408) 727-0182
http://www.php.com/

National Fathers' Network supports fathers and families raising children with special health-care needs and developmental disabilities.
Tel.: (206) 747-4004
http://www.fathersnetwork.org/

The National Information Center for Children and Youth with Disabilities is a referral center that provides information on disabilities and disability-related issues for families, educators, and other professionals.
P.O. Box 1492
Washington, DC 20013-1492
Tel.: (800) 695-0285
(202) 884-8200
Fax: (202) 884-8441
http://www.nichcy.org/

PREEMIES

Preemies.org offers resources, chats, and support for parents of children born prematurely.
http://www.preemies.org/

Emory Regional Perinatal Center is a great source of info on developmental milestones, medical concerns, and other issues.
Neonatal Section
P. O. Box 26015
80 Butler Street SE
Atlanta, GA 30335
http://www.emory.edu/PEDS/NEONATOLOGY/DCP/

Preemie Store offers anything you could possibly need to buy for your preemie.
17195 Newhope St., Suite 105
Fountain Valley, CA 92708
Tel.: (800) O-SO-TINY (676-8469)
(714) 434-3740
Fax: (714) 434-7510
http://www.preemie.com/

TWINS (AND MORE)

M.O.S.T. (Mothers of Supertwins) provides information, resources, empathy, and support to families with triplets and more.
P.O. Box 951
Brentwood, NY 11717-0627
Tel.: (631) 859-1110
http://www.mostonline.org/

National Online Fathers of Twins Club is a member-run organization that provides support and info for dads of multiples.
c/o Jeff Maxwell
2804 NW 163rd
Edmond, OK 73013
http://www.nofotc.org/

The National Organization of Mothers of Twins Clubs, Inc. (NOMOTC) promotes the special aspects of multiple-birth children.
P.O. Box 438
Thompson Station, TN 37179-0438
Tel.: (877) 540-2200
(615) 595-0936
http://www.nomotc.org/

Triplet Connection
P.O. Box 99571
Stockton, CA 95209
Tel.: (209) 474-0885
http://www.tripletconnection.org/

Prenatal Communication/ Enrichment

The BabyPlus Company
301 East Carmel Drive
Building G, Suite 300-2
Carmel, IN 46032
Tel.: (800) 330-6944
E-mail: management@babyplus.com
http://www.babyplus.com/

Work and Family

The Entrepreneurial Parent is a resource for home-office entrepreneurs and career professionals who are looking for alternative work options. It offers information, professional assistance, and a strong "Entrepreneurial Parent" community.
P.O. Box 320722
Fairfield, CT 06432
Tel.: (203) 371-6212
E-mail: office@en-parent.com
http://www.en-parent.com/

Families And Work Institute provides information on the changing nature of work and family life.
330 Seventh Avenue, 14th Floor
New York, NY 10001
Tel.: (212) 465-2044
Fax: (212) 465-8637
http://www.familiesandwork.org/

Work/Family Directions offers practical ideas on how to stay ahead of emerging personnel and workplace issues and provides employers with innovative ways to achieve maximum commitment from their employees.
200 Talcott Avenue West
Watertown, MA 02472
Tel.: (800) 447-0543
Fax: (617) 926-6443
http://www.wfd.com/

Index

Cartoon Credits

© Edgar Argo from The Cartoon Bank: pp. 35, 109; © Donna Barstow from The Cartoon Bank: pp. 2, 66; © Dave Carpenter from The Cartoon Bank: p. 152; © Tom Cheney from The Cartoon Bank: p. 169; © Michael Crawford from The Cartoon Bank: p. 125; © Leo Cullum from The Cartoon Bank: pp. 34, 85; © Joe Dator from The Cartoon Bank: p. 80; © Liza Donnelly from The Cartoon Bank: p. 124; © Ed Frascino from The Cartoon Bank: pp. 74, 167; © Mort Gerberg from The Cartoon Bank: p.22; © John Greer: pp. 8, 28, 70, 133, 144, 148; © Liza Haberfeld from The Cartoon Bank: p. 76; © Bill Haefeli from The Cartoon Bank: p. 223; © Bob Mankoff from The Cartoon Bank: p. 114; © Brian Savage from The Cartoon Bank: p. 232; © Bernie Schoenbaum from The Cartoon Bank: p. 31; © Danny Shanahan from The Cartoon Bank: p. 247; © David Sipress from The Cartoon Bank: p. 243; © Peter Steiner from The Cartoon Bank: p. 240; © Mick Stevens from The Cartoon Bank: pp. 38, 160; © Mike Twohy from The Cartoon Bank: p. 107.

About the Author

A nationally recognized parenting expert, **Armin Brott** is also the author of *The New Father: A Dad's Guide to the First Year*, *The New Father: A Dad's Guide to the Toddler Years*, *The Single Father: A Dad's Guide to Parenting without a Partner*, and *Father for Life: A Journey of Joy, Challenge, and Change*. He has written on parenting and fatherhood for *The New York Times Magazine*, *The Washington Post*, *Newsweek*, and dozens of other periodicals. He also writes a nationally syndicated column, "Ask Mr. Dad," and hosts "Positive Parenting," a weekly talk show. Armin lives with his family in Oakland, California. To learn more, please visit his Web site, www.mrdad.com.

ARMIN BROTT:OVER 1,000,000 FATHERHOOD BOOKS IN PRINT!

THE EXPECTANT FATHER BOXED SET
FATHER KNOWS BEST
ISBN 0-7892-0824-5 · $39.95

EXPECTANT FATHER
Facts, Tips, and Advice for the Dad-to-Be

NEW FATHER
A Dad's Guide to the First Year

NEW FATHER
A Dad's Guide to the Toddler Years

EXPECTANT AND FIRST-YEAR FATHER BOXED SET
ISBN 0-7892-0840-7 · $27.50

EXPECTANT FATHER
Facts, Tips, and Advice for the Dad-to-Be

NEW FATHER
A Dad's Guide to the First Year

THE NEW FATHER SERIES BOXED SET
ISBN 0-7892-0825-3 · $27.50

NEW FATHER
A Dad's Guide to the First Year

NEW FATHER
A Dad's Guide to the Toddler Years

THE EXPECTANT FATHER
SECOND EDITION
Facts, Tips, and Advice for Dads-to-Be
By Armin A. Brott and Jennifer Ash
30 black-and-white illustrations
272 pages · 6 x 9"
Paper · 0-7892-0538-6 · $11.95
Hardcover · 0-7892-0537-8 · $16.95

THE NEW FATHER
SECOND EDITION
A Dad's Guide to the First Year
By Armin A. Brott
30 black-and-white illustrations
320 pages · 6 x 9"
Paper 0-7892-0815-6 · $12.95
Hardcover · 0-7892-0806-7 · $18.95

THE NEW FATHER
A Dad's Guide to the Toddler Years
By Armin A. Brott
35 black-and-white illustrations
224 pages · 6 x 9"
Paper · 0-7892-0396-0 · $11.95
Hardcover · 0-7892-0480-0 · $16.95

Available from your favorite bookstore, or at abbeville.com, or by calling 1-800-ARTBOOK